*The Craft and Art
of Dylan Thomas*

The Craft and Art

of Dylan Thomas

WILLIAM T. MOYNIHAN
University of Connecticut

Cornell University Press

ITHACA, NEW YORK

CORNELL UNIVERSITY PRESS

First published 1966

Library of Congress Catalog Card Number: 65–28600

PRINTED IN THE UNITED STATES OF AMERICA
BY KINGSPORT PRESS, INC.

To Ruth

Preface

THIS book is a study of the artistry and meaning of Dylan Thomas's poetry. It deals with the prose and drama in so far as they are relevant to the poetry and is concerned with Thomas's life only "in the light of the very obvious truth," as Henry James put it, "that the deepest quality of a work of art will always be the quality of the mind of the producer." All of Thomas's work, then, falls within the scope of this study, but its focal point from beginning to end is *Collected Poems*.

Thomas was an acclaimed lyricist, a difficult poet, and a phenomenal public personality. Thus, while he provides engrossing copy for the journalist and the biographer, he provides added difficulties for the critic. The critic, like any reader, is mysteriously enticed by the lyric beauty of some of the poems and exasperated by the opacity of others. Unlike the reader, the critic must constantly face the fact that the lyricism of Thomas remains in the poetry and cannot be captured in a book about his poetry, and must reluctantly admit that the attempt to dispel one kind of obscurity almost necessarily entails other kinds of obscurity.

Moreover, because the combination of lyricism and opacity is further compounded with the public personality, Thomas seems to arouse laudations and deprecations with remarkable ease. Thomas's is the "voice of origins," he is a "wild boy," he exercised a "mesmeristic flair," he was the victim of "verbal compulsions," he created a meaningless "hot sprawl of mud," he wrote the "most pure poetry of our age." No critic can ignore these charges and claims; no critic can possibly deal with them fully.

The critical dilemma is manifested on the proverbial horns of "too much" and "too little." I doubt that any modern poet, even Eliot, has been so fully explicated as Thomas. At one extreme Thomas's obscurity invites what is often called the "lemon squeezer" technique, or what William James would describe as invoking "the zodiac to account for the fall of the sparrow." At the other extreme there is always the temptation to say too little, to provide a too facile summation of a Thomas poem. I do not imagine that I shall escape this dilemma entirely, but I have written this study in hopes of escaping it.

I make one all-important assumption; I have assumed the reader is convinced that Thomas wrote at least a handful of great lyric poems and that I do not have to define what I mean by great lyric poem. Thomas's worst detractors have granted him the *occasional* gift of lyric genius. I try, therefore, at the outset, to concentrate on areas of confusion and controversy. I address myself especially to the problems of Thomas's formative years, problems of his imagination and of his obscurity. I try, first, to show some of the ways Thomas sought to exploit the emotional potential of language and, second, to suggest some of the completely unpredictable qualities of his imagination. Fully one half of this study is devoted to the growth of Thomas's imagination and to his auditory, rhetorical, and metaphorical craftsmanship.

My method at times in dealing with these techniques amounts to bold-faced enumeration of examples of Thomas's amazing versatility. In discussing rhetorical and auditory techniques I know no better method than citing a convincing number of specific instances, for these instances not only demonstrate Thomas's esthetic practices but also provide occasions to comment on the meaning of obscure passages. Furthermore, it seemed to me that sheer verbal facility was one of Thomas's major claims to literary attention. What he demanded of himself, and what he demands of his reader, is an almost insatiable curiosity about language and about the potency of poetic language.

The examination of rhetorical and auditory practices is preliminary to a consideration of the thematic and symbolic meaning of Thomas's work. The rational or, if understood in a general sense, the logical relationship among Thomas's ideas and themes is a subject which has not been much discussed in previous studies. I try to right that situation here. Although many of Thomas's themes contradict one another and their emphasis is, finally, alogical, they do establish certain norms and values and their very confusion is in itself meaningful.

It becomes clear from a study of Thomas's themes and images that there is an inner contest in the work between the rational and the emotional, and that those things Thomas could not bring himself to formulate in logical terms he nevertheless strove to express symbolically. The final stages of this study thus move from the thematic to the imagistic, or symbolic, content of the work—from artistry through statement to vision, from what Thomas could not rationally resolve to what he was able to symbolize. Logically, the work of Thomas may be mired in confusions and contradictions, but, symbolically, it reveals a mythic unity.

This brings us to the vexing problem of Thomas the "religious poet." I touch on this later at several points, but I feel that the reader is entitled to my opinion as early as possible. I find the problem vexing only because critics have tried to make Thomas into a Christian poet on one hand and into a pagan poet on the other. If we don't mind including a bit of polytheism and a good deal of magic under the idea of "religious poet," Thomas would certainly be one of the most religious poets of the modern period. For, as I shall later show, there are in his poetry many gods, many Christ-figures, and much magic. He believed in them as deeply as a poet has to in order to earn the title "religious." This is the necessary distinction, of course; a theologian must define and distinguish, an ordinary person must make his actions give evidence of faith, or piety, but the poet needs only a vague "reverence for life," has only to use certain images and situations. Thomas's work abounds in religious images and themes; to determine what meaning these had in his life is the province of the biographer.

As far as the work itself goes, I think Thomas put it as well as he could in the prefatory note to *Collected Poems:*

I read somewhere of a shepherd who, when asked why he made, from within fairy rings, ritual observances to the moon to protect his flocks, replied: "I'd be a damn' fool if I didn't!" These poems, with all their crudities, doubts, and confusions, are written for the love of Man and in praise of God, and I'd be a damn' fool if they weren't.

Like the Athenians,[1] Thomas was taking no chances; he'd be sure to have a place reserved for the unknown God. And it is Man whom he loves, not God; God is something to be praised. God is something to take into consideration the same way a shepherd takes storm, wolf, and pasture into consideration; and the way to note this phenomenon is by making ritual observations from within fairy rings or by writing poems of love and praise. For all of its "crudities, doubts, and confu-

[1] See *Acts* 17:22–23.

Preface

sions," this is a religious impulse as old as the rites of Nemi, or as Genesis itself.

The paradoxes Thomas's work, its lyric directness and verbal opacity, its contrived rhetoric and emotional simplicity, its intellectual limitations and its mythic universality—these are the "cunning passageways" that must be traced in Thomas's artistry. Tracing them—as involved as that process is— seems the only way the meaning and quality of Thomas's achievement can be revealed.

ACKNOWLEDGMENTS

In conceiving and writing this book I have become indebted to many—none of whom is responsible for its shortcomings, but all of whom are responsible to some extent for whatever merits it may possess. My former colleague Frederick S. Kiley was the first to whet my critical appetite for Thomas's work by challenging me to "make sense" of some obscure lines from "Author's Prologue." I am not sure that I ever satisfactorily met his challenge, but I continued to try to make sense out of the rest of Collected Poems, first under the direction of John Malcolm Brinnin and later under Edward Bloom and Edwin Honig. For enlightenment of both a general and a specific nature I am indebted to Constantine FitzGibbon, Vernon Watkins, Lady C. P. Snow (Pamela Hansford Johnson), Wyn Henderson, Bill Read, Donald C. Freeman, Rex Warner, Jack Grant, Kenneth Wilson, Daniel Hughes, and Kent Thompson. A postdoctoral Fellowship from the Lilly Foundation in 1964–1965 enabled me to complete this book; the University of Connecticut Research Foundation, and Leslie Duer and Harriet Taylor, provided typing and clerical assistance. My debt to previous Thomas critics, which I try to acknowledge in my text, is considerable—even when I may disagree on particular details. Finally, the assistance of my wife at every stage has been invaluable.

Earlier versions of portions of this book have appeared in *Explicator, Journal of Aesthetics and Art Criticism, Texas Studies in Language and Literature,* and *PMLA* (*Publications of the Modern Language Association*).

I was greatly hampered by the refusal of New Directions to allow me to quote from Thomas's Notebooks or his unpublished correspondence. Hence, I regrettably had to employ more paraphrase, I hope not circumlocution, than I would have liked. In all instances I have scrupulously retained the substance of what Thomas originally wrote.

My quotations from Thomas's poetry are from *The Collected Poems of Dylan Thomas,* copyright 1953 by Dylan Thomas, © 1957 by New Directions; used by permission of New Directions, Publishers, J. M. Dent & Sons Ltd., and the literary executors of the Dylan Thomas estate.

Quotations from Thomas's prose are from *Portrait of the Artist as a Young Dog,* copyright 1940 by New Directions; *Adventures in the Skin Trade,* copyright 1955, copyright © 1964 by New Directions; *Under Milk Wood,* copyright 1954 by New Directions, all rights reserved. All material is used by permission of New Directions, Publishers.

Quotations from the works of other poets are as follows: From *The Complete Poems of D. H. Lawrence,* edited by Vivian De Sola Pinto and F. Warren Roberts, copyright 1933 by Frieda Lawrence, all rights reserved; reprinted by permission of The Viking Press, Inc., Laurence Pollinger Limited, and the estate of the late Mrs. Frieda Lawrence. From *Collected Poems 1909–1962,* by T. S. Eliot, by permission of Harcourt, Brace & World, Inc., and Faber and Faber, Ltd. From *Poems of Gerard Manley Hopkins,* by permission of Oxford University Press. From *The Collected Poems of Hart*

Preface

Crane, by permission of Liveright, Publishers, N.Y., copyright © R, 1961, by Liveright Publishing Corp. From *The Collected Poems of W. B. Yeats,* reprinted with permission of The Macmillan Company (also by permission of Mr. M. B. Yeats and Macmillan & Co., Ltd.), copyright 1903 by The Macmillan Company, renewed 1931 by W. B. Yeats. A quotation from Dylan Thomas's letter to Marguerite Caetani, printed in *Botteghe Oscure,* is used by permission of Lelia Caetani Howard.

WILLIAM T. MOYNIHAN

Storrs, Connecticut
April, 1965

Contents

Contents

CHAPTER ONE

"The Tree of Nettles": The Man and the Poet

I with the wooden insect in the tree of nettles,
In the glass bed of grapes with snail and flower,
Hearing the weather fall.
                    "I, In My Intricate Image" [1]

"NO one can deny that the most attractive figures in literature are always those around whom a world of lies and legends has been woven, those half mythical artists whose real characters become cloaked forever under . . . the bizarre." [2] So the eighteen-year-old Dylan Thomas wrote in his local newspaper, and, true to his analysis, so he became. Largely because of the legends and lies woven around his real character, he is today one of the most attractive figures in modern literature. Regrettably, the misconceptions about the man have too often carried over into judgments of his work.

[1] *The Collected Poems of Dylan Thomas* (New York, 1953), p. 41. All page numbers in parentheses following quoted poems are to this volume, unless otherwise noted. The augmented edition, 1957, is identical in pagination but adds "Elegy."

[2] "Tragedy of Swansea's Comic Genius: The Story of Llewelyn Pritchard," *Herald of Wales* (January 23, 1932), 6.

Craft and Art of Dylan Thomas

The poetry, like the man himself, has occasioned extreme and contradictory responses. Some have seen Thomas's work as an esthetic orgy, others as the expression of a deeply religious mind. Kenneth Rexroth said that Thomas "hits you across the face with a reeking, bloody heart, a heart full of worms and needles and black blood and thorns, a werewolf heart." [3] W. S. Merwin saw Thomas as a "religious poet trying, at times desperately, to find and come to grips with his subject, finding it, and making it into a poetry of celebration." [4] Geoffrey Grigson called Thomas's work a "meaningless hot sprawl of mud," while Herbert Read said it was "the most absolute poetry . . . written in our time." [5] Thomas himself touched on one of the most pervasive of all contradictions in his work when he said he wrote "in praise of God's world" although he did not believe in God. [6] "Dylan Thomas," concluded Vernon Watkins in the London *Times* obituary for his friend, "presents, in retrospect, the greatest paradox of our time."

It is, in fact, sometimes difficult to determine whether Thomas's detractors are attacking the man or the work; the artist and the public personality become one. There is a perceptible desire on the part of a few, most of whom are English critics or people who were for a brief time personally acquainted with him, to drive Thomas off the stage of literary history because he embodies attitudes and values that they feel

[3] Kenneth Rexroth, "From the Introduction to *The New British Poets*," in *A Casebook on Dylan Thomas*, ed. John Malcolm Brinnin (New York, 1960), p. 128. Future references to this volume will be to *A Casebook*.

[4] W. S. Merwin, "The Religious Poet," *A Casebook*, p. 60.

[5] Geoffrey Grigson, "How Much Me Now Your Acrobatics Amaze," *A Casebook*, p. 119; Herbert Read's remark is quoted in Marshall W. Stearns's "Unsex the Skeleton" in *Dylan Thomas: The Legend and the Poet*, ed. E. W. Tedlock (London, 1960), p. 113.

[6] Quoted by John Malcolm Brinnin, *Dylan Thomas in America* (Compass, New York, 1957), p. 128.

are antithetical to the higher aspirations of "civilization." As
the wife of an English clergyman clearly expressed it to me,
"Dylan Thomas may have been a very clever poet, but he had
a dirty mind."

The sophisticated elaboration of such a judgment is David
Holbrook's book, *Llareggub Revisited: Dylan Thomas and the
State of Modern Poetry*. Holbrook feels that modern poetry
no longer satisfies and that little, if any, of the verse written
since the turn of the century possesses the true rhythms of
English poetry; nor does modern poetry, in general, express
the mind of "civilized" man. These feelings of dissatisfaction
"centered round the work of Dylan Thomas," says Holbrook.
He then goes on, "I felt that only by a rejection of Thomas's
poetry, his attitude to poetry, and the attitudes of his audience
to poetry could this essential activity of the civilized consciousness, poetry, regain health, prestige and effectiveness."
What is most unhealthy about Thomas's poetry, according to
Holbrook, is its immaturity. Thomas failed "to come to terms
with adult sex, with death, time and circumstances." His work
"yields no feeling of achieved pattern or structure," he appeals
to the salacious, he is "childish." [7] It has become almost a part
of the climate of opinion in Thomas criticism to concede that
the poet was not much concerned with meaning. From such a
premise it has become all too easy to see any number of his
poems as irresponsible creations—most likely the least appeal-
ing ones. And the conclusion has very naturally followed that
the poetry says little or nothing, that it has no "content," that
Thomas had only "a few young things to say," that he began
on some fringe of surrealism and ended as a "windy fake."

George Steiner is one of the more recent critics to go so far
as to claim that Thomas was a poetic impostor. After pointing
out that "only genius can elaborate a vision so intense and so

[7] See David Holbrook, *Llareggub Revisited* (London, 1962), pp. 16,
238, 239, 247, 248.

3

specific that it will come across the intervening barrier of broken syntax or private meaning," Steiner comments on the followers of Rimbaud and Mallarmé by saying:

In the hands of lesser men or impostors, the attempt to make language new is diminished to barrenness and obscurity. Dylan Thomas is a case in point. He realized with the flair of a showman that a wide, largely unqualified audience could be flattered by being given access to a poetry of seeming depth. He combined a froth of Swinburnean rhetoric with cabalistic devices of syntax and imagery. He showed that one could have one's Orphic cake and eat it too. But barring certain eloquent exceptions there is in his poetry less than meets the dazzled eye.[8]

Steiner provides an even better catalogue of misconceptions about Thomas than Holbrook does. The one thing that Dylan Thomas's language is rarely reduced to is barrenness, and the one thing that Thomas's poetry does at its most private and most obscure level is to "communicate." It is not that the poetry lacks meaning but rather that it has too many possible meanings. Thomas himself said everything that can be said about his attitude toward "cabalistic devices" when he wrote that the most prized expressions should be eliminated if meaning demands it, that conscious obscurity should never be allowed to smother poetry. But, he contended, all good poetry need not be simple, the great truths of life and the great artistic variations of these truths cannot be reduced to the level of the most naive reader. Some things, he concluded, are so involved that even the poet may not always understand what he is writing.[9]

The image of Thomas as "impostor," as showman, poetic

[8] George Steiner, "The Retreat from Word," *Kenyon Review*, XXIII (Spring, 1961), 207.
[9] From Thomas's letters to Pamela Hansford Johnson, which are now in the Lockwood Memorial Library, Buffalo, New York. The letters

charlatan, barker without poetic bite, or what have you, is, it would seem, based to a large extent on the confusion of man and poet. It is axiomatic in all critical evaluation that, as George Whalley says, "the poet, mystic, and the rest are properly so called only when engaged in some activity that entitles them to the name. No system of classification is sensitive enough to accommodate the variations in attitude and activity of a single individual; an individual may well be—and most individuals are—a poet for an hour, a scientist for a week, and an 'ordinary man' for the rest of his life." [10]

Thomas himself remarked, "A poet is a poet for such a very tiny bit of his life; for the rest, he is a human being, one of whose responsibilities is to know and feel, as much as he can, all that is moving around and within him, so that his poetry, when he comes to write it, can be his attempt at an expression of the

---

comprise 200 pages and cover a period extending from the autumn of 1933 to the late summer of 1934. Most of the letters are undated. Future references to this collection will be to P.H.J. Correspondence. Where this correspondence is identified in the text, no footnote will be used.

[10] George Whalley, *Poetic Process* (London, 1953), p. 27. This essential separation of the man and the function (the office and the officeholder, the sin and the sinner) is also acutely drawn by Northrop Frye: "In the artist the difference between the time-bound ego and the imaginative state in which great things are done is even more sharply marked than it is in the ordinary man. The artist may be conceited, irritable, foolish, or dishonest, but it makes no difference what he is: all that matters is his imagination." *Fearful Symmetry* (Princeton, 1947), p. 112.

Robert Lowell has drawn the same distinction in a different way: "So much of the effort of the poem is to arrive at something essentially human, to find the right voice for what we have to say. In life we speak with many false voices; occasionally, if we are lucky, we find a true voice in our poems." Stanley Kunitz, "Talk with Robert Lowell," *New York Times Book Review* (October 4, 1964), 36.

summit of man's experience on this very peculiar and, in 1946, this apparently hell-bent earth." [11]

This was not a new idea with Thomas. All his life he seems to have been aware of a dichotomy between the world of artistic creativity and the world of ordinary events. To his early friend Trevor Hughes, Thomas wrote that there were two worlds for an artist—the outer world in which one suffered and enjoyed, despaired and made money, loved, mated and died, because one must, and the artist's unique inner world of creative splendor. [12]

The public man and the poet, of course, can never be separated. Dylan Thomas must, I suppose, always remain a semblance of what he himself described as "a bombastic adolescent provincial bohemian with a thick-knotted artist's tie made out his sister's scarf—she never knew where it had gone—and a cricket-shirt dyed bottle green; a gabbing, ambitious, mock-tough, pretentious young man." [13] He will always to some degree remain the tragic, roaring boy genius with the lilting and soaring voice who wove his own net of "lies and legends" and who wrote a kind of epitaph for himself when he announced, "I've had eighteen straight whiskies. I think that's the record." [14] But this man is very indirectly involved in the poetry. The biographical catch phrases are exciting eavesdroppings from backstage, but they are not the poetry—the high mimesis that was performed upstage. They are hardly more valuable than rent receipts, barroom bills, or laundry slips when it comes to dealing with the man *as poet*.

Poetry of great emotion proceeds from lives of great emo-

[11] *Quite Early One Morning* (New York, 1954), p. 193.
[12] Letter to Trevor Hughes (January, 1933), Lockwood Memorial Library, Buffalo, New York.
[13] *Quite Early One Morning*, p. 71.
[14] Quoted by John Malcolm Brinnin, *Dylan Thomas in America*, p. 272.

tional pitch—whether that pitch be public or private, interior or exterior; whether the poet be Dylan Thomas or Emily Dickinson. This is the source of the traditional comparison between the oyster's grain of sand and a poem's gestation. The most recent elaboration of this germinal analogy is the theory of "symbolic extrication," which holds that the poet extricates himself from situations of intolerable reality in the process of poetic creation.[15]

Yeats said it best when he wrote that "only an aching heart/ Conceives a changeless work of art." And, as Yeats also reminds us, in "Adam's Curse," this painful task is always liable to ridicule:

> A line will take us hours maybe;
> Yet if it does not seem a moment's thought,
> Our stitching and unstitching has been naught.
> Better go down upon your marrow-bones
> And scrub a kitchen pavement, or break stones
> Like an old pauper, in all kinds of weather;
> For to articulate sweet sounds together
> Is to work harder than all these, and yet
> Be thought an idler by the noisy set.

Rather than seeing Thomas's excessive and perhaps immature behavior reflected in his literary productions, it would seem more accurate to see his literary creations as escapes from or sensitive reassessments of orgiastic behavior. It is more than plausible that there would have been no art without his life of

[15] "A poem," George Whalley says, "springs from a paradeigmatic event [an event of knowing characterized by vivid perception.] . . . A poem is in some sense the resolution of an event in reality. A germ, a catalyst, a quantum of 'poetic energy,' intrudes into consciousness; the associative function of memory which we call imagination is stimulated, and orients itself in a particular manner. The activity that proceeds between the paradeigmatic event and the finished poem I have called *symbolic extrication*." *Poetic Process*, pp. 104–105.

7

maladjustment. Perhaps the kind of poetry he wrote had to come, in George Whalley's terms, from conditions of "intolerable reality." Like the boy in Graham Greene's short story "The Revolver in the Corner Cupboard" who could find purpose in life only by repeatedly playing Russian roulette, Thomas evidently felt life most rich when most threatened. "Damocles never danced better than beneath the sword." [16] As Thomas wrote of Lawrence, his creativity and his illness grew side by side and were indispensable to one another.[17]

Thomas was the very opposite of a poetic impostor. He was a man devoted to poetry from childhood, a man who saw in poetry a means of apprehending truth and of helping others to apprehend it. Whether the public role he assumed in order to express this truth makes him a showman is problematical. For if he can be so called, it is only in the sense that many of the greatest artists are showmen. Granted, Thomas was a rhetorician, he was an irrepressible performer, he apparently enjoyed nothing more than entertaining—publicly or privately. From his grammar school days he was interested in acting and was never very far from the stage, actually and metaphorically. But the desire and ability to perform do not make Thomas a charlatan; they help to explain some of the characteristics of his poetry, but not his sincerity or the lack of it.

We can go further than this. We can say that Thomas was an incomparable verbal craftsman, and that his obsession with craft is inherent in every line he wrote. Technically he experimented with numerous styles and rhythms. Almost every poem is an example of a verse form that he laboriously developed, perfected in that one poem, then dropped. True,

---

[16] Albert Camus, *The Rebel*, trans. Anthony Bower (Vintage, New York, 1956), p. 72.
[17] P.H.J. Correspondence.

8

his dexterity sometimes resulted in metrical stunts. He wrote his 102-line "Author's Prologue" in what would have to be called chiasmatic rhymed couplets. The first line rhymes with the last, the second with the next to the last, and so on up to the center of the poem, where the two middle lines are rhymed. In the poem "I, in My Intricate Image," Thomas uses seventy-two variations of the letter *l,* one for every line-ending in the poem.[18] The indisputable fact of the matter is that Thomas "was the very opposite of a careless writer; his poems are not eccentric; his relationship to any one of his poems was not a trance-relationship; it was rather that of a chess master to a piece." [19] We know, for instance, that one of his poems exists in more than two hundred separate and distinct versions.[20]

I do not pretend that it is possible either to dismiss or to answer completely all of the charges made against Thomas. Indeed, if one were able to resolve fully the difficulties implied by his critics, much of the power and magic of poetry would yield its secrets as quickly as the last chapter of a Sherlock Holmes mystery. What is barren language?—in what sense are poems and stories that move and excite millions examples of barrenness? Why are audiences who are moved by Thomas "largely unqualified"? How does one bake an Orphic cake, never mind eat it? Or when does metaphor cease to become responsible criticism and become instead the concealment of the lack of close analysis?

We know too much about the man, especially about the carnival of excess that marked his public life, and too little

[18] Thomas points this out to Watkins. *Dylan Thomas: Letters to Vernon Watkins,* ed. Vernon Watkins (London, 1957), p. 15.

[19] "The Writings of Dylan Thomas," *Times Literary Supplement* (July 27, 1956), 451.

[20] Brinnin, *Dylan Thomas in America,* p. 125. The poem is "Fern Hill."

about Dylan Thomas the poet. What Thomas's *enfant terrible* strut across the stage of literary history and his *symboliste* and verbal excesses have most seriously distorted is his genuine devotion to poetry, his conception of poetry and of the role of poet. Holbrook felt uneasy about Thomas's "attitude to poetry"; Steiner saw in Thomas something of the charlatan. We might do well to begin by considering the early development of Thomas's imagination—in the years before he strutted the "ivory stages." Then it would seem sensible to examine precisely Thomas's concept of the role of poet—what he had to say about poetry; what, in Holbrook's phrase, constituted his "attitude to poetry." The paradoxes and confusions of Thomas's work will never be fully resolved, but they will become more understandable, and his work better appreciated, when we realize that they are all part of an unrelenting attempt to express "the summit of man's experience," to find the "inner splendour."

I
GROWTH OF THE IMAGINATION

A poet's first book often seems to spring forth full-grown from some brow of inspiration. In 1934, when Thomas's *18 Poems* appeared, readers were delighted, confused, disturbed; many were, as Dr. Johnson said in describing the appearance of *Gulliver's Travels,* "caught in wonder." No one was able to understand with any precision what process of intellectual and artistic gestation preceded such a volume, or to guess what intellectual and artistic development would follow such a volume. To emphasize, as many critics did then and have since, that Thomas was a Welsh poet, was to grope in the direction of an explanation, to hint at some of the forces of tradition and individual talent which helped to shape his poetry. It is only slightly easier today to give an account of the growth of the imagination which culminated in *18 Poems,* and developed from *18 Poems.*

The beginnings of Thomas's art rest as much in the traditions of English poetry as in racial or environmental conditioning, and it is not possible to keep the two influences distinct. Indeed, English poetry and Welsh background meet in one overriding influence on Thomas—the Bible. The few distinctions discernible in tracing the growth of Thomas's imagination seem best stated simply at the outset, if only to provide some sense of direction: Thomas's poetic talents were nurtured by a childhood rich in the experience of Wales and its traditions, and richer still in reading. The first clearly marked period of writing—Thomas's juvenilia from the age of about eleven to sixteen—provides a marvelous pastiche of imitative verse. Around the age of sixteen there began the four years of his most intensive imaginative and intellectual searching (c. 1930–1934), chiefly revealed in four poetry Notebooks. These Notebooks lead directly to the *18 Poems.* Of even more help than the Notebooks for understanding the processes of Thomas's thought and imagination, in all stages of his formative period, are the detailed analyses and commentaries Thomas himself provided in letters during the years 1933–1934—primarily in correspondence with Pamela Hansford Johnson.

To begin with, Wales. Wales meant for Thomas home, country, countryside, particular traditions, residual characteristics of race, and a cast of mind that may loosely be called romantic. Granted that Thomas's Welshness is amorphous and indefinable; it is also inescapable. A whole book has been devoted, rightly, to Thomas and Wales,[21] but one of the most sensible general comments remains that of Geoffrey Moore:

[21] John Ackerman, *Dylan Thomas: His Life and Work* (London, 1964).

Craft and Art of Dylan Thomas

For all Dylan Thomas's disclaimers . . . , the mere fact of being born in a country so small, so clannish, and so fiercely nationalistic as Wales is meaningful in itself. . . . The harp of Wales sounds in the ears of Welshmen whether they are arch druids from Bangor or boyos from the back streets of Cardiff. Without being hopelessly mystical about race, one can with some confidence assert that both it and environment have an effect on the nature of a people and the art that springs from them. The Welsh are lively, quick-tempered and proud. They talk to you in railway carriages and they sing together spontaneously, musically and unselfconsciously. And if this sounds like *How Green Was My Valley*, it is none the less true. You can find Welshmen who are as phlegmatic-seeming as the average Anglo-Saxon, but get them in an argument, or on a platform, or in a pub, and you will likely as not discover that quality of passion and attack which in the Welsh preacher is called *hwyl*.

In the "natural" qualities of his poetry—its high emotional charge and sonorous rhetoric, and the lilt and exaggeration of its phrasing—Dylan Thomas reveals himself as a true son of the Cymry.[22]

Thomas frequently and eloquently recognized his debt to Wales. He praised it and condemned it; but he always returned there. His praise is usually found in his torrential prose: "Naturally, my early poems and stories . . . came out of a person who came willy-nilly out of a particular atmosphere and environment and are part and parcel, park and castle, lark and seashell, dark and schoolbell, muck and entrail, cock, rock and bubble, accent and sealap, root and ribbon of them."

"I gladly accept the fact," Thomas was accustomed to

---

[22] Geoffrey Moore, in Tedlock, pp. 254–255. See "The Peaches," *Portrait of the Artist as a Young Dog* (New York, 1940), pp. 9–28, for interesting aspects of Thomas and Welsh fundamentalism, especially the sermon on pp. 18–19.

telling his audiences, "that I first saw the light and screamed at it in a loud lump of Wales. . . . Of course my writing could not now be what it is—always experimental and always completely unsuccessful—if it had not been for the immortal fry of the town in which I simmered up."[23] His "Reminiscences of Childhood" begins:

> I was born in a large Welsh industrial town at the beginning of the Great War; an ugly, lovely town (or so it was, and is, to me), crawling, sprawling, slummed, unplanned, jerry-villa'd, and smug-suburbed by the side of a long and splendid-curving shore where truant boys and sandfield boys and anonymous men, in the tatters and hangovers of a hundred charity suits, beachcombed, idled, and paddled, watched the dock-bound boats, threw stones into the sea for the barking, outcast dogs, and, on Saturday summer afternoons, listened to the militant music of salvation and hell-fire preached from a soap-box.
> This town was my world.[24]

One thing Thomas was not, of course, was a "professional Welshman." He was not a nationalist, he did not know Welsh, he did not consciously try to adopt Welsh forms. He once remarked, "There are a number of young Welshmen writing poems in English who, insisting passionately that they are Welshmen, should by rights be writing in Welsh, but who, unable to write in Welsh or reluctant to do so . . . , often give the impression that their writing in English is only a condescension to the influence and ubiquity of a tyrannous foreign tongue. I do not belong to that number."[25]

Thomas hated the industrial towns of Wales, which he described as festering sores "on the body of a dead country."

[23] "A Few Words of a Kind," Caedmon Records, Vol. 3.
[24] *Quite Early One Morning,* p. 3.
[25] *Ibid.,* p. 97.

When young and struggling with his words and starving for recognition, he sometimes turned fiercely on his native land. He said he had a friend who wrote poetry about Wales that began: "What are you, Wales, but a tired old bitch?" and "Wales my country, Wales my sow"—phrases that respectively bring to mind Pound's lines about England in "Hugh Selwyn Mauberley" and, more appropriately, Stephen Dedalus's view of Ireland as a sow who eats her own farrow. Like Joyce, the young Thomas longed to be an exile. He complained of the ugliness, dirtiness, and narrowness of Wales and its people; he even irritably complained of his mother's pettiness.[26] But Thomas got only to London, whence it was easy enough to return to his Dublin, Wales.

Speaking on one occasion about the Welsh poet Edward Thomas, he gave a description that, with only slight modification, might apply to the poet he himself eventually became as well: "He loved the fields, the woods, the winding roads; he knew a thousand country things: the diamonds of rain on the grass-blades, the ghostly white parsley flower, mouse and wren and robin, each year's first violets, the missel-thrush that loves juniper, hawthorn berry, hazel-tuft, new-mown hay, the cuckoo crying over the untouched dew, churches, graveyards, farms and byres, children, wild geese, horses in the sun. . . . Edward Thomas was a faithful and solitary lover of the lovely that is not beloved by most of us, at much expense."[27] In Thomas's poetry, too, there is much of the countryside: "a wood's dancing hoof," "sheep white hollow

[26] P.H.J. Correspondence.

[27] *Quite Early One Morning*, p. 104. In *Dylan Thomas in America*, pp. 120–121, Brinnin discusses what appears to Americans as the "exotic unfamiliarity" in Thomas's imagery. "While we think, as a rule, of the exotic as something rarefied, and out of reach, and perhaps slightly bogus, the exotic in Dylan Thomas's poems is something that intrigues and charms us because . . . he is giving us a vision of the world he sees and knows."

farms," "Tom tit and Dai mouse" ("Prologue"); "water-/Birds and the birds of the winged trees," "pale rain over the dwindling harbour/ And over the sea wet church the size of a snail" (pp. 113, 114); the "ancient minutes in the cuckoo's month" (p. 58); "the smell of hay in the snow," "the blinding byres alone" (pp. 131, 132); "the spellbound horses walking warm/ Out of the whinnying green stable" (p. 179). He too was "a faithful and solitary lover of the lovely." And his images, as he wrote in "I, in my Intricate Image" (p. 41), "climb the country pinnacle."

Rustic and sea-beset Wales saturated Thomas's imagination and eventually provided a symbolic resolution for the complexities that were slowly denying him life. It is from the country that he derived the pastoral archetypes of season, country things, and the malignant and benign figures of the green world, just as the relatively simplified world of rural New England enabled Robert Frost to symbolize many of the tensions of a more complicated contemporary life.

The presence of rustic Wales is less apparent, however, before 1938 than after—although the "country" and the processes of nature are everywhere present in the earlier work. The early mechanistic metaphors—man and God depicted as machines[28]—certainly owe a good deal to the fact that Thomas was brought up in an urban center like Swansea. To this day the derricks and booms of Swansea docks suggest a source for the metaphoric levers of such a poem as "All All and All the Dry Worlds Lever" (p. 33). Rhossili—a beach eighteen miles from Swansea where Dylan often wrote—more obviously suggests the geography of "We Lying by Seasand" (p. 91).[29]

[28] See Jacob Korg, "Dylan Thomas's '18 Poems,'" *Accent*, XVII (Winter, 1957), 3-15.
[29] The short story "Extraordinary Little Cough," *Portrait of the Artist as a Young Dog*, pp. 65-76, deals with a trip to Rhossili.

Craft and Art of Dylan Thomas

Thomas was born into an upper-middle-class Welsh home on October 27, 1914. The son of a doting mother, made more doting by her son's sickly childhood, and of a father who was senior English master at Swansea Grammar School, he lived and acted the role of "poet" from early youth. Thomas, who described himself as a "sweet baby, a precocious child, a rebellious boy, and a morbid youth," claimed that "poetry first unveiled herself" to him when he was six or seven. In his father's study, as thousands of Americans remember him recounting, he read "everything and anything." The study contained all the masters of English poetry since Chaucer.[30] His schoolmates recall him indulging in other less elevated endeavors, such as avoiding all school subjects except English literature, keeping his own schedule of classes, and, in the natural order of things, keeping faithful hours along the promenade and in the parks—and still later in the local pubs.

Even these preliminary remarks about Thomas's back-

[30] In a letter to P.H.J. begun Christmas Day, 1933, Thomas makes these observations about his reading habits and the books available to him. He had received these as presents: Blake's complete works, the Koran, a 1923–1933 anthology of poems by Mrs. Munro, and two pamphlets by James Joyce.

Later he writes that he had read *Look Homeward, Angel* and liked it especially well.

He also described the books in his home. His father's library included all the usual writers of English literature, all sorts of reference books, and numerous critical works and books on literary theory. Dylan's books were more specialized—mostly poetry and mainly modern poetry. Poets represented were Auden, Crane, Eliot, Hopkins, de la Mare, Wilfred Owen, Osbert Sitwell, and Yeats in their respective collected poems; Aldous Huxley, D. H. Lawrence, Edna St. Vincent Millay, Harold Munro, Sassoon, Edith and Sacheverell Sitwell, and Humbert Wolfe. He also owned anthologies such as the *Best Poems of the Year*, Georgian and Imagist collections, *Whips and Scorpions*, Cambridge and Oxford undergraduate verse. Other books were the Greek translations by Gilbert Murray, some of Shaw's plays, and novels by Virginia Woolf and E. M. Forster.

ground bring us face to face with some of the countless paradoxes of both his life and his work. The son of a school master, Thomas never went beyond Swansea Grammar School; the implacable iconoclast of received literary values, Thomas probably was as widely read and as knowledgeable about English poetry as any young boy ever was. But, like most of the paradoxes of his life and work, the paradoxes of his youth are more apparent than real, and their antinomies are explicable. The disparate elements form, in the terms of Lupasco's new logic, a "contradictory complementarity"; that is, the contradictions complement one another. There was in Thomas's life (as in the lives of many men), and there remains in his art, what might be described, in an application of Lupasco's terms, as a constant movement between contradictory forces of personality and genius, one now potential, now actual, another now potential, now actual—without any possibility of a Hegelian synthesis. The basis of Thomas's creativity perhaps depended on the potential-kinetic alternation of forces which at first glance seem not only contradictory but even destructive. Thomas often saw things in dialectical terms and there is evidence of an Hegelian influence in his themes (as will be seen in Chapter Four), but there is little point in applying the dialectic either to his life or to his imagery.

Thus, although young Dylan Thomas always stood at, or near, the bottom of his class, his extraordinary literary abilities were constantly in evidence and steadily developing. And even though Dylan's father, D. J. Thomas, was many times embarrassed by his son's behavior—as Mrs. Thomas told a B.B.C. interviewer—he actually shared many affinities with Dylan and helped to shape the course of his poetic development. The father passed on to his son his enthusiasm for poetry, and early in Dylan's life he saw to it that the boy had elocution lessons. Until his death, he and Dylan shared a delight in crossword puzzles—often working on them together. The *Swansea Grammar School Magazine*, reminiscing about the father and son, reported of Dylan: "Like his father he was fascinated by the sounds of words." [31] Hetty Owen, a friend of the Thomas family during the Swansea years, has in her possession a number of Dylan's juvenile poems—some of which are in Dylan's hand, some in a hand similar but more mature.[32] It seems certain that an older member of the Thomas family copied over Dylan's earliest poems before they were submitted to newspapers—and if D. J. himself did not act as amanuensis for the child poet, he certainly had a dominant influence.

As a boy Dylan was much exposed to the Welsh Chapel and to the strong Nonconformist ethos of the farming districts of Carmarthenshire. On his mother's side, there was a long clerical heritage. Bill Read, a Thomas biographer, gives this account of clerical relatives:

Dylan's grandfather was a deacon, his Uncle Tom Williams was a Swansea preacher, and his Uncle David Rees became a well-known figure as minister of the Church of the Paraclete in Newton, a position he held from 1898 until 1933.[33] Dylan, his mother, and his older sister Nancy all attended the Congregational Church, where Dylan earned the Sunday School certificate he kept on the wall of his room. When they went to visit Aunt Dosie and Uncle Dai on week ends, as they often did, everyone went to church services three times a day at the Paraclete: morning services at eleven, Sunday school at two-thirty, and evening services at six-thirty.[34]

[31] *Swansea Grammar School Magazine*, LI (December, 1953), 5.
[32] These poems were shown to me by a friend of Mrs. Owen, Kent Thompson, of University College, Swansea, Wales.
[33] In the *Herald of Wales* (November 5, 1932), 6, Thomas wrote an article dealing with his uncle's church.
[34] Bill Read, *The Days of Dylan Thomas* (New York, 1964), p. 24.

"Tree of Nettles"

Adding to Dylan's consciousness of religion was the obvious difference in outlook between his mother and his father. His mother was described as "extremely devout"[35] while Dylan himself called his father an atheist (albeit an idiosyncratic one, as we shall shortly see). Young Dylan's imagination, like that of many an artist before him, was immediately and strongly drawn to the Bible. "The Bible . . . I had, of course, known from very early youth," wrote Thomas in 1951. "The great rhythms had rolled over me from the Welsh pulpits; and I read, for myself, from Job and Ecclesiastes; and the story of the New Testament is part of my life."[36]

The similarity between D. H. Lawrence and Thomas in this respect is instructive. Lawrence remarked on his own fundamentalist upbringing:

I was brought up on the Bible, and seem to have it in my bones. From early childhood I have been familiar with Apocalyptic language and Apocalyptic image: not because I spent my time reading Revelation, but because I was sent to Sunday School and to Chapel, to Band of Hope and to Christian Endeavor, and was always having the Bible read at me or to me. I did not even listen attentively. But language has a power of echoing and re-echoing in my unconscious mind. . . . The sound of Revelation had registered in me very early.[37]

Revelation has no "meaning" for the child, but it is full of magical incantations and apparently wild statements. It does not mean; it elicits meanings, numerous, indefinable, illimitable meanings. It is a book which verges on the irrational and

[35] Letter to me from Constantine FitzGibbon, Thomas's authorized biographer.

[36] Dylan Thomas, "Poetic Manifesto," *Texas Quarterly*, IV (Winter, 1961), 49.

[37] D. H. Lawrence, *Selected Literary Criticism* (London, 1956), p. 164.

excites all the multitudinous latency of the unconscious. It is suggestive beyond reason. "The orthodox critics will say: Fantasy! Nothing but fantasy! But then," concludes Lawrence, "thank God for fantasy, if it enhances our life." [38]

The influence of the Bible would continue to grow on Thomas throughout the whole of his imaginative life. What had been heard from God-intoxicated men ("tipsy from salvation's bottle," p. 82) would take on new meaning for him after he read the Romantic visionaries (especially Blake) and saw in his own physical processes parallels with the great events of scripture. But the suggestiveness of Revelation, the single-mindedness of the pulpit, the love of word-sounds for their own sake—such things could be immediately imitated. And Thomas, completely absorbed in poetry and the creation of poetry at a very young age, did imitate them.

In his story "The Fight," based to some extent on the actual boyhood fight which began his friendship with Daniel Jones, Thomas described himself, at what appears to be the age of ten, walking in the streets reciting poetry. Here is an example:

> My mind is fashioned
> In the ways of intertissue
> Veiled and passioned
> Are the thoughts that issue
> From its well of furtive lust
> Raptured by the devil's dust.[39]

Critics have often pointed to poetry as a kind of serious game—from Aristotle, who saw the child at play practicing mimesis, to Eliot, who called poetry a superior amusement,

[38] *Ibid.*, p. 166.
[39] *Portrait of the Artist as a Young Dog*, p. 53. Ralph Maud, *Entrances to Dylan Thomas' Poetry* (Pittsburgh, 1962), p. 123, writes: "Thomas quotes from five of his early poems (c. 1929) in his story 'The Fight.'" Presuming these were written in 1928 or 1929, this would make Thomas fourteen or fifteen, rather than ten.

"Tree of Nettles"

"amusement *pour distraire les honnêtes gens.*" Thomas's boyhood demonstrates such theories. Daniel Jones has recorded a childhood collaboration with Thomas which not only seems to describe poetry originating in babble, as Frye would have it, but also seems to foreshadow Thomas's adult working methods as well:

In poetry collaboration . . . we always wrote alternate lines; I had the odd-numbered lines and Dylan the even-numbered, and we made it a rule that neither of us should suggest an alteration in the other's work. These poems . . . are . . . what I would call serious play. The poetic style of Walter Bram, as we called ourselves, is bafflingly inconsistent; it is fragile, furious, laconic, massive, delicate, incantatory, cool, flinty, violent, Chinese, Greek, and shocking. One poem may begin "You will be surprised when I remain obdurate," and the next, "I lay under the currant trees and told the beady berries about Jesus." Some of the poems are very, very beautiful. . . .

They had come from the place high on the coral hills
Where the light from the white sea fills the soil with ascending
   grace.
And the sound of their power makes motion as steep as the sky,
And the fruits of the great ground lie like leaves from a vertical
   flower.
They had come from the place; they had come and had gone
   again
In a season of delicate rain, in a smooth ascension of grace.[40]

[40] Jones, "Memories and Appreciations," *A Casebook*, pp. 280–281. Jones says further, "We had word obsessions: everything at one time was 'little' or 'white'; and sometimes an adjective became irresistibly funny in almost any connection: 'innumerable bananas,' 'wilful moccasin,' 'a certain Mrs. Prothero.' [She appears in "Memories of Christmas."] These word games, and even the most facetious of our collaborations, had a serious experimental purpose, and there is no doubt that they played an important part in Dylan's early poetic development."

Craft and Art of Dylan Thomas

Although Thomas never published a piece of automatic writing, there are indications that he did for a time believe in a closely related kind of inspired poetry; this belief, however, slowly disappeared, to be replaced by a belief in the magic of auditory organization. Thomas "apparently felt that he 'received' whole images and lines. E. F. McInerny, who was editor of *The Swansea Grammar School Magazine* when Thomas was a lower-form schoolboy, recalls that on one occasion Thomas was discussing his latest poem with one of the masters when the master challenged Dylan to explain the meaning of the line, 'They toil powdered with a white music.' Dylan replied that he didn't know what it meant, that 'It simply came into my head and I think it's the best line I've written.' " [41]

While the young Dylan waited for other lines and images to come into his head, he read all the writers and books in reach. In later years he listed them: "Sir Thomas Browne, de Quincey, Henry Newbolt, the Ballads, Blake, Baroness Orczy, Marlowe, Chums, the Imagists, the Bible, Poe, Keats, Lawrence, Anon., and Shakespeare" (whom he "heard, read, and near-murdered in the first forms of my school").[42] In the upper forms Dylan went on to read the "moderns," of course: Yeats, Eliot, Hopkins, Housman, the Sitwells, Hardy, and Auden. In addition there were always the more obscure heroes of poetry that he discovered for himself—such as Thomas Lovell Beddoes, whom Thomas was constantly talking about when he first met Pamela Hansford Johnson. He was twenty at the time, and Beddoes was the perfect companion for his frustration. As F. L. Lucas wrote in the introduction to his selection of Beddoes that Thomas read (probably in 1933):

[41] Kent Thompson, "An Approach to the Early Poems of Dylan Thomas," *The Anglo-Welsh Review*, 14 (Winter, 1964–1965), 84.
[42] "Poetic Manifesto," 47, 48.

"*Tree of Nettles*"

"There are dawns, indeed, when to be young is 'very heaven'; the morning after is apt to be less celestial. Then the young pass from excessive enthusiasm to excessive melancholy, feeling they have been born out of due time." [43] But we are ahead of ourselves. It would be some years from the first forms, from green Cwmdonkin Park, before Thomas would "see the boys of summer in their ruin" (p. 1). He was still trailing Wordsworthian "clouds of glory" in grammar school, writing light, entertaining schoolboy verse, imitating all the poets he found congenial.

Thomas entered Swansea Grammar school when he was approaching eleven years of age and left about five and a half years later. He contributed to the school magazine every term, sometimes as many as three poems in a single issue. Occasionally he published poems in local newspapers, and toward the end of his schooldays he began the first of four extant poetry Notebooks.[44]

"The writers . . . who influenced my earliest poems and stories were, quite simply and truthfully, all the writers I was reading at the time," Thomas told a student in 1951.[45] He was seldom more simple or truthful. Particularly notable is the narrative influence of Thomas Hardy and A. E. Housman, extending back to the publication of "His Requiem" in the

[43] *Thomas Lovell Beddoes: An Anthology,* ed. F. L. Lucas (Cambridge, England, 1932), pp. xi–xii. This volume was shown to me by Pamela Hansford Johnson, who recalled receiving it from Thomas in June of 1934.

[44] Books kept mainly during the years 1930–1934 and containing versions of more than two hundred poems in various stages of completion—most in very rudimentary form. The Notebooks, in possession of the Lockwood Memorial Library, Buffalo, New York, are these: (1) 1930 Notebook, (2) 1930–1932 Notebook, (3) February, 1933, Notebook, (4) August, 1933, Notebook, and (5) a Red Prose Notebook. For detailed descriptions see Maud, pp. 121–148.

[45] Thomas, "Poetic Manifesto," 47.

Craft and Art of Dylan Thomas

Western Mail (January 14, 1927), when Thomas was twelve years old (and "Missing" published July, 1928). "His Requiem" tells of a "wicked old man" who had no friends or relatives and who went to his grave without a mourner, "Or so folks thought." But as the coffin passed through the old man's garden a bird's requiem

> Stole over the silence,
> And someone said:
> " 'Tis the little brown linnet the old man fed."

"Missing" opens:

> Seek him thou sun, in the dread wilderness
> For that he loved thee, seek him thou, and bless
> His upturned face with one divine caress.[46]

The veiled presence of the Romantic poets is constantly evident. One wonders whether Thomas's later antagonism to Wordsworth, for example, may not have sprung from an earlier infatuation—this is demonstrably the case with Rupert Brooke, a poet Thomas several times berated in his correspondence, but whom he imitated (with subsequent regret) when only twelve:

> Rose-red banners across the dawn,
> Brown sails at sea on a misty morn,
> Racing shadows across the corn,—
> These are the things I love.[47]

In the poems he published in *The Swansea Grammar School Magazine* during his early teens, Thomas often shows a style strangely compounded from various and indefinable Romantic poets. In March, 1928, for example, he published a poem beginning: "Calm and strange is this evening in the forest/

[46] *Swansea Grammar School Magazine*, XXV (July, 1928), 43.
[47] *Swansea Grammar School Magazine*, XXIV (July, 1927), 44.

24

"Tree of Nettles"

Carven domes of green are the trees." Occasionally the imitation is more specific. There is a Shelleyan touch in December, 1928: "Their pale, ethereal beauty seems to be/ The frail delicate breath of even-time"; and something of Keats in "Summer is heavy with age, and leans upon autumn,/ All the land is ripe" (March, 1928). The influence of Poe appears several places in the poetry, but nowhere as clearly as in a short story called "Brember" which obviously derived from "The Fall of the House of Usher."

By fifteen Thomas was analyzing modern poetry for his school magazine and showing a precocious knowledge of contemporary trends. In one essay he emphasized the influence of Hopkins, the Sitwells, and Eliot.[48] Modern poetry, he wrote, had its roots in Hopkins's "compressing the already unfamiliar imagery" and in the realism of Eliot's "Preludes." It seems somehow significant that Thomas should stress Hopkins's imagery rather than his rhythmic and auditory techniques. For Thomas himself would first absorb the image-making technique of Hopkins before he would attempt auditory effects like Hopkins's.

In his Notebooks, begun around the age of sixteen, Thomas began to record more individual ideas and poetic efforts. Most of these were inevitably childish, but they do show a new originality of mind, and many are embryonic versions of the most successful poems that were to appear in both *18 Poems* (1934) and *Twenty-Five Poems* (1936).[49]

[48] *Swansea Grammar School Magazine*, XXVI (December, 1929), 82–84.

[49] Cf. Maud, pp. 121–148. The Notebooks attest to the precocity of Thomas; as Maud says: "Before Thomas left school at sixteen and a half he had written 'The Spire Cranes' in a form close to its final published state in *The Map of Love* eight years afterwards." p. 122. But Maud has a tendency to make too much of the Notebooks. A few tentative jottings toward a poem do not constitute a poem, and the rela-

One of the most startling things that the Notebooks reveal is how Thomas could take an unpromising fragment, or a garbled beginning, and eventually come up with a fine poem. Poem 42 in the 1930 Notebook, for example, is an embryonic version of his later "How Shall My Animal." In terms of diction, image, rhythm, sound manipulation, and meaning, in all important aspects, the two poems are vastly different. The poet of sixteen with his "bitter certainty" and "bantering philistine" was certainly not the poet of twenty-four who could describe himself in terms of a "drunk . . . vineyard snail, flailed like an octopus." The immaturity of the early poem stands out in its every line and in its one-level theme. It is concerned only with poetry, whereas the later poem is concerned not only with poetry but also with the horror and implacable decay of death's "weird eyes."

From one view the Notebooks are the testings of a young poet seeking his own voice; from another view they are a series of passionate introspections into the conditions of existence. The poet of the Notebooks is obsessed with his body, with the potency of creation, with the horror of death, with the abolition of time and space in dream and in the creations of the imagination—all concerns that remained important throughout Thomas's work. Typically, the view of the Notebooks is that of

> the ascending boy
> The boy of woman and the wanton starer
> Marking the flesh and summer in the bay.
>
> (p. 54)

Although a "wanton starer," he is a frightened and horrified agent in the business of life. Caught between his wantonness

---

tionship between the Notebooks and *Collected Poems* is generally little more than that.

and his dread, he records a series of reactions—from delight to disgust, from faith in the purpose of the universe to blasphemy against any idea of terrestrial or cosmic order.

In a Notebook poem written in 1933 that summarizes his years from ten to fifteen, he makes clear the basic sexual tensions of his youth. He speaks of years hanging between heaven and hell, of dreams like those of Anthony in the desert, of going to sleep every night with the same old thoughts in his head. And the effect of Thomas's early environment, even that most publicly rejected, always persisted in his work. When, for example, in "A Prospect of the Sea" (1937), he described (in a series of Gordian metaphors) a young boy's initiation into sex, he placed in the mind of the boy these fears and warnings of childhood:

Now on the world-sized hill, with the trees like heavens holding up the weathers, in the magnified summer weather she leaned towards him so that he could not see the cornfield nor his uncle's house for her thick, red hair; and the sky and far ridge were points of light in the pupils of her eyes.

This is death, said the boy to himself, consumption and whooping-cough and the stones inside you and the death from playing with yourself.[50]

Along with opening exalted doors of the imagination, the formative influence of Bible and Chapel also helped to inculcate semblances of puritanism and God-consciousness.

These aspects of Thomas's character seldom showed themselves in his public life, although shortly before he died, in a moment of excruciating self-awareness, he did say to Elizabeth Reitell, "I am a Puritan!" [51] Caitlin Thomas, in her grim and wailing book, partially explains this attitude when she says:

[50] *Adventures in the Skin Trade and Other Stories* (Signet, New York, 1956), p. 131.
[51] Brinnin, *Dylan Thomas in America*, p. 263.

"There was one part of him that nobody could get at, that was impregnable, untouchable, not of his own making, but handed down from generations of close-tied, puritanical, family tradition." [52] After "three dark days in London," Thomas told Watkins, the city filled him with terror, and one of the causes of the terror was that in the city "there's no difference between good & bad." [53] The poem that followed this visit to London, "Because the Pleasure-bird Whistles" (p. 86), seems rightly read as Tindall reads it: "a Puritan's vision of Vanity Fair, the wicked city of destruction." [54]

Thomas provides a more horrible vision of Vanity Fair in the short story "Prologue to an Adventure":

As I walked through the wilderness of this world, as I walked through the wilderness, as I walked through the city with the loud electric faces and the crowded petrols of the wind dazzling and drowning me that winter night before the West died, I remembered the winds of the high, white world that bore me and the faces of a noiseless million in the busyhood of heaven staring on the afterbirth. [55]

The narrator is a man, a spirit, a hopeless man-spirit in a truly godless world: "See now, you shining ones, how the tuner of harps has fallen, and the painter of winds like a bag of henna into the gutter." There is no prophet to preach doom and damnation. Daniel rather "lurched after a painted shadow that led him, threading through smoke and dancers, to the stained window." The end of the story is apocalyptic consummation: "The sea of destruction lapped around our feet. We saw the

[52] Caitlin Thomas, *Leftover Life to Kill* (Boston, 1957), p. 58.
[53] Watkins, p. 49.
[54] William York Tindall, *A Reader's Guide to Dylan Thomas,* (New York, 1962), p. 145.
[55] *Adventures in the Skin Trade and Other Stories,* p. 146.

starfall that broke the night up. The glass lights on iron went out, and the waves grew down into the pavements." [56]

Thomas's Nonconformist upbringing also manifests itself in the intransigent Deity that lurks in the background of his early poetry and in a Manichean attitude toward sex. The Deity in Thomas is often an aloof, distant force, a Being to be associated with Job's tormentor, or with John's apocalyptic beast that comes

> Down . . . four padding weathers on the scarlet lands,
> Stalking my children's faces with a tail of blood.
>
> (p. 58)

Rhys Rhys, in the story "The Burning Baby," succinctly expresses Thomas's Manichean tendencies when he says, "The devil is . . . flesh." [57] This sentiment lies just beneath the surface of many of Thomas's poems and stories. "In their good bodies they saw evil for the first time," says the madman in "The Mouse and the Woman." [58] If the truth of life were known, "any boy of love," writes Thomas, perhaps thinking of his own Chapel days, would "look twice before he fell from grace" (p. 72). The lovers of "In My Craft or Sullen Art," who are in bed with "all their griefs" (p. 142), epitomize what happens to most lovers in Thomas's works when they go to bed: they find grief.

In the Notebooks, Thomas complains (at sixteen) about the stale actions of love and longs for a new dimension of love beyond sex. He says the animal is not sufficient and expresses the desire to dispense with animality (May 10, 1930). But neither is any other kind of love sufficient. Once rid of Eve he finds that the new love calls for sacrifice and yields no pleasure. Devoid of religious certainty, he longs for new certainty, new truth. At eighteen he laments that "truth" once lost is never

---

[56] *Ibid.*, p. 150.   [57] *Ibid.*, p. 96.   [58] *Ibid.*, p. 116.

again found. In a Notebook entry for August, 1932, Thomas regrets the loss of that truth that could make the deaf hear and the blind see. He says he will remember until he dies the moment he lost that truth. In an entry on February 17, 1933, he cries for belief although he has no faith. The certainty he craves he will build from myth and symbol, spending twenty years in the building, and the more desperate becomes his craving the heavier he will lean upon his symbolic universe.

Paradoxically, Thomas depended for his new symbolic universe on a structure he rejected—the Chapel. Although he rejected the message, he did not reject the terms of that message. Nor did he believe in the definitions usually given the words, but he believed in the words. God-devil, heaven-hell, spirit-flesh, preacher, sermon, message, dogma, word—these, above all the sense of dichotomy imparted by the first of these terms, are the cells out of which Thomas's imagination developed. They are equivocal terms in that Thomas often used them inconsistently and paradoxically. The terms are always viewed as symbols, that is, as representations of unseen and incomprehensible forces. Most often they have direct reference to the body—thus God could be a moment of love, the devil the absence of love. The directing power of chromosomes was to Thomas a god; the madness that accompanied sterile attempts at writing he felt to be the devil.

Although Thomas's imagination can be reduced to a few sets of antinomies, it is of course not his imagination when thus reduced, any more than a critical analysis of *King Lear* is Shakespeare's play; any more than it is life when we say man exists between love and hate, fear and desire, freedom and necessity. But the view of Thomas as a naif is not entirely wrong. What becomes more clear the better one knows Thomas is that both intellectually and artistically he is more complicated when young than when old. His lyrical gift matured early, as is common among romantic poets. That he could expand so competently on his early work is, in a sense, testimony of a particular kind of poetic genius. There is, on the other hand, the feeling that Thomas as a young man confronted the contradictions of life with great intelligence and enthusiasm. At twenty he lectured in print an elder writer, Alfred Haffenden, telling him to

read more and read deeper, clean up his diction, and forget the hyphen. He must learn, not through the protests of reviewers, but through the literature of the mind of Europe . . . , that poetry which is written for "all time" is written in and out of its own time. . . . There must be no compromise. His living message must be in living language. Let him read Yeats and Rilke, reach his phrasing independently, and have no fear of the blue pencil.[59]

Introduced to the Chapel by his mother, Thomas was introduced to atheism by his father. He once described his father, for whom he had great love and respect, as a "militant atheist." But the father's atheism, like many of the son's attitudes, was strangely inconsistent. Thomas explained that it "had nothing to do with whether there was a god or not, but with a violent and personal dislike for God. He would glare out of the window and growl, 'It's raining, blast Him!'" [60]

This inverse theology resembles several of Thomas's own statements about God. In "A Prospect of the Sea," Thomas writes of the boy: "He did not believe in God, but God had made this summer full of blue winds and heat and pigeons in the house wood." [61]

[59] Dylan Thomas, in a review of a poetic tract by Alfred Haffenden, *Adelphi,* IX (February, 1935), 317–318.

[60] Marjorie Adix, "Dylan Thomas: Memories and Appreciations, IV," *Encounter,* II (January, 1954), 16.

[61] *Adventures in the Skin Trade and Other Stories,* p. 130.

Craft and Art of Dylan Thomas

Whether from his own father, or from the circle of unortho-
dox intellectual friends of his middle and late teens, Thomas
must have had some knowledge of Nietzsche. (Constantine
FitzGibbon, Thomas's authorized biographer, once told me
that the elder Thomas was a Nietzschean.) The "death of god,"
the *Übermensch* (in the sense of the man who overcomes,
the man of self-realization, of higher states of consciousness),
and recurrence: these Nietzschean commonplaces are clearly
evident in Thomas's writings. At the age of fifteen Thomas
was already tending toward the *Übermensch*. Man, he wrote in
his 1930 Notebook, will be aware of his divinity when the
right moment in history arrives. Curiously, Thomas saw his
own emphasis on the physical, proceeding as it did from a frail
adolescence and a sickly childhood, as comparable to
Nietzsche's condition. In his correspondence he develops the
idea that the physically weak tend to emphasize what they
lack.[62] A fearful self-consciousness, he explained, prevented
him from developing this thought further.

But of more importance than either Nietzsche or his own
frailties in dramatizing his own and man's mortality was the
progressively worsening cancer of the throat and tongue that
afflicted the elder Thomas during Dylan's late teens. The
prescience of death imbedded itself deeply in the imagination
of the young poet and never left him. Knowledge, enlightenment, pleasure, the passing of all superstitious and moral
fear, none of these would overcome the dread of death. A
Notebook entry of July, 1933, which, again, I am unfortu-
nately not allowed to quote, equates Mother Goose tales and
the story of God walking with Adam in the evening as fibs told
to children. Although free from these fibs, there is still one

---

[62] P.H.J. Correspondence.

ghostly tale that binds—the tale of death—which makes the hair of boys and girls stand on end.

When one looks back from the vantage point of the complete work, Blake's influence looms large in Thomas's attempt to find fresh symbols for the old forms of Chapel and country. Although many of Thomas's ideas and attitudes —from anagrams to mysticism—could have been influenced by any number of poets, only Blake could have provided models for so many of Thomas's interests. It is Blake's name alone and Blake's words that one finds in the crucial formative years. The exact extent of Thomas's knowledge of Blake is open to conjecture, but Thomas evidently read Blake off and on throughout his youth and young manhood. In 1951 he could recall Blake as an "incomparable and inimitable" master.[63] One of the first things he wrote to Pamela Hansford Johnson twenty years earlier was: I am in the path of Blake, but so far behind him that only the wings of his heels are in sight. Ruthven Todd supplies the rather unexpected information that Thomas not only read Blake deeply and intelligently, but that he also read S. Foster Damon's superb study of Blake's ideas and symbols.[64]

The first clear signs of Blake's influence appear sometime between 1929 and 1931. In the 1930 Notebook there are journeyman imitations of the "Songs of Innocence." The fifteen-year-old Thomas wrote of the shepherd blowing upon his reed and of all the creatures in the forest that feed on the music of golden throats. In the 1933 Notebook there are more

[63] Thomas, "A Poetic Manifesto," 47.
[64] S. Foster Damon, *William Blake: His Philosophy and Symbols* (Boston, 1924). This was told to Lita Hornick by Ruthven Todd and is quoted in her dissertation, "The Intricate Image: A Study of Dylan Thomas," (Columbia University, 1958), p. 5.

polished imitations, including one that uses such Blakean images as lepers and lambs, babes and dams. Even before this, in 1931, there were clear signs of a new searching of the imagination, a searching, again, with Blakean overtones:

> These thousand pebbles are a thousand eyes.
> Each sharper than the sun;
> These waves are dancers;
> Upon a thousand, pointed toes
> They step the sea,
> Lightly, as in a pantomime.[65]

One of Blake's most famous descriptions of the living universe is contained in his letter to Thomas Butts (October 2, 1800):

> Each grain of sand
> Every stone on the Land
> Cloud, Meteor and Star
> Are men seen afar.

This is in Keynes's 1927 edition of Blake, which was readily accessible to Thomas and was most likely, in fact, the book that he received as a Christmas present in 1933.

The world of Thomas's poetry, early and late, is an animated world in which he would speak to the heavens and the heavens would speak to him in return. The known, received, accepted norms of knowledge and evaluation have been discarded in favor of unknown means of perception. Blake, says Joyce Cary, recalling his own encounter with that poet, demolishes the material universe "into imaginative construction and states of feeling where matter, mind and emotion become simply different aspects of one reality."[66] For Thomas the Blakean destruction of the material universe was finally a

---

[65] This example is quoted by Suzanne Roussillat in Tedlock, pp. 4, 5.
[66] Joyce Cary in an unpublished essay, quoted in Andrew Wright, *Joyce Cary: A Preface to His Novels* (New York, 1958), p. 22.

means of overcoming the dread of death—a means, his letters to Trevor Hughes reveal, not completely successful: In one letter, for example, he remarks how easy it is for him *to say*, as Blake did, "Death to me is no more than going into another room." But how difficult for him to believe it.[67]

The physical limitations of man and the possibility of human capabilities in all parts of the inanimate world fascinated Thomas throughout his career, but especially during his formative years. His letters repeatedly comment on the limitations of his senses. He complains specifically about man's partial vision. When a man sees a tree, he sees only one aspect of the tree, whereas the appearance of the tree to a star or to an insect can only be conveyed by the imagination. For Thomas, the materialist was the man who believes that his vision of the tree is the whole reality, whereas the spiritualist believes in a great deal more than what is revealed to the physical eye.[68]

Pantheism seemed to Thomas an involvement with life at a lesser stage of being, at a lesser stage of intensity. In pantheism, Thomas felt, all the potentialities of man were not realized. In Thomas's canon there had to be thought, not a rational process but some vital activity which, to Thomas, was equivalent to thought. It is not possible to discern this distinction in Thomas's later poetry, and we would be hard put to demonstrate it convincingly even in his earlier poetry if it were not for the correspondence and critical dictums contained in his reviews.

Perhaps the beginning of Thomas's antipantheism is a misconception, an identification of pantheism with the pathetic fallacy. But of more importance in shaping his thought was an unalterable conviction that man makes the world, the world does not make man. As one of Blake's proverbs states: "Where

[67] Letter to Trevor Hughes (January 12, 1934), in Lockwood Memorial Library, Buffalo, New York.
[68] P.H.J. Correspondence.

man is not nature is barren." Nature is not to be worshiped, Thomas insisted to Pamela Hansford Johnson. Nature is what we make it. Man, Thomas claimed, tells the sun to stop and tells the sun to go on. Thomas occasionally so emphasized the supremacy of man that he once surmised he might think through the medium of rain, as he then thought through the medium of cells.

According to these terms, Thomas was a spiritualist. He seems even to have endeavored to appraise visionaries according to whether they were "pantheistic" or "mystic." He condemned Wordsworth as a "human nannygoat with a pantheistic obsession." Although not too precise about the refinements of pantheism, Thomas makes it clear that he disliked Wordsworth because he was a "moralizer," and because he "hadn't a spark of *mysticism*." [69]

Thomas distinguished between "moralizing" and dogmatism. He felt the great poet should be a dogmatist and praised Blake for being dogmatic. Dogmatism was desirable for Thomas when it derived from a private searching and evaluation unrelated to the received laws of society or religion. One moralized when one depended on received opinions; one dogmatized when one was willing to build his rational frame on an irrational base. Mysticism for Thomas as for Blake was a kind of radical pragmatism; a mystic, he said, is the man who takes the world exactly as it is. And what the world "is" to Thomas was mysterious, not a series of laws based on materialistic and rationalistic deceptions. Life, Thomas stressed, was not proved by thinking but by being. For Thomas the proof of existence lay in the answer to one question, and that question had nothing to do with the mechanics of living, but only with

[69] These phrases were recalled by Lady Snow, the former Pamela Hansford Johnson, in conversation with me.

Being. Man, Thomas said, is overly concerned with action and does not believe Blake's "Thought Is Action." [70]

Thomas has always been identified with the pantheistic vitalism of D. H. Lawrence, and it would seem that he inclined that way in his life and in many of his poems. Lawrence, however, is one of the few writers whom Thomas attacked with violence. In a 1935 review, Thomas linked together many of his favorite ideas to reject the Lawrentian ethos. He dismissed Lawrence because "he was primarily concerned with achievement of a pagan content. There is no pagan literature." [71] This sounds curiously like something written from an orthodox religious viewpoint, but such is not the case. Underlying Thomas's condemnation is no Christian orthodoxy, at least none that Thomas would have admitted or recognized. Although he wrote to Trevor Hughes on January 12, 1934, that he held paganism a great evil, his correspondence makes clear that his rejection of paganism, which he defined as sex and sun, is based on the feeling that paganism denied an unseen but real world and that Lawrence would have *written nothing* if he had not been prevented by disease from following a life of complete sensuality. Thomas, with no small amount of Puritanism and a good deal of self-knowledge, resented Lawrence because he felt that phallic consciousness, star and sex equilibrium, would mean the death of art. Thomas wanted to see creativity perpetuated, not phased out, by sexual bliss; Thomas sensed that art is born in pain and loved art more than the elimination of that pain. Thomas's argument, of course, does not allow for the complexities of Lawrence; it is, Thomas would be the first to admit, a dogmatic judgment. Thomas resented Lawrence on other grounds, however;

[70] P.H.J. Correspondence.   [71] Thomas, "Review," *Adelphi*, 317.

namely, economic. With an almost prophetic insight Thomas saw that Lawrence's world was based on a kind of totalitarian capitalism. In the early thirties Thomas was passionately, if sporadically, devoted to the Revolution, and in a strange fusion of Communism, Christianity, and Blake he envisioned a new state which, following Haffenden, he calls the state of Christhood. It is in this state that the sovereign law, "the law of libertarian love, is fulfilled." Thomas explains this fulfillment as coming "through the communism, the spiritual immediacy of the Christ in man. The state of pagan bliss produces nothing but pagan children, a brood contented with the social purpose of any civilization so long as their hot and seedy streams do not dry up. The state of Christhood produces a love-dictated progeny and a communal art." [72]

Through Blake, Thomas came to believe in the possibility of finding this Christhood in symbology. He cared nothing for Christ in a theological sense, he said, but cared very much for Christ as a symbol. And he praised Blake not for his wisdom, or his "message," but for his poetry and especially for his "monstrous mythology."

If we pursue the relationship between Lawrence and Thomas one step further, we shall discover one of the essential outlines not only of Thomas's emergent imagination but of his mature imagination.

Despite Thomas's rejection of Lawrence's "paganism," one can find in the works of the two men passage after passage that are in near-perfect accord. Here, for instance, is a passage from Lawrence's *Apocalypse* which could be cited as the *fons et origo* of a major part of Thomas's work:

For man, the vast marvel is to be alive. For man as for flower, beast and bird [a trinity Thomas invokes in his "Refusal to

[72] *Ibid.*

Mourn"], the supreme triumph is to be most vividly, most perfectly alive. Whatever the unborn and dead may know, they cannot know the beauty, the marvel of being alive in the flesh. The dead may look after the afterwards. But the magnificent here and now of life in the flesh is ours, and ours alone, and ours for only a time. We ought to dance with rapture that we should be alive in the flesh, and part of the living incarnate cosmos. I am part of the sun as my eye is part of me. That I am part of the earth my feet know perfectly, and my blood is part of the sea. My soul knows that I am part of the human race, my soul is an organic part of the great human soul, as my spirit is part of my nation. In my very own self I am part of my family. There is nothing of me that is alone and absolute except my mind, and we shall find that the mind has no existence by itself, it is only the glitter of the sun on the surface of the waters.[73]

While Thomas and Lawrence were one in their veneration of the *life force*, important differences separate the degree and the end of their veneration. These differences are evident in several particulars, most clearly in their respective attitudes toward death. Lawrence accepts death and looks forward to it as a release. Thomas, in his work, never admits the existence of death as it is generally understood—a state of nonexistence. "Furious/ Drunk as a vineyard snail, flailed like an octopus" (p. 100), Thomas strove with all his creative strength to reveal creativity in death. The Lawrentian view of death, except in such rare instances as Birkin's enigmatic remark in *Women in Love* about the perpetuity of life through love, is of rest, a desirable quietus. Two of Lawrence's poems are fine expressions of this reaction.

> Build then the ship of death, for you must take
> The longest journey, to oblivion.
> ("The Ship of Death," Part V)

[73] *Apocalypse* (London, 1931), p. 223.

If there were not an utter and absolute dark
of silence and sheer oblivion
at the core of everything,
how terrible the sun would be,
how ghastly it would be to strike a match, and make a light

. . . . .

But dipped, once dipped in dark oblivion
the soul has peace, inward and lovely peace.

("The End, The Beginning")

Such attitudes do not exist in Thomas. There is neither rest
nor peace in his vision of death; there is rather an alleluia of all
the earth's potential energy. When Thomas builds his ark of
death ("Prologue"), which is a refutation of Lawrence rather
than an imitation of him as most critics claim, the conclusion of
the poem is a burst of "Huloo," and "Ahoy"; the ark *sings* and
the flood tide of death *flowers*. Again, in his final birthday
poem, "Poem on His Birthday," Thomas cried out:

> the closer I move
> To death, one man through his sundered hulks,
> The louder the sun blooms
> And the tusked, ramshackling sea exults.

(p. 193)

Death in Thomas is not simply a matter of "Huloo" and
"Ahoy," a rousing cheer and "into the breach." It is a matter of
ultimate dread and loathing at one extreme ("If I Were
Tickled by the Rub of Love") and a refusal to admit to death,
a mysticism of perpetuity, at the other extreme. It is the
loathing of death, in conjunction with the leftover life of
Christianity and Blake's symbol-making, that begot, in
Thomas's work one of the most individual and clear expressions of the infinitude of man in modern poetry.

Thomas's ideas on the indestructibility of matter and, by

40

extension, of man were fully developed by the age of twenty.
[All around him, he said, he could feel a spirit creating and
destroying and resurrecting a body. He did not believe in the
Christ of tradition, but he saw Christ as a symbol of victory
over death.[74] Put that baldly, it sounds too much like something from the rejected sermons of the Chapel. Thomas found
a poetic way of expressing it when he wrote, "My Jack of
Christ born thorny on the tree" (p. 15). The only tree on
which Christ was "born" was the tree of Calvary. Here we
have [Thomas working with a favorite paradox, one that he
will use again in the first sonnet of the "Altarwise" sequence:
the moment of birth ushers in the moment of death; even more
paradoxically, the moment of death is a new kind of birth.]

In the same year, 1934, Thomas was emphasizing that he
believed in basing his poetry on the flesh—especially on dead
flesh. He accused other modern poets of making the living
flesh into a carcass, and proudly stated that his object was to
take the dead flesh and, with the optimism born of an un-
quenchable faith in life, to fashion something living from the
dead.[75] Thomas did not always retain the same degree of
"positivity," but he always retained a sufficient amount of belief and faith to achieve, eventually, a vision of symbolic regeneration.

[74] P.H.J. Correspondence.
[75] *Ibid.* Thomas's association of birth and death coupled with his
anthropomorphic view of the world (primarily in sexual terms) led
him not only to view the grave as a Freudian womb, but, further, to see
the grave as a lover and death as the "lyrical/ Aggression of love in a
bridal broth"; in this depiction the earth is the bed in which the slow
copulation of decay is consummated—"continent-sheeted . . . with
animal rails/ And a tucked crust of fossils." Thomas commented to
Watkins on these lines from an early version of "Unluckily for a
Death": "I am not sure of the word 'animal' . . . ; it says more or
less what I mean, that the rails, the frame if you like, of the bed of the
grave is living, sensual, serpentine." Watkins, p. 63.

These, then, are some of the influences on and the dimensions of Thomas's art. For Wales, the Chapel, Blake, traditions of English poetry—such influences not only helped shape *18 Poems* but were of equal importance in defining the whole scope of Thomas's work. The identity of man and his world, the sense of perpetual Genesis where man is each moment discovering fresh wonder and fresh horror, the craving for old order in a new disorder, the immensity of physical and imaginative potency, the uncharted wonder of dreams and passion—these, with constant modification, remained the great concerns of Thomas's art. Such concerns, and they will be amply demonstrated in all their variety in *Collected Poems*, must inevitably have affected Thomas's "attitude toward poetry." It is now time to consider that attitude, not only as it was in 1934, but as expressed throughout his poetry and prose.

II
THOMAS'S CONCEPTION OF POETRY

Thomas's ideas on poetry and his conception of the role of poet are fully developed in his prose and in his poems. A poet's critical statements, as Eliot has reminded us, may be of little esthetic importance, but they are of great interest in revealing what kind of work the poet himself desired to produce.

Thomas saw poetry in the most varied perspectives. At one extreme it was simply "work," at the other it was an inspired act of love; at one time it was "the inner splendor," at another it was a "passion for self-glorification." [76] "Poetry, to a poet," said Thomas, "is the most rewarding work in the world." [77] He once wrote to Vernon Watkins, "The one thing that's saving me—saving me, I mean, not from any melodramatic issues but

[76] Dylan Thomas, letter of November 6, 1952, to Marguerite Caetani, in "Three Letters," *Botteghe Oscure*, XIII (1954), 100.
[77] *Quite Early One Morning*, p. 192.

just from sheer unhappiness—is lots and lot of work." [78] Perhaps the most idealistic statement he makes in the poems themselves is in the justifiably popular "In My Craft or Sullen Art." [79] Here poetry is

> Exercised in the still night
> When only the moon rages
> And the lovers lie abed
> With all their griefs in their arms,
> I labour by singing light
> Not for ambition or bread
>
> .   .   .   .   .
>
> But for the common wages
> Of their most secret heart.

(p. 142)

Of course, Thomas did write for ambition and bread, and probably he would have agreed with Samuel Johnson's judgment that "no man but a blockhead ever wrote except for money." But he constructed this romanticized view of the poet in order to describe an ideal devotion to the craft and art. To convey the poet's loneliness and sacrifice, the lovers must lie abed and the writer's heart must be devoid of ambition. The "truth" of the poem lies not in its depiction of life as it is lived, certainly not as Thomas lived it, but in its portrayal of life as it might be lived. The truth of the portrayal lies in the glimpse it gives us of one who sees the poet singing for the grieving lovers of the world.

Though no more valid as an expression of Thomas's attitude toward his work, it balances the picture to see his poetry as

---

[78] Watkins, p. 25.

[79] Perhaps another romantic aspect of this poem is implied in Watkins's remark that Thomas never wrote at night but "in the day, usually in the afternoon, . . . never in the evening which he regarded as the social time of the day." *Ibid.,* p. 13.

sullenness rather than as a plaintive song sung for "lovers lying abed." Even if we had no biographical evidence, the poetry itself would tell of the sullenness, of the "unruly scrawl/ That utters all love hunger/ And tells the page the empty ill" ("My Hero Bares His Nerves," p. 11). There is in Thomas the bitterness of the poet who spends himself, who "sheds [his] syllabic blood" (p. 19), and that of the poet who is unable to spend himself:

On no work of words now for three lean months in the bloody
Belly of the rich year and the big purse of my body
I bitterly take to task my poverty and craft.

(p. 104)

Thomas provides an illuminating gloss on this "dejection ode" in an early 1934 letter—if the anachronism can be overlooked. In this letter Thomas said writing poetry was a physically painful task, and from this real, screaming pain often resulted only a line, meaningless as Sanskrit. At times like this Thomas felt himself a freak, and compared himself to a hyena sitting up all night in pain, writing poetry that was only a strange noise in his bowels.[80]

Thomas's art is also sullen because it requires something more than seriousness. The process by which the poet draws "from the treasures of man" is not a carefree process. For, "to take [in order] to give is all," and it is a task which Thomas could not lightly shirk because it is part of life "which is each man's work" (p. 104).

Thomas's "work" was poetry, which he felt was a contribution to reality. When he said it was the responsibility of the poet "to know and to feel . . . all that is moving around and within him," he was expressing a variant of Keats's notion of "negative capability." He was choosing a way of arriving at

[80] P.H.J. Correspondence.

truth. He could say with Blake, and most poets since Blake, "I will not reason and compare; my business is to create" ("Jerusalem," Part 10). Thomas's *means* were much less those of Blake than of Keats, with whom he would have asked, "Oh, for a life of sensation rather than of thought." For Thomas, as for most poets, abstract speculation upon the primary relationships into which man enters—birth, suffering, love-sex-reproduction, death—only teased him "out of thought," but the senses, the truth of the heart's affections, told him immediately and directly what is real, what is worthwhile, what is lasting about existence. "When logics die,/ The secret of the soil grows through the eye" (p. 30). The medium in which this sensuous apprehension of reality was expressed, the only medium in which it could be expressed, was poetry. It is in this sense that Thomas could claim, "A good poem is a contribution to reality. The world is never the same once a good poem has been added to it. A good poem helps to change the shape and significance of the universe, helps to extend everyone's knowledge of himself and the world around him." [81]

Everywhere in the prose and poetry we see the artist at work with his insights, but from slight modification in his treatment of similar subjects we can infer some difference between Thomas's attitude toward poetry and his attitude toward prose.

In the prose there are numerous stories about writers and writing, not only Thomas's most hilarious work, *Portrait of the Artist as a Young Dog,* but a number of stories symbolically exploring the creative process, such as "The Orchards," "The Visitor," and "The Mouse and the Woman." Nearly all of *Adventures in the Skin Trade and Other Stories* is concerned with the subconscious, dream symbolism, the relation-

[81] *Quite Early One Morning,* p. 192.

ship between the inner and the outer worlds. But in none of these stories is there the exhaustive comprehensiveness of "I, in My Intricate Image," (pp. 40–44) which treats of his methods and intentions in writing. This poem is so finely wrought intellectually that almost everything this book has thus far said may be conceived of as a direct or indirect commentary on that one poem.

Perhaps a better example, because much more readily observable, is Thomas's treatment of childhood. In his prose, childhood is rendered with warmth, humanity, touches of Dickens and Rabelais under a new dispensation. Here is a typical episode from a 1939 story:

One afternoon, in a particularly bright and glowing August, some years before I knew I was happy, George Hooping, whom we called Little Cough, Sidney Evans, Dan Davies, and I sat on the roof of a lorry travelling to the end of the Peninsula. It was a tall, six-wheeled lorry, from which we could spit on the roofs of the passing cars and throw our applestumps at women on the pavement. One stump caught a man on a bicycle in the middle of the back, he swerved across the road, for a moment we sat quiet and George Hooping's face grew pale. And if the lorry runs over him, I thought calmly as the man on the bicycle swayed towards the hedge, he'll get killed and I'll be sick on my trousers and perhaps on Sidney's too, and we'll all be arrested and hanged, except George Hooping who didn't have an apple.

But the lorry swept past; behind us, the bicycle drove into the hedge, the man stood up and waved his fist, and I waved my cap back at him.[82]

Contrast this to Thomas's most famous poetic depiction of childhood, "Fern Hill" (1945). In the poem the child is

[82] "Extraordinary Little Cough," *Portrait of the Artist as a Young Dog*, p. 65.

mythic; in the prose the child is realistic, Welsh, and of the twentieth century.

There is, furthermore, a nightmare effect of dread and madness in his prose which is far less frequent in his poetry. Many of his stories were struck off quickly, he allegedly dictated some, and the stories in his notebooks were published with only a few minor changes. In the working and reworking of his poems Thomas exorcized a certain amount of nightmarish reality. As he wrote in one of his letters, polishing words removes their madness and preserves their bluntness.[83]

The symbols in his early stories are chaotic; the symbols in his early poetry seem ordered and subdued by comparison. In the former he seems more content to leave an impression of chaos; in the latter he seems struggling with a puzzle that he has not completely mastered, but the pieces of which do have a rational order—if it be only the closer order of words and sounds. Although the poetry may be agonizingly opaque, there is always the sense of an exquisitely finished form; the prose, on the other hand, is often an experimental reaching—and Thomas seemed willing to leave it at just that stage. This is true, it must be stressed, only of the prose up to 1939; that prose is a kind of trial poetry. Or, as Thomas explained it: "When you are young you are liable to write this bastard thing, a prose-poetry. When you get a bit older you find they get separated, and prose becomes more clean and spare." [84]

In his scattered and unsystematic comments on his own poetry and on the poetry of others, Thomas employed a handful of related words which carried the burden of his thought. Words such as *freshness, intensity, concentration,*

[83] P.H.J. Correspondence.
[84] Harvey Breit, "Talks with Dylan Thomas," in *A Casebook*, p. 196.

and *magic* suggest both Thomas's thematic obsessions and desiderata of style. They are, in Coleridge's sense of the word, "incantations."

Thomas's poems, he felt, would be "fresh" if they contained frequent and actual accounts of physical life. It was from life at the fingertips that not only freshness stemmed but truth as well. For Thomas's mind, in fact, freshness and truth were synonymous. The poetry which Thomas felt lacked freshness he also felt lacked truth, and the reason for the shortcoming was the same in both instances—the failure to render life from a physical perspective. In his correspondence, Thomas stressed that all ideas and actions began in the body. As a result, he insisted, the best way to render a thought or action, however abstract, was to express it in as physical a way as possible. Every thought, for him, could find an equivalent in blood, flesh, or gland. He saw it as his particular task to find and express all the equations between body and world, between body and idea.[85]

There are grave limitations in simply feeling one's way through the world, of course, and Thomas was well aware of them. When we talk about a poet living the life of sensation, we mean that the physical, sensuous awareness merges with the intellectual, cognitive awareness. The poet really says neither "I feel" nor "I think," he says "I both feel and think." This is, at least, what Thomas meant when he praised the epistemological value of the senses. In a series of New Year's resolutions for 1934, he resolved not to distinguish between the rational and the irrational, but to try to create through his imagination a single attitude.[86] Even earlier he had dichotomized young writers into those stressing the body and those stressing the intelligence. He recognized the need for both tendencies, but

[85] P.H.J. Correspondence.   [86] *Ibid.*

if he had to make a choice, he said, he would choose intelligence over flesh. In his correspondence he clearly recognizes the difficulty of achieving a flesh-not flesh equilibrium, and, while admitting that the more direct pleasure is derived from the body, he praises the life of the mind and spirit—even if physically unsatisfying—as having a capability for development, for creating art, for achieving infinity.[87] What Thomas meant exactly by infinity he did not explain. But a poet's sensations, as Colvin says of Keats, not only are of the body but are "intuitions of the mind and spirit . . . independent of consecutive stages and formal processes of thinking." [88]

Thomas's poetry would struggle for freshness not only in the ordinary fashion of revitalizing language but also in its stress on the identity of body and spirit, in its examination of the world through the senses as enlightened by poetic insight. His mind stalks "the trees and the slant sap's tunnel/ . . . the green steps and spire," where he abides, like a Buddhist in the surrender of *satori:*

> with the wooden insect in the tree of nettles,
> In the glass bed of grapes with snail and flower;
> Hearing the weather fall.

(p. 41)

It is Blake's admonition that we should see through the eye, not with the eye (as well as world–human body identifications), that sums up recurrent perspectives in Thomas's work. Thomas knew that a total perception, not the perception of any one sense, would reveal the secrets of man's mysterious existence. As Blake expressed it in *The Marriage of Heaven and Hell* (Plate 14):

[87] *Ibid.*
[88] Sir Sidney Colvin, *John Keats: His Life and Poetry* (New York, 1917), p. 155.

If the doors of perception were cleansed everything would appear to man as it is, infinite.

For man has closed himself up, till he sees all things thro' narrow chinks of his cavern.

To see through the eye and not with it meant for Thomas to see with his whole body, with all his senses, especially with his "heart." The witness of the heart for Thomas, as for all true romantics, is the supreme witness:

> My one and noble heart has witnesses
> In all love's countries, that will grope awake;
> And when blind sleep drops on the spying senses,
> The heart is sensual, though five eyes break.
>
> (p. 90)

When one sees the world from the inside, a true awareness is attained, as the word *insight* itself implies. For Thomas, *intensity* was a synonym for *insight*, and both words meant a quality of vividness that made itself most apparent in a sense of conflict. His most famous description of this quality is contained in a letter to Treece in which he talked about his warring images. "Any sequence of my images," he said, "must be a sequence of creations, recreations, destructions, contradictions. . . . Out of the inevitable conflict of images—inevitable, because of the creative, recreative, destructive and contradictory nature of the motivating centre, . . . —I try to make that momentary peace which is a poem." [89] He once applied the same principle of struggle or conflict to words

[89] Henry Treece, *Dylan Thomas: "Dog Among the Fairies"* (London, 1956), p. 37. This statement to Treece has proved to be one of the most celebrated statements on the image-making process ever made by a poet. I shall return to it several times in the course of this study, but I would like to emphasize here, at the outset, that this statement does not make Thomas a "surrealist." Just the opposite; the statement and the letter reaffirm the importance of the critical function of poetic intelli-

when he cryptically complained to Watkins that the words in one of Watkins's poems did not strive against each other: "They do not cancel each other out." [90] Another time he complained that a certain poem was "literary," not fresh and living, and concluded, "I don't ask you for vulgarity, though I miss it; I think I ask you for a little creative destruction, destructive creation." [91]

This sense of vibrant life was something Thomas felt that the poetic craftsman could impart to his work if he took the pains to do so. It was not the sufficient cause of that "magic of poetry" which Thomas repeatedly talked of, but it was a necessary cause. Sheer labor expended would impart some of the sense of intensity. "Poetry," he said early in his career, "depends in its intensity on the strength of the labour put into the creation. . . . The laziest workman receives the fewest impulses." [92]

If we consider that the end of all Thomas's struggle and conflict was "that momentary peace which is a poem," we can

gence. Immediately following the passage quoted by Treece (the whole letter is in Lockwood Memorial Library) are these lines: "Reading back over that, I agree it looks preciously like nonsense. To say that I 'let' images breed and conflict is to deny my critical part in the business." In his "Poetic Manifesto," Thomas goes into great detail to explain Surrealism and to disassociate himself from their beliefs and practices. "One method the Surrealists used in their poetry was to juxtapose words & images that had no rational relationship; and out of this they hoped to achieve a kind of subconscious, real, imaginative world of the mind. . . .

"This is, very crudely, the credo of the Surrealists, and one with which I profoundly disagree."

[90] Watkins, p. 29.

[91] Watkins, p. 38. In this same passage he said, "I can see the sensitive picking of words, but none of the strong, inevitable pulling that makes a poem an event, a happening, an action perhaps, not a still-life or an experience put down, placed, regulated."

[92] *Quite Early One Morning*, pp. 188, 189.

see that his ideas about intensity are not really so unusual. The activity that springs from Coleridge's secondary Imagination is, like Thomas's intensity, guided by a "synthetic and magical power." And Coleridge's Imagination, *"laxis effetur habenis,* reveals itself in the balance and reconcilement of opposite and discordant qualities," much as Thomas felt his warring images were "reconciled for a moment." What should be immediately apparent, furthermore, is the link between Thomas's attitude toward poetry and his latter-day Coleridgean strictures regarding ambiguity, polysemy, paradox, and tension.

In his remark that his poetry is obscure because of "rigorous compression" Thomas comes close to putting his poetic dialectic into terms relevant to practical criticism. It was this rigorous compression to which he was referring when he wrote that his words contained no "diffusion or dilution" and that everything was being tightly packed away in "a mad-doctor's bag." [93] He reached a point where his language implied so much that it seemed to say nothing, and he complained of this fact in April, 1936—just about the time he was completing the last of the sonnets, which were the most ambiguous poems he ever wrote.

Intensity in Thomas's mind was not simply a means for evoking the magic of poetry, the emotional responses. Though he always sought to convey the original impulse—"what in a poem makes you laugh, cry, prickle, be silent"—he insisted that only close examination could do justice to the full meaning of the poem. He expected his poems to create some kind of immediate emotional response, but, even more important, he expected sincere readers to take time to work through his "artifices and obscurities." "Only the printed page, or the interior monologue, or private discussion is able to give the

[93] Watkins, p. 25.

poem the time it is justified in asking," [94] Thomas insisted. In brief, what Thomas praised in other poetry and what he sought in his own was not breadth of incident and theme but intensity of vision, what he once described as the "immense, momentous scrawl on the leaf—the peculiar power of minute concentration." [95]

For a time Thomas fostered obscurity as a structural device. Obscurity was a formal sign of struggle, and struggle was in turn a metaphor for life. This attitude may have sprung in part from a youthful disdain for the established poets. If newness or freshness could not be achieved by a statement of immediate force and compelling strength, as in his "straight poems" (The Hand That Signed the Paper"), then freshness might be achieved by a sense of verbal, thematic, or imagistic struggle. When the intensity of a particular poem was contained, when the conflicting imagery was "reconciled," when the complex emotions that gave rise to the poem were somehow ordered—even if only by their expression in words—then the magic of poetry was achieved. "And the best poem," Thomas explained, "is that whose worked-upon unmagical passages come closest, in texture and intensity, to those moments of magical accident." [96]

Among other things, intensity meant shock and implication to Thomas. The shock, as we have seen, could be conveyed by choice of subject matter, by use of unexpected words and points of view. But how did one convey implication? When Thomas told Treece that much of the obscurity in his poems was "due to rigorous compression; the last thing they do is to flow; they are . . . rather hewn," [97] he was describing a com-

[94] "A Few Words of a Kind," Caedmon Records, Vol. 3.
[95] Watkins, p. 25.　　[96] *Quite Early One Morning*, p. 192.
[97] Treece, p. 121.

mon method of achieving esthetic effects. A similar concept of compression lies behind Poe's dictum against "long poems." Aristotle announced a version of the same principle when he praised tragedy over epic on the grounds that tragedy achieved its end in briefer time. Of tragedy he said, "The concentrated effect is more pleasurable than one which is spread over a long time and so diluted." [98]

The concentrated effect that Thomas sought to attain varied, of course, from poem to poem, depending on the subject he was dealing with and the period in which he was writing. Toward the end of his career he came more and more to rely on repetitive devices to convey emotion. But throughout his work there is at the end of almost every poem a curious climactic moment. After the packing away and compression which has been described as intensity, there occurs a statement, or an image, which either resolves the struggle or marks the continuation of the struggle. There is, it seems, a conscious effort to form "a watertight section" against the flux of time. There is, in brief, a *stasis* at the conclusion of almost every Thomas poem.

What generalizations, Robert Penn Warren asks, can we safely make about the nature of poetic structure? He answers: "First it involves resistance at various levels. A good poem to be good must earn itself. It is a motion toward a point of rest, but if it is not resisted motion, it is motion of no consequence." [99]

If the clash of word, letter, and idea represented to Thomas the hue and passion of life, then it logically followed that language was for him comparable to life. One of the most

[98] *Criticism: The Foundations of Modern Literary Judgment,* ed. Mark Schorer *et al.* (New York, 1948), p. 217.

[99] Robert Penn Warren, "Pure and Impure Poetry," *Criticism: The Foundations of Modern Literary Judgment,* p. 377.

interesting creations in his poetry is, in fact, that of a world which is entirely verbal and entirely capable of replacing the ordinary material world. Thomas stressed the idea of a verbal universe in his correspondence as well as in his poems, but it is in the poetry that the world-poetry metaphor is fully developed.

The evangelist's gospel was in Thomas's mind when he wrote:

> In the beginning was the word, the word
> That from the solid bases of the light
> Abstracted all the letters of the void;
> And from the cloudy bases of the breath
> The word flowed up, translating to the heart
> First characters of birth and death.
>
> (p. 27)

Life is equated with light and thus the beginning of language in light is comparable to the origins of life in the first fiat of Genesis.

The meaning of this light-life-language identification is manifested in the sounds and in the shapes of words. Thomas reasoned that, just as existing entities have shapes, language as an existing entity must likewise have this attribute of "reality." The sound-shape metaphor naturally enough begins in Thomas's synesthetic imagination:

> blood blessed the heart,
> And the four winds, that had long blown as one,
> Shone in my ears the light of sound,
> Called in my eyes the sound of light.
>
> (p. 24)

But when we discover that light in Thomas's poetry has the obvious value of *awareness* or understanding, we realize there is something more than synesthesia going on here.

It is this sound-shape sense that lies behind his seeing spring as the sound of huntsmen on the chase, and behind his hearing the hill as "four-stringed":

> the horns of England, in the sound of shape
> Summon . . . snowy horsemen, and the four-stringed hill,
> Over the sea-gut loudening.
>
> (p. 58)

The flesh of man is the declension by which all this confused jumble of shape-sound is sorted out and yields whatever meaning it is capable of yielding. This is the poet's source of knowledge:

> And from the first declension of the flesh
> I learnt man's tongue, to twist the shapes of thoughts
> Into the stony idiom of the brain,
> To shade and knit anew the patch of words.
>
> (p. 25)

Man himself is "wordy," he is a "tower of words," and the poet as well as nature is bound by this restriction of language. Like Merlin, the word magician is bound in his tree-prison, in his flesh-tower—he who would make all the world meaningful in words. Thomas expresses this thought most clearly in "Especially When the October Wind" (p. 19), where he talks through his "busy heart"; he talks by the mere fact that he lives, and in writing he sheds his "syllabic blood." He can see life speaking, he marks "the wordy shapes of women," and he tells his readers that he could make other words for them from the world he sees:

> Some let me make you of the vowelled beeches,
> Some of the oaken voices, from the roots
> Of many a thorny shire tell you notes,
> Some let me make you of the water's speeches.

"Tree of Nettles"

His senses attuned to the world tell him all, the hour's word is the "neural meaning," and

> The signal grass that tells me all I know
> Breaks with the wormy winter through the eye.

The winter is wormy because it, like the slug, teaches the poet destruction. (We see this even more clearly in "The Force That through the Green Fuse," page 10, where in the first stanza, "My youth is bent by the . . . wintry fever," and in the last stanza, "at my sheet goes the . . . crooked worm." The work of winter and worm is analogous; namely, destruction.)

Thomas makes it quite clear that in this verbal world the role of the poet is of the utmost importance. From the outset he presents a picture of the poet as a word magician imaginatively conjuring visions whereby the stubborn alienation between man and nature, as Hegel perceived it, may be overcome. The reconciliation begins by imaginatively viewing the world as only the poet can view it. But the abolition of the distinction between word and reality is only part of the poet's function. In order to realize more fully an imaginative view of existence, Thomas, like other romantics, assumed a variety of roles, most consistently, those of Adam and Christ. Like Adam he continually sees the world afresh; like Christ he suffers from his vision—the vision of the biting serpent, death.

> I, in a wind on fire, from green Adam's cradle,
> No man more magical, clawed out the crocodile.
>
> (p. 44)

"The Hunchback in the Park" is, on one level, a description of the power and value of the imagination in finding sufficient beauty to persevere in the struggle. All day the hunchback is abused and cruelly treated, but his imagination draws from

57

these agonies the materials for a finer existence—in dreams. In
the midst of personal and public deformity, the hunchback
creates his new world. He suffers, to be precise, so that he may
create; out of the world of chains, keepers, and abuse he selects
that by which he may find eventual release:

> A woman figure without fault
> Straight as a young elm
> Straight and tall from his crooked bones
> That she might stand in the night
> After the locks and chains.

(p. 124)

In the inner, creative life of poetry, life "after the locks and
chains," Thomas reveals a variety of prophetic and patriarchal
roles—prophetic in the Blakean and Shelleyan sense, not of
predicting the future but of imaginatively seeing deeper realities. The prophetic poet sees and knows only the same events
and objects as other men, but for the poet the grain of sand is
infinity, an hour eternity. "The 'seer' has insight, not second
sight: he is not a charlatan but the contrary of one, an honest
man with a sharper perception and a clearer perspective than
other honest men possess." [100]

The notion of Thomas assuming prophetic or patriarchal
stances perhaps seems too magniloquent for a poet who sati-
rized himself as a "middle-class, beardless Walt." [101] But
Thomas's prose and poetry are full of pronouncements and
exhortations, prayers and lamentations, which find no better
parallel than in the Biblical rhetoric of malediction and bene-
diction. One can open the prophetic books of the Bible almost
at random and find parallels to Thomas, both in imagery and
theme. Tailor, worm, and womb images are all found in Isaiah,

[100] Frye, *Fearful Symmetry*, p. 59; cf. S. Foster Damon, *William
Blake: His Philosophy and Symbols*, p. 61.

[101] Watkins, p. 85.

"*Tree of Nettles*"

for example: "I have cut off like a weaver my life" (Isaiah 38:12); "And they shall go forth, and look upon the carcases of the men that have transgressed against me: for their worm shall not die, neither shall their fire be quenched" (Isaiah 66:24); "The Lord hath called me from the womb; from the bowels of my mother hath he made mention of my name" (Isaiah 49:1).[102] It was because of his prophetic role that Thomas considered himself also a Christ figure and his work a "cross of tales."

> "Adam I love, my madmen's love is endless,
> No tell-tale lover has an end more certain,
> All legends' sweethearts on a tree of stories,
> My cross of tales behind the fabulous curtain."
>
> (p. 48)

When Thomas wanted to select one of his early poems as an example of what he felt most important in his work, he chose "Before I Knocked and Flesh Let Enter" (pp. 8–9). This is a poem written from the viewpoint of Christ. It traces Christ's awareness of life from the "felt thud" of God's "rainy hammer" on the "leaden stars," through the tapping "with liquid hands . . . on the womb," to the crucifixion. This poem by the nineteen-year-old Thomas is a brief but incomparable imaginative achievement.

Thomas saw the poet not only as a kind of Christ, as a celebrator, and bard, "Ann's bard on a raised hearth" who calls "all/ The seas to service" (p. 96), but also as a man fated to destroy himself in his role as poet, "Now my saying shall be my undoing" (p. 98). Finally, in the poem written to introduce *Collected Poems*, "Author's Prologue," he becomes the Noah of Wales, gathering all the creatures of his country. He

---

[102] Thomas's concern with the Bible is explored in greater depth in Chapter Five.

sees himself, somewhat self-consciously, as "the moonshine/ Drinking Noah of the bay" outfitting in his poetry a "patch/ Work ark" with which to ride toward death.

Thomas's attitudes toward poetry and toward the role of poet are nowhere stated more clearly than in two of his definitions of poetry. Poetry, Thomas said when he was twenty, expresses the unchanging through the changing, the spirit through the flesh.[103] Nearly twenty years later he responded to the question "What is your definition of Poetry?" by writing:

All that matters about poetry is the enjoyment of it, however tragic it may be. All that matters is the eternal movement behind it, the vast undercurrent of human grief, folly, pretension, exaltation, or ignorance, however unlofty the intention of the poem. . . . The joy and function of poetry is, and was, the celebration of man, which is also the celebration of God.[104]

So much for the ends of poetry that Thomas sought; now to consider some of the ways in which he achieved those ends.

[103] P.H.J. Correspondence.
[104] Thomas, "Poetic Manifesto," 53.

CHAPTER TWO

"The Churning Bulk":
Artifice and Obscurity

Now I'm almost afraid of all the once-necessary
artifices and obscurities, and can't, for the life or
the death of me, get any real liberation, any diffusion or dilution or anything, into the churning
bulk of the words.

Dylan Thomas to Vernon Watkins
April 20, 1936

IN 1934 Thomas voiced an idea that would remain constant
throughout his career. Poetry, he said, must drag into "the
clean nakedness of light, more even of the hidden causes than
Freud could realise." [1] Thomas sought to fulfill this desire by
an unbounded exercise of imagination, and, curiously, by an
absolute craftsmanship. "I am a painstaking, conscientious,
involved and devious craftsman in words," Thomas explained
to a student in 1951, quickly adding, "however unsuccesful
[sic] the result so often appears, and to whatever wrong uses I

[1] "Replies to an Enquiry," *A Casebook,* pp. 102–103.

61

may apply my technical paraphenalia [sic]." Thomas went on to specify aspects of his craftsmanship:

I use everything & anything to make my poems work and move in the direction I want them to: old tricks, new tricks, puns, port-manteau-words, paradox, allusion, paronomasia, paragram, cata-chresis, slang, assonantal rhymes, vowel rhymes, sprung rhythm. Every device there is in language is there to be used if you will. Poets have got to enjoy themselves sometimes, and the twistings & convolutions . . . are all part of the joy.[2]

Thomas's list of artifices, his technical paraphernalia, sug-gests two general kinds of devices, rhetorical and auditory, and it seems useful to observe this division in examining the "churning bulk." Thus the rhetorical devices of language, persona, and metaphor—viewed mainly in terms of obscurity—are the subject of the present chapter. The audi-tory techniques—rhythm, rhyme, vowel and consonant manipulation—will be discussed in Chapter Three.

I
OBSCURITY

Any consideration of Thomas's craftsmanship ought to be prefaced by some attention to the problem of obscurity in his work. It is difficult to generalize about obscurity, but since Thomas himself is responsible for a number of such generali-zations, some of which have already been touched on in discussing his ideas on poetry—especially his desire for concentration—it is almost impossible to avoid the subject.

Late in his career Thomas habitually dismissed his opacity as a youthful aberration. He often characterized his early work as "explosive bloodbursts of a boily boy," and, in 1952, told an interviewer: "At first I thought it enough to leave an impression of sound and feeling and let the meaning seep in

---

[2] "Poetic Manifesto," *Texas Quarterly*, IV (Winter, 1961), 50.

later but [now] . . . I find it better to have more meaning at first reading."[3]

The general validity of such remarks is obvious enough, but they can be very misleading if we try to apply them to *Collected Poems*. Several of the earlier poems (composed mostly in 1933, published in 1934) are quite straightforward; some of the poems in the second book (published in 1936) like the "Altarwise" sonnet sequence[4] are even more difficult. Many of the later poems, "In the White Giant's Thigh" (1950), for example, are far more obscure than poems such as "A Process in the Weather of the Heart" (1934) or "And Death Shall Have No Dominion" (1936).

Considering the order of *Collected Poems* as an accurate chronological representation of Thomas's poetry—and there is little reason why we cannot accept it as such[5]—we must conclude that obscurity in Thomas follows a parabolic pattern, with the height of the opacity occurring during the years 1936–1938. If we go beyond *Collected Poems* and examine everything from juvenilia to *Under Milk Wood* for obscurity, we see further evidence of this pattern. The Thomas of the Notebooks is a relatively straightforward poet, but as he experimented with various subjects and styles, as he sought

[3] Marjorie Adix, "Dylan Thomas: Memories and Appreciations, IV," in *A Casebook*, p. 285.

[4] It was at this time that Thomas complained about his words containing no "diffusion or dilution" and that everything he wrote was being tightly packed away in "a mad doctor's bag." He went on: "All you can see is the bag, all you can know is that it's full to the clasp, all you have to trust is that the invisible and intangible things packed away are—if they *could* only be seen and touched—worth quite a lot." *Letters to Vernon Watkins*, ed. Vernon Watkins (London, 1957), p. 25.

[5] For an account of whatever doubts there are see Ralph Maud, "Dylan Thomas' *Collected Poems*: Chronology of Composition," *Publications of the Modern Language Association*, LXXVI (June, 1961), 292–297.

more freshness and intensity, the more obscure his poetry became. Then, with B. B. C. broadcasts and public appearances, his work grew slowly more lucid, reaching a music-hall norm of clarity with *Under Milk Wood*. As Vernon Watkins was first to observe, the year 1939 marked a fairly definite turning toward greater clarity in both prose and poetry, and as will be shown later, marked major stylistic changes also. In the poems there is more clarity following "After the Funeral" and in the stories beginning with "Extraordinary Little Cough."

Youthfulness, at least in the sense of age rather than attitude, does not adequately account for very many of the characteristics and alternations in Thomas's work. If a single word were capable of accounting for large areas of interests and style, *imagination, vision,* or *enthusiasm* would be more accurate than *youthfulness*. When Thomas remarked that there is "in many people a need to share enthusiasm," [6] he was describing himself, and he might well have added that there is likewise a need to share misery, confusion, and wonder. He was a man who felt poetry had saddled him to the dazzling horse of Pegasus.[7]

Thomas's imaginative enthusiasms usually manifested themselves in his projecting onto ordinary events great cosmic, terrestrial, spiritual, or physiological significance, or in portraying ordinary events in the most extraordinary circumstances. It seems probable that Thomas did not so much try to dress up his experiences in outlandish garb as he attempted to perceive the ordinary in hyperverbal and hyperimaginative ways. Accustomed, apparently from earliest childhood, to verbalize every activity and thought, and to see these activities and thoughts in trees, winds, sea, animals, insects, physical processes, dreams, and the Bible, Thomas seems to have as-

[6] *Quite Early One Morning* (New York, 1954), p. 161.
[7] P.H.J. Correspondence.

sumed that the reader could enter intelligently and appreciatively into the spirit of the language and the projection if he so desired.

To what degree these imaginative constructions were a part of Thomas's normal modes of perception is suggested by his use of almost the same constructions in his letters as in his prose and poetry. A few of these letters are, furthermore, helpful in revealing the workings of Thomas's imagination insofar as they sometimes provide enlightening parallels with the poetry. Thomas, for example, wrote to Pamela Hansford Johnson that he wanted to live under the sea and behold the moon from beneath the waters. In his poetry he says of his images: "They suffer the undead water where the turtle nibbles, come unto sea-struck towers" (p. 43). Another time he wrote Miss Johnson that he was enjoying the companionship of beetles, much as he wrote in his poetry: "My images stalk the slant sap's tunnel" (p. 41). He wrote to Marguerite Caetani that he was winding "brass music around me"—meaning by "brass music" the words of his letter and his poetry. Similarly he describes himself in his poems as "Forged in man's minerals, the brassy orator/Laying my ghost in metal" (p. 40). (Perhaps laying the ghost in metal means putting the spirit in print—a notion Thomas could have been struck by as a schoolboy editor watching his magazine being set in type.) In one of the last letters he ever wrote, Thomas described his feelings of guilt as sewing him in a sack, weighting him with "guilt and pig-iron" and pitching him "squealing to sea, so that time and time again I must wrestle and unravel in a panic . . . and ooze and eel up wheezily, babbling and blowing black bubbles, from all the claws and bars and breasts of the mantrapping sea bed." [8] It is a similar sea of guilt and

[8] Letter to Marguerite Caetani, "Three Letters," *Botteghe Oscure,* XIII (1954), 101.

entrapment that Thomas describes himself rising from in "Once Below a Time":

> Then swift from a bursting sea with bottlecork boats
> And out-of-perspective sailors,
> In common clay clothes disguised as scales,
> As a he-god's paddling water skirts,
> I astounded the sitting tailors,
>
> . . . . .
>
> Hopping hot leaved and feathered
> From the kangaroo foot of the earth,
> From the chill, silent centre
> Trailing the frost bitten cloth,
> Up through the lubber crust of Wales
> I rocketed. . . .
>
> (p. 147)

Thus the most valid generalizations we can make about Thomas's obscurity are about the quality of his imagination—that faculty which, as we have seen in a variety of ways already, combined Blake and "boily boy," idealism and agnosticism, surrealism and pastoralism. What is first necessary in considering Thomas's obscurity is an awareness that he was always capable of making untraceable imaginative leaps. It is of little use to say that Thomas was the perfect romantic, that his own existence was the whole subject matter of his poetry, that he was only interested in the basic conditions of life. Although all of these remarks are true, they are of little help when the imagination of Thomas takes flight. At that moment, at the moment of the poem, the commonplace disappears in a series of statements and images that seem to bear no relation to the commonplaces the poem is dealing with. Suddenly, as he said in his letters to Pamela Hansford Johnson, the mortar holding the bricks together *is* opium, which the bricklayers carry in their small pipes. No word, Thomas once complained to Miss Johnson, could describe the scenes he beheld. For him the muscles of a cockle's legs seemed large as hills, the prints in the sand deep as the abysses of hell, clouds like the ears of donkeys. The moon seemed to be plowing the Towy River and the stars were, somewhat like Blake's angelic tree, the bright eyes of urchins.

Thomas's imaginative leaps are naturally more extensive, and language is put to a greater strain, in his poetry than in his letters. "I Make This in a Warring Absence," for example, is a cosmic experience described in a sexual metaphor. The poem tells of a wife's denial of marital favors, the husband's anger, his persistence, "conquest," and finally the release and reconciliation following the consummated act. Thomas here sees a domestic occurrence as having immense implications. The universe is involved in the actions of the couple, and the couple is involved in the actions of the universe. It is doubtful that any detailed comment on this poem will be very enlightening without both a thorough knowledge of Thomas's imagination and the poem itself. Yet some brief comment should be worthwhile inasmuch as Thomas himself "explained" the last stanza of the poem. That stanza reads:

> Now in the cloud's big breast lie quiet countries,
> Delivered seas my love from her proud place
> Walks with no wound, nor lightning in her face,
> A calm wind blows that raised the trees like hair
> Once where the soft snow's blood was turned to ice.
> And though my love pulls the pale, nippled air,
> Prides of to-morrow suckling in her eyes,
> Yet this I make in a forgiving presence.

(p. 89)

The relationship completed, the speaker says, the woman (the cloud) is now at peace. She has been transported from her "proud place," she now feels no hurt, "wound," nor anger,

"lightning." The fourth and fifth lines are ingenious exten-
sions of the metaphysical wife-cloud metaphor. The cloud,
having "delivered" her storm ("seas"), now contains no thunder or lightning. What was ice in the storm cloud has, in falling, changed its "blood" to soft snow and the winds are calm.
In the last three lines the poet says that although his wife, his
"love," already is beginning to teat on the infant prides of
tomorrow, although he knows the same troubles will occur
again, she is now content, and as he writes this poem she is
forgiving, "Yet this I make in a forgiving presence," or in the
absence of warring.

"I Make This in a Warring Absence" is typical of the
difficult poems of Thomas's middle period, 1936 to 1940, and
typical of the allegorical paraphrase one devolves upon in
order to talk about the "meaning" of the most complicated
Thomas poems. The pattern of metaphor is based on a series of
parallels and juxtapositions. The man's anger at being refused,
for instance, is earlier treated in terms paralleling Samson's
fury against the Philistines:

> I make a weapon of an ass's skeleton
> And walk the warring sands by the dead town,
> Cudgel great air, wreck east, and topple sundown.
>
> (p. 88)

The two lines Thomas chose to comment on reveal further
metaphoric parallels. The lines in question are these: "A calm
wind blows that raised the trees like hair/ Once where the soft
snow's blood was turned to ice." Certainly on a verbal level
Thomas's lines parallel those of two clichés: my hair stood on
end, my blood froze. Thomas's own mind, however, was also
working on a more complicated metaphoric parallel. He offers
this explanation of these lines:

They say exactly what I mean them to. Are they clear? Once
upon a time, before my death & resurrection, before the "terrible"

world had shown itself to me . . . a wind had blown that had frightened everything & created the first ice & the first frost by frightening the falling snow so much that the blood of each flake froze. This is probably clear, but, even to me, the lines skip (almost) along so that they are taken too quickly, & then mainly by the eye.[9]

It is inconceivable that any reader of Thomas could ever have devised such an interpretation for these two lines. Armed with Thomas's comment, however, the reader is encouraged to make further equations. By death Thomas means ungratified desire; by resurrection, consummated love. Snow, one would logically continue, an almost universal symbol of frigidity, is here (anticipating "A Winter's Tale," pp. 131–137) a symbol of sexual need. And whatever life, or blood, that is in this need was frozen by the indifferent woman, the cold wind that created ice and frost. To conceive of snow as possessing blood, or to conceive of ice and frost being caused by an indifferent woman, are rather common flights of the Thomasian fancy. Man thus is the world, he is part of the trees, the storms, the ice ages, all the while remaining man.

Thomas would consider his explanation of this marital

[9] Watkins, pp. 30–31. A good deal of what I discuss here as Thomas's "imaginative leap" is closely related to Maud's idea of "Distancing the Intimate." "To express the important and intimate facts of experience without seeming to blurt them out—this is the task the poet sets himself. Thomas in his youth made several important poems from the personal, and dangerously bathetic, subject of onanism. He did so by stating sexual waste not in terms unbearably close to the subject but in remoter images such as night-mare and graveyard figures." *Entrances to Dylan Thomas' Poetry* (Pittsburgh, 1963), p. 81. Maud's discussion of "A Grief Ago" is an excellent illustration of his point. I think Maud and I differ in one important sense. I see the winged horse of Thomas's imagination as primary and all-powerful, and I see much of Thomas's problem as making this runaway imagination intelligible to his reader. Maud seems to see the problem in just the reverse manner. He sees the common experience as coming first and Thomas's poetic function as being to make this common experience esthetically rich.

experience in terms of wind, ice, and snow a literal explanation. What Thomas tells us about particular poems, however,
does not usually help us to understand the literal meaning of
the poems, in the ordinary sense of the term "literal." But his
readings do give us insights into how his imagination worked.
The usefulness of Thomas's criticism on Thomas is perhaps
best illustrated in his comments on Dame Edith Sitwell's
reading of these lines from the first "Altarwise" sonnet:

> The gentleman lay graveward with his furies;
>
> . . . . .
>
> And, from his fork, a dog among the fairies,
> The atlas-eater with a jaw for news,
> Bit out the mandrake with to-morrow's scream.
>
> (p. 80)

Dame Sitwell commented on these lines by saying that they
referred to "the violent speed and the sensation-loving, horror-
loving craze of modern life." Thomas corrected her view by
saying:

She doesn't take the literal meaning: that a world-devouring
ghost-creature bit out the horror of tomorrow from a gentleman's
loins.
A "jaw for news" is an obvious variation of "a nose for news,"
and means that the mouth of the creature can taste already the
horror that has not yet come, or can sense its coming, can thrust
its tongue into news that has not yet been made, can savour the
enormity of the progeny before the seed stirs, can realise the
crumbling of dead flesh before the opening of the womb that
delivers that flesh to tomorrow.[10]

If we take Thomas's explanation at face value, the poem is
even more baffling than it was before. If, however, we take his

---

[10] Henry Treece, *Dylan Thomas: "Dog Among the Fairies"* (1949
edition), pp. 149–150.

description as providing other metaphors for the "dog among the fairies" and the "atlas-eater," we will find his explanation helpful. The only creature that "devours" an atlas (a book of maps, here a metaphor for the world) is the poet. There is also a biographical reason for the former "Herald of Wales" reporter seeing the poet as having "a jaw for news." (Further, see *Collected Poems*, page 70, where Thomas says he has "made/ A merry manshape" out of the world; page 65, where he describes the poet as "the biting man"; page 44, where the poet is depicted as one who claws out the serpent creature; and page 6, where the poet tells us "the womb/ Drives in a death as life leaks out.") Savoring "the enormity of the progeny before the seed stirs" is a magical and unpleasant task. It is thus analogous to grubbing up the mandrake root. The mandrake is a medicinal, narcotic, forked, carrotlike herb, and death was the penalty attached to digging it up. For this reason a dog was traditionally assigned the job. (Thus it is that Thomas called the poet "a dog among the fairies" and later played with the mandrake tradition and Joyce's *Portrait of the Artist as a Young Man* when, at the suggestion of a friend, he called his own autobiographical collection of prose *Portrait of the Artist as a Young Dog.*)

In brief, then, Thomas's "literal" reading is based on two things: metaphor and artifice. He begins, in fact, by exposing one of his most common devices, the rejuvenated cliché: "A 'jaw for news' is an obvious variation of a 'nose for news.'" Such a device is common to many poets, but examination of the particular use of a common device shows how an individual poet makes it his own. And, perhaps more important, every close analysis (even when threatening to take the clock apart to see how it works) helps to clarify the poetic imagination.

What these generalizations mean in terms of practical criticism, then, can best be determined by considering a few lines of poetry. Various critical reactions to the opening of " 'If My Head Hurt a Hair's Foot' " conveniently suggest practical approaches to the difficulties of Thomas's imagination and artifices, and, curiously, these same reactions provide a kind of summary for the varying critical reactions to a difficult Thomas poem.

The lines in question are these:

"If my head hurt a hair's foot
Pack back the downed bone. If the unpricked ball of my breath
Bump on a spout let the bubbles jump out.
Sooner drop with the worm of the ropes round my throat
Than bully ill love in the clouted scene. . . ."

(p. 108)

Shortly after the poem was published, Treece, who must be considered sympathetic to Thomas, wrote, "Such a passage . . . seems to me a *verbal compulsion*, almost a psychopathic phenomenon, musical-rhythmic automatism, with a possibly unconscious sexual reference thrown in to emphasise the primitive source of the word group." [11]

Robert Graves called the stanza "nonsense" and offered a one-pound reward to anyone who could make sense out of it. M. J. C. Hodgart replied to Graves. He pointed out that the dramatic frame of the poem was a dialogue between an unborn child and its mother. (This point was also made by Olson and Stanford.) [12] Graves summarizes Hodgart's reading and gives his counter-reading as follows:

He suggests that the child about to be born is here addressing his mother. The child cries out that if he is to cause her any pain by

[11] *Ibid.*, p. 131.
[12] Elder Olson, *The Poetry of Dylan Thomas* (Chicago, 1953), pp. 43–44; Derek Stanford, *Dylan Thomas* (New York, 1954), p. 85. The Graves-Hodgart exchange is given in Graves's *The Crowning Privilege* (London, 1955), pp. 140–141.

his birth, let him not be born at all. "If I were to hurt so much as a hair of your head in process of birth push my downy, but bony, head back into the womb." . . . Birth (Mr. Hodgart adds) is represented here as a violent movement like a bouncing ball; and the child's breath before birth is compared to an unpricked bubble. Therefore: "If even this soft bubble of breath should hurt you by bouncing on your spouting blood, prick it and let my life run out in bubbles." And: "I would sooner be born hanged with my navel-string coiled around my throat than bully you when I appear on a scene made wretched by baby-clouts, or clouts on the head."

To this reading Graves replies:

The hair's foot, misleadingly identical in sound to hare's foot, is not a hair's *root*. Also, the physical situation is blurred by the apparent contact of the baby's downy head with the mother's hairy one, and by the description of the navel-string as "the worm of the ropes"—why "ropes" in the plural? And by the metaphor of an unpunctured ball bouncing on the top of a spout—as in pleasure fountains; how the bubble of breath could bounce on the flow of lochial blood is not easy to see (blood is not mentioned in the poem). And why should the unpricked bubble become "bubbles"? And is the infant experienced or ignorant? If ignorant, how can it anticipate baby-clouts, and balls bouncing on fountains? If experienced, how can it make so absurd a suggestion as that the mother should push its head back again to relieve her labour pains? And if it is so considerate and saintly as Mr. Hodgart suggests, why should it ever turn bully?

Needless to say, Hodgart did not get his reward.

Most recently, Tindall—following Hodgart and Olson in seeing the speaker as an infant—says, "Nothing by Thomas could be plainer." He paraphrases the lines:

Hair and foot, anatomical extremes, find reconciliation in "hair's foot" at the pubic middle. Promising no harm to this, the em-

bryo, still "unpricked" in several senses, also promises no inter-
ference with father's "spout." This imagery is at once familiar
and extravagant—but so, after all, a speaking embryo. Compare
the "bubbles" of unpricked breath with the "swag of bubbles in
a seedy sack" (76). "The worm of the ropes" seems umbilical,
phallic, and deathly. Better polite death than playing the bully
to parental loving, however "ill" or ill-timed. "Clouted," which
echoes "out," involves amatory striking and, by anticipation,
swaddling.[13]

We seem to have here a reaction of shock and dismay
(Treece's), one of apparent hostility to Thomas's methods and
temperament (Graves's), one which accepts the lines on their
own terms and tries to make them intelligible (Hodgart's), and
one which, at points, becomes over-imaginative and over-
ingenious (Tindall's). All of these critical responses can un-
doubtedly be defended, but some are obviously more valuable
than others in trying to understand Thomas. What should be
immediately apparent is that the two critics who were familiar
with Thomas's use of voices (Hodgart and Tindall) were
better able to cope with the obscurity of the stanza. Tindall's
imaginative boldness provided—with his reference to the
"father's spout"—a possible explanation for what Treece saw
as an "unconscious sexual reference" and what Hodgart
vaguely identified as "spouting blood." We should further
notice that Hodgart, in exploiting common knowledge of
Thomas's verbal devices, makes the "hair's foot" reference
most intelligible. Hodgart, however, is not exactly right in
implying "hair's foot" means the child will not "hurt so much
as a hair of your head in process of birth." Though it may be
possible to connect the expression to "hair of your head," the
sense of it is "the least measurable amount" and is more closely
related to the folk expression "hair's breadth." There is an

[13] William York Tindall, *A Reader's Guide to Dylan Thomas* (New
York, 1962), pp. 173, 174.

intentional confusion of homonyms, "hair" and "hare," in order to impart another level of meaning. For the thinness of "hair" has its counterpart in the swiftness of "hare," and the idea of least measurable amount is paralleled by the notion of swiftest possible instant.

Besides an understanding of the verbal artifices and of the persona or voice in the poem, there is also a need to understand certain of Thomas's metaphorical practices. Tindall alludes to one aspect of this latter necessity when he refers to other poems in which Thomas used "bubbles." We cannot, as Hodgart tries to do, adequately explain the bubble metaphor without recourse to the body of Thomas's work.

In Thomas the ball is a metaphor for the world, and, in so far as the world is life, the ball often means life. Obviously, a ball is also a plaything generally associated with youth; thus "ball," having these two links, may not only mean life but young life. A ball which is pricked loses its bubbles of air. Life, too, may be seen as a process wherein we eventually come to lose our air, our breath. (Yeats uses this view several times in his poetry—most notably in "In Memory of Major Robert Gregory.") "Bubble" is metaphorically related to "ball" in Thomas; it too is a synecdoche for life. More specifically, it is a metaphoric substitute for breath. Life is pictured as being created by nature out of "blood and bubble" ("I, in My Intricate Image," p. 40), and time is depicted as a thief who brings death by stealing bubbles ("Grief Thief of Time," p. 76):

> the time-faced crook
> Death flashing from his sleeve,
> With swag of bubbles in a seedy sack.

Thus the unborn child can say, "If the unpricked ball of my breath/ Bump on a spout let the bubbles jump out." This reference to the body of the work does not, of course, exclude the possibility that Thomas, in the manner of Joyce, also meant to use these words as sexual slang, but there seems little point in piling up *possible* readings—individual readers may easily enough do that after the poem has been made coherent on a single level.

Hodgart's interpretation of "the worm of the ropes" seems more accurate than Tindall's because it is based on the facts of the poem rather than on an attempt to incorporate *all* the meanings which Thomas has previously implied by "worm." Although a word is often used symbolically, it may still be used in an ordinary way where it fits the particular context. If this worm is "phallic" and "deathly" here, it is so only in addition to being "umbilical." "Ropes," it might be added, is most likely plural because Thomas knew that the umbilical cord is often wrapped around an infant's neck several times.

Thomas's "churning bulk" is a product of imagination and wit, and, ideally, the reader should delight in constant discoveries of ingenious artistry. The joy of the poet in his "twistings & convolutions" should come through to the reader. But a reader who is bored by this kind of literary gamesmanship will find only confusion and irritation in much of Thomas's work—especially in the prewar work. It is not justified to exalt Thomas's verbal play (or Shakespeare's or Joyce's) as an end in itself, nor is it justified to see this kind of craftsmanship as a low-grade entertainment, one rank below detective stories and crossword puzzles. Verbal wit is an integral part of emotional pitch, of sensibility, and of vision—not only in Thomas but in all poets. The only useful gradations would seem to depend on critical demonstrations: on a demonstration that such imaginative exuberance does not exist, a demonstration that whether or not it exists (a moot point) it is ineffective because of obscurity, or a demonstration that imaginative exuberance is present, but defective. If any conclusions can be drawn from even such a brief demonstration as that concerned with "If My Head Hurt . . . ," it would seem to be that there is a marvelous abundance of imagination in Thomas, but its obscurity often mars our esthetic appreciation of it. To examine specific artifices of diction, persona, and image is to examine this abundance and its limitations and, at the same time, to find out something about what Thomas's poetry means.

II
REFURBISHING LANGUAGE

Like most poets, Thomas was "in love with the shape and the sound of words." "When I experience anything," he once told Alastair Reid, "I experience it as a thing and a word at the same time, both equally amazing." He said the writing of the "Ballad of the Long-legged Bait" had been "like carrying a huge armful of words to a table he thought was upstairs, and wondering if he could reach it in time, or if it would still be there." [14] This prehension of awareness, native to all poetic perception, is what George Whalley describes as "a double concern and excitement, not only for the thing or event perceived but also for the medium. . . . This excitement— often a sense of loathing as well as one of delight or enthusiasm —helps to sustain the state of feeling throughout the activity of composition." [15] Thomas's verbal devices also enabled him to sustain states of emotion in his reader by demanding attention and concentration, by keeping his reader's mind in a state of excitement and effort comparable to his own in the throes of creation, by constantly drawing his reader's mind

[14] Alastair Reid, "A First Word," *Yale Literary Magazine* (November, 1954), 20.
[15] George Whalley, *Poetic Process* (London, 1953), p. 97.

back to obsessive concerns through verbal repetition and variation.

To Thomas's own catalogue of means by which he sought to hold his reader, "puns, portmanteau-words, paradox, allusion, paronomasia, . . . slang," we must add dialectal words, clichés, words based on hidden metaphors, common words with uncommon meanings, grammatical shifts and wrenched syntax. These were the building blocks of his poetic structures—and stumbling blocks to his poetic meaning.[16] And yet to call them stumbling blocks is not quite accurate, since, when they are finally properly interpreted, they usually provide vividness and clarity.

Some of Thomas's more startling expressions come from slang, such as his reference to "my cherry capped dangler" (p.

[16] Because the unit and sometimes the total poem is the key to Thomas's use of words, it is not always necessary to catalogue or analyze his vocabulary. What has already been done along this line seems sufficient. Maud, for example, has classified a few of his dialectal puns ("Obsolete Dialect Words as Serious Puns in Dylan Thomas," *English Studies*, XLI, 28–30); Treece, *op. cit.*, has listed the hyphenated words (Appendix III, pp. 155–157); and Josephine Miles has examined the most frequently repeated words and the proportionate frequency of parts of speech (*Continuity of Poetic Language*, Berkeley, Cal., 1948). This type of analysis is primarily mechanical. Although it has to be done, its value lies chiefly in reinforcing statistically the impression we have probably already received from a close reading of the poetry. And although we may index Thomas's puns, specialized diction, and dialectal words, such a catalogue will not help us overcome the most serious obstacles to comprehending his poetry. It will serve only to amplify, perhaps with slight variations, Miss Miles's conclusions, p. 448: "Thomas' is a most bodily universe, for all its scope. *Blood, eye, hand, heart, bones, face, head, mouth, tongue* keep it expressive, and *water, house, tower, stone, bell* are analogues for it, in addition to other traditional and special terms. Most of the rainbow colors make the major qualities of this world. Against color the verbs play with unusual vigor of body, in *make, lie, fall, break, drive, hold, drop, turn,* and with much verbal individuality."

148), his description of Sodom as the "bum city" (p. 86), or his statement that the "rotating halves are horning as they drill/ The arterial angel" (p. 35). He speaks of the "ninnies' choir" (p. 69), the "cuckoo lovers" (p. 98), and a "swag" of bubbles (meaning loot or stolen property, p. 76). He effectively substitutes "snap," which suggests both "break" and "seize" (as in "snap up"), to give a profane ring to his parody of the Eucharist—"My wine you drink, my bread you snap" (p. 45).

The "chucked bells" of "A Saint About to Fall" are the discarded bells, the thrown-away bells. In the same poem he says, "Heaven fell with his fall and one crocked bell beat the left air" (p. 105). It is possible that "crocked" is being used in the dialectal sense of "dirty," but it seems more probable that Thomas also intended the slang meaning, "drunken."

The word "lammed," meaning "beaten," also has the slang usage of the flight or getaway of a criminal, and thus adds, with marvelous economy, new dimensions of meaning to "A Grief Ago":

> A grief ago,
> She who was who I hold, the fats and flower,
> Or, water-lammed, from the scythe-sided thorn,
> Hell wind and sea,
> A stem cementing, wrestled up the tower.
>
> > (p. 63)

The implication is that the woman whom he holds has, by the processes of evolution, escaped from the water, the sea, but as a criminal, a marked person. This idea is further developed in the next two stanzas, and she is described even more specifically as having the "brand of the lily's anger on her ring."

The source of the lively humor in "Lament" is puns and slang expressions—the "old ram rod," the "wick-/Dipping

moon," the "black sheep with a crumpled horn," the jawing of
the bells (pp. 194–196). "When, Like a Running Grave" is
another poem built on numerous slang expressions and puns,
such as "love in her gear," meaning apparatus or equipment as
well as apparel; "dusters in my glove," meaning brass
knuckles; "Cadaver's trap," meaning the corpse's mouth;
"boxy shift," meaning undershorts as well as pine coffin (pp.
21–22).

Fortunately, such slang is easy to identify, as are the few
unusual or dialectal words which appear in Thomas's poetry.
With the help of a standard dictionary we can find that
"wynds" (p. 190) are narrow lanes, that "parhelion" (p. 36) is
"a spot of light," a "mock sun," that the "widdershin earth"
(p. 55) means the earth moving in a direction contrary to the
apparent course of the sun, that "stammel feather" (p. 37) is a
red feather, that "dingle" (pp. xvii and 184) means a small,
deep wooded valley or dell. We would probably require the
Oxford English Dictionary, unabridged, however, to learn that
"gambo" means farm cart—"butter fat goosegirls, bounced in
a gambo bed" (p. 198)—or that "folly" as it is used in several
poems, notably "Hold Hard, These Ancient Minutes" (p. 58),
means steeple or the goal in a steeplechase. But most of
Thomas's vocabulary is deceptive in that it *seems* to be made
up almost entirely of perfectly familiar words. It is the way in
which he uses the words that causes the difficulty.

One of Thomas's favorite tricks is to use familiar words in
unfamiliar senses. As he told Harvey Breit, "I like to put down
the word blood. It's a curious kind of word; it means insanity,
among other meanings." [17] It seems possible that this is one of
the meanings he had in mind when he wrote, in "I Fellowed
Sleep":

> There grows the hours' ladder to the sun,
> Each rung a love or losing to the last,

[17] Harvey Breit, in "Talks with Dylan Thomas," *A Casebook*, p. 196.

"The Churning Bulk"

The inches monkeyed by the blood of man
An old, mad man still climbing in his ghost,
My fathers' ghost is climbing in the rain.

(p. 32)

The idea of "blood" meaning insanity in this context is reinforced by the reference to the "old, mad man" in the next line.
And its double entendre cleverly matches the double meanings
of evolution and meddling in the word "monkeyed." The
ladder has been tampered with, has been made more difficult to
climb by man's foolishness. (But this "ghost," or spirit, this
"mad man," man devoid of his senses, man made up of all
previous generations, is still climbing toward the sun through
the rain.)

Perhaps the fullest explanation of Thomas's attitude toward
using words in rare and unusual senses is contained in his
earliest letter to Pamela Hansford Johnson (autumn of 1933),
in which he comments on the phrase "unquiet mouse" that
Miss Johnson had used. He complains that "unquiet" does
nothing for "mouse." Explaining that other people's private
associations have a crucial effect on their interpretation of
particular words and phrases, he says that a poet must choose a
qualifying adjective from one of two possibilities. One must
either find or make an adjective that will include all associations or that will replace previous associations, thereby revealing "mouse" in a completely new way. This was advice that
Thomas himself attempted to follow, although not always
with perfect success.

"How Soon the Servant Sun" (p. 65) uses the word "fog" in
its primitive or dialectal sense to mean "grass." In "Do You
Not Father Me" (p. 54), Thomas refers to "the Abraham-
man," using the name not only as a Biblical allusion (Abraham's proposed sacrifice of Isaac is seen as "madness" for
God's sake) but also in its literal Hebrew meaning, "father of

many." Those who hack down the tower, who crucify Christ, are, like Abraham, the people of God, fulfilling God's will and at the same time preparing the way for future generations. In the same poem the word "wrack" means not only destruction and wreck but also very appropriately to this poetic context, seaweed or weeds cast on the shore:

> Up rose the Abraham-man, mad for my sake,
> They said, who hacked and humoured, they were mine.
> I am, the tower told, felled by a timeless stroke,
> Who razed my wooden folly stands aghast,
> For man-begetters in the dry-as-paste,
> The ringed-sea ghost, rise grimly from the wrack.

This unexpected meaning is the basis for the word "seaweedy" in the next stanza:

> Do you not father me on the destroying sand?
> You are your sisters' sire, said seaweedy.

"Seaweedy," the speaker, is one of the progeny who rose from the "wrack."

The word "grave" near the end of "Over Sir John's Hill" actually means 'engrave":

> and I who hear the tune of the slow,
> Wear-willow river, grave,
> Before the lunge of the night, the notes on this time-shaken
> Stone for the sake of the souls of the slain birds sailing.

> (p. 189)

Numerous other words in this same poem have been used as different parts of speech, for example, "wrestle of elms" and "white cranes stilt." When Thomas says "the gulled birds hare/ To the hawk on fire," he means that the "duped" birds are like hares in a game of hound and hares. ("Hare" is used in the same way in a line from "I, in My Intricate Image"—"The haring snail go giddily round the flower," p. 41.)

The syntax, and thereby the meaning, of the whole first sentence (comprising twenty-four lines) of "Unluckily for a Death" (p. 120) turns on the usage of the word "dedicate" in the sixth line. The reader naturally takes it to be a verb, whereas it is really an archaic adjective meaning "dedicated."

Thomas, then, often throws us off the track of the real meaning or implication of the words he uses. For example, he describes

> The stream from the priest black wristed spinney and sleeves
> Of thistling frost
> Of the nightingale's din and tale!
>
> (p. 184)

Since "spinney" means "thicket," what Thomas is really describing is a thicket, not a stream, which looks as though it had black wrists and sleeves of frost. The syntax may have been wrenched in order to maintain the rhythm and the tight rhyme scheme.

In Part II of "I, in My Intricate Image," (pp. 41–42) the stanza

> As they dive, the dust settles,
> The cadaverous gravels, falls thick and steadily,
> The highroad of water where the seabear and mackerel
> Turn the long sea arterial

can be understood only when we get the syntax and metaphor of "cadaverous gravels" straight. The word "cadaverous" is an adjective used as a noun meaning "cadaverous persons," i.e., the dead, while "gravels" is a verb meaning "covers with gravel" or dust in this context. The verbs "settles," "gravels," and "falls" are parallel to each other, while the object of "gravels" is "the highroad of water."

Although Thomas tolerated, even fostered, syntactical congestion in order to convey a sense of struggle and involvement, that sense is certainly not always conveyed to the reader. Faced with piled-up phrases and clauses so characteristic of many Thomas poems, the reader must patiently search for subject, verb, object, and so forth until the riddle of syntax is solved or until boredom or irritation concludes the search. When the effort is successful there is a sense of discovery, but sometimes the discovery seems hardly worth the effort. Consider, for example, the opening of "When, Like a Running Grave":

> When, like a running grave, time tracks you down,
> Your calm and cuddled is a scythe of hairs,
> Love in her gear is slowly through the house,
> Up naked stairs, a turtle in a hearse,
> Hauled to the dome,
>
> Comes, like a scissors stalking, tailor age.
>
> (p. 21)

Study reveals that the clauses "time tracks you down," "Your calm and cuddled . . . ," "Love in her gear . . . ," and "Comes . . . tailor age" are objects of the adverb "when." The other phrases can then be assigned to their appropriate positions and the whole six lines seen as an adverbial clause leading to the simple imperative statement "Deliver me." The rest of the poem can be analyzed in the same way—and must be, if we are to come to any understanding of it. In this instance, as in the case of "Now," "How Soon the Servant Sun," and "Unluckily for a Death," among others, such effort hardly seems rewarded. In these poems obscurity results in esthetic failure.

Some complaints about Thomas's obscurity, however, are not fully justified. When, for example, Olson learned that there was a real geographical landmark behind the poem, "In the White Giant's Thigh," [18] he suggested: "A reader is perhaps entitled, in instances of this sort, to complain that a matter of such special, indeed local, information, especially if it makes the difference between understanding and not understanding, might have been supplied in a note." [19] Actually, if we study the syntax of the lines in question, we can get enough information about "the white giant's thigh" to understand the passage satisfactorily.

> Through throats where many rivers meet, the curlews cry,
> Under the conceiving moon, on the high chalk hill,
> And there this night I walk in the white giant's thigh
> Where barren as boulders women lie longing still
> To labour and love though they lay down long ago.
>
> (p. 197)

The first two lines describe the curlews crying in the moonlight "on the high chalk hill." Then Thomas says, "And *there* this night I walk in the white giant's thigh." What else can "there" refer to but the "high chalk hill"—a large white hill? The image of a hill as a giant is a very common one, and if Thomas is walking in the "thigh" of the "white giant" he must be on the side of the hill. The only further information we need is supplied in the next two lines—the particular place must be a cemetery. If the phrase "through throats where many rivers meet" confuses the picture, the syntax certifies that it can only refer to the curlews.

But Thomas's syntactical complexities are, finally, one of his serious defects. If we are to count as part of the genius of Thomas that he could turn commonplace words into something fresh and original, then we must count as one of his

[18] "Salute to a Poet," *Times Literary Supplement* (October 28, 1952), 776.
[19] Olson, p. 46.

deficiencies that he was sometimes unable to achieve syntactical clarity. For example, how can we interpret these lines from Sonnet VII (p. 83)?

> Now stamp the Lord's Prayer on a grain of rice,
> A Bible-leaved of all the written woods
> Strip to this tree.

It would seem that Thomas was describing the woods as a Bible, a sacred text. But the confusion caused by the use of a hyphen instead of a comma between "Bible" and "leaved," making the word an adjective without any noun referent, cannot be resolved.

In the same way, when Thomas says in "After the Funeral" (p. 96) that he shall

> call all
> The seas to service that her wood-tongued virtue
> Babble like a bellbuoy over the hymning heads,
> Bow down the walls of the ferned and foxy woods
> That her love sing and swing through a brown chapel,
> Bless her bent spirit,

it is never precisely clear who or what will "bow down the walls" or "bless her bent spirit." Is it his call that will bow down the woods, or is it her virtue that will babble and bow down? One presumes that it is his calling, his voice, that will perform these acts, but there is only the overall import of the poem to support this contention. The syntax does not settle the matter for us.

The phrases that open this same poem do not follow a simple grammatical pattern either. But in this case, an apparent illogicality is clearly appropriate to the subject; one usually does not speak or perceive reality in a neat appositive fashion at the funeral of one deeply loved.

"The Churning Bulk"

After the funeral, mule praises, brays,
Windshake of sailshaped ears, muffle-toed tap
Tap happily of one peg in the thick
Grave's foot, blinds down the lids, the teeth in black,
The spittled eyes, the salt ponds in the sleeves,
Morning smack of the spade that wakes up sleep,
Shakes a desolate boy who slits his throat
In the dark of the coffin and sheds dry leaves,
That breaks one bone to light with a judgment clout.

This stacking of phrases is an illustration of one of Thomas's favorite devices for imparting intensity. He uses appositives *within* appositives, piling them on top of one another to such an extent that they become a tangle of loosely connected phrases. Here the first nine lines are made up of numerous objects of the preposition "after," all in loose apposition with "funeral." These objects include "mule praises," "windshake . . . ," "muffle-toed tap . . . ," "eyes," "ponds," "smack." Within this pattern, "brays" is in apposition with "praises," "blinds" is the predicate for "tap," "shakes" is in apposition with "wakes" and "breaks" (or a predicate for "smack"). The tenth line sums up everything that has been said in the previous nine lines—"After the feast of tear-stuffed time and thistles."

A glance at the poet whom Thomas most resembles stylistically, Hopkins, may help to clarify some of the points being made about Thomas's language. Here are the first four lines of Hopkins's "The Caged Skylark":

As a dare-gale skylark scanted in a dull cage
Man's mounting spirit in his bone-house, mean house, dwells—
That bird beyond the remembering his free fells;
This in drudgery, day-labouring-out life's age.

The emotional impulse of the language, the alliterations, assonances, and consonances, immediately link the two poets. Hopkins' syntax, however wrenched, however unexpected the verbs and modifiers, maintains precise syntactic control. Thomas makes the reader's mind dart and search not among pieces of scattered syntax but among pieces of ambiguous syntax. Even when we find what goes with what we can never be sure of the meaning. For example, he says that the Thief in "In Country Sleep"

> comes to take
> Her faith that this last night for his unsacred sake
> He comes to leave her in the lawless sun awaking
> Naked and forsaken to grieve he will not come.
>
> (p. 186)

We have grammatical units starting and ending here without any certain idea of just where they go or what they mean. The passage apparently means that the Thief comes to take the child's faith so that on the last night he can come "to leave her in the lawless sun . . . ," where she will grieve "he will not come." This example is typical of the syntactical difficulty in Thomas in that the source of the confusion usually is clausal; Thomas's clauses tend to get detached from his sentences. This is not the case with Hopkins, where in the most hectic headlong rush of his language the proper subordination usually remains clear. (Obviously this is a stylistic distinction which has great semantic and thematic significance for the two poets.)

The effect of the word "mean" in Hopkins "Skylark" is very similar to the effect of surprise and density Thomas achieves with puns or with double and triple levels of ambiguity. The phrase "mean-house," of course, implies both "half-way house" and "lowly house."

In numerous cases Thomas built whole poems around the various and ambiguous meanings of a certain word or phrase.

"The Churning Bulk"

The well-known poem "If I Were Tickled by the Rub of Love" (p. 13) is an example. The word "rub" is used both as a noun and a verb, but it is also related in meaning throughout the poem to Hamlet's use of the word—"Aye, there's the rub." In Hamlet's soliloquy, however, the word means "obstacle" or "difficulty," whereas for Thomas it has taken on the connotation of death as well, because of the way Shakespeare used it. The changing meaning of the word "tickle" in this poem is almost as significant. In the first four stanzas it has to do with a pleasurable sensation, but in the last two stanzas it means "moved," "affected by."

In "Do You Not Father Me" (p. 54) there is an intricate and almost indecipherable play on the word "tower." The word has the broad Yeatsian implication of "Man"—the tower of words. Further, it is not only a tall structure, which may be both a church steeple and a prison, but also a phallic "lover's house." It represents Christ, the Savior, who is like a tower in strength and dominance, but it seems possible that Thomas also intended a concealed pun on the word "magdalena," meaning "tower" in Latin, so that his first stanza has a partial reference to Mary Magdalen and the woman taken in adultery:

> Do you not father me, nor the erected arm
> For my tall tower's sake cast in her stone?
> Do you not mother me, nor, as I am,
> The lovers' house, lie suffering my stain?
> Do you not sister me, nor the erected crime
> For my tall turrets carry as your sin?
> Do you not brother me, nor, as you climb,
> Adore my windows for their summer scene?

Since Christ is seen here as an androgynous figure, these two references are not mutually exclusive. The word "tower" in this poem also has to do with time because of Thomas's association of steeples and towers with the clocks often found on them. This association explains the phrase "the tower told" (the clock told), the irony of "felled by a timeless stroke," and "my wooden folly" (meaning steeple).

> I am, the tower told, felled by a timeless stroke,
> Who razed my wooden folly stands aghast.

And because of death's association with time it too can be called a tower—"the tower death"—in the last stanza.

A much simpler example of a poem turning on a particular word or words is the beautiful but seldom noticed "We Lying By Seasand" (p. 91). This Audenesque poem describes two people marooned on a point of land separated from the mainland by the high tide. Its significance is largely connected to the meaning of the words "yellow" and "grave." In the first two lines,

> We lying by seasand, watching yellow
> And the grave sea,

the words "yellow" and "grave" are both used with purposive ambiguity. By its syntax, "yellow" modifies "watching" but it also applies to "sea." In either case, it implies "melancholy." The word "grave" here means somber in color—gray. (It may likewise mean ominous, while "yellow" may also imply some fear.) The "yellow grave" of the fifth line refers to the color of the sand and the metaphorical grave in which they are lying. Thomas goes on to describe the "wind/ That's grave and gay as grave and sea," thereby giving "grave" all its meanings in the space of one line (and adding to the ambiguous effect by the use of the assonantal antonym "gay"). The poet continues to play with these meanings and their ramifications, describing the coming of the storm tide, the wish for death and deliverance,

> for wind to blow away
> The strata of the shore and drown red rock;

but, he says, the wishes are useless because the rock will reappear when the tide goes down, and we cannot just lie waiting for the good weather to begin (an analogy for heaven and death). The word "breaks" in the last line is also worth noting as an example of Thomas's multiple meanings:

> But wishes breed not, neither
> Can we fend off rock arrival,
> Lie watching yellow until the golden weather
> Breaks, O my heart's blood, like a heart and hill.

"Break" means begin or come into being in regard to the "golden weather"; it means shatter in regard to "heart"; it means disintegrate in regard to "hill." By this multiple usage, Thomas conveys his ambivalent feelings toward death.

Unlike Hopkins, but like the whimsical and ironic Ransom, Thomas made the refurbished cliché one of his foremost artifices, perhaps his single most important device. There is, as Robert Penn Warren tells us in his essay "Pure and Impure Poetry," always a sense of shock involved in putting worn-out language to fresh use.[20] In Thomas's creative hands even the cliché finds new life. The "dead of night" quickens as "the quick of night" (p. 132), "a nose for news" becomes more energetic as "a jaw for news" (p. 80), the worn out "young and gay" is refreshed as "young and easy" (p. 178), "cocksure" becomes more sure as "cockshut" (p. 21), and the "man in the moon" takes on a Shelleyan or Daliesque hue as "man in the wind and the west moon" (p. 77). Thomas forces his reader to pay attention by using clichés and familiar words in new arrangements or as different parts of speech. In "Once Below a Time" (p. 147), he refers to his body as his

> pinned-around-the-spirit
> Cut-to-measure flesh bit,

[20] In *Criticism: The Foundations of Modern Literary Judgment,* ed. Mark Schorer *et al.* (New York, 1948), p. 371.

Suit for a serial sum
On the first of each hardship.

In "Prologue" (xvi) he says that he has written all his poetry "to the best of my love." The force of a phrase like "Sundays of the dead" (p. 199) is derived from its echo of "a month of Sundays," while the grim humor of the last stanza of "Lament" (p. 196) is partly based on its parody of all the familiar clichés about old age and death.

In some cases Thomas seems to be trying to achieve an apparent simplicity, a conversational tone, as well as to establish a sense of conflict between what we expect and what he is actually saying. "Once Below a Time," for example, employs these verbal approximations: "common clay clothes," "lubber crust of Wales," "My silly suit, hardly yet suffered for" (instead of paid for), "boy of common thread," and "ready-made handy water."

"To Others Than You" (p. 118) also uses this wrenching of expectations in order to convey Thomas's disgust with a false friend—"You with a bad coin in your socket," "While you displaced a truth in the air." The first of these two quotations not only suggests "pocket" but also the dangerous coin in the socket of a fuse box (also Thomas's own "coins on my eyelids," p. 151, and "penny-eyed" from Sonnet I, p. 80). The second example comes from the jargon of science in which one substance is said to displace another—water displaces air in a jar, a ship displaces water in the ocean. In "Fern Hill" (p. 178) almost every phrase is based on some such familiar turn of speech.

The echo of familiar idioms often serves to add extra depth to an otherwise ordinary idea, as when the poet says that the dying man in a bomb raid "will dive up to his tears" (p. 129) in death. The echo of diving up to one's ears implies a deep dive, while the variation, "tears," conveys the idea of suffering as

well. "Rain wringing/ Wind" (p. 114) renews "rain-bringing
wind," while "shall I let pray the shadow of a sound" (p. 112)
indicates a far greater intensity than "shall I let fall . . ."
would have. In the line "love in the frost is pared and wintered
by" (p. 90), the use of the homey reference to canning and
preserving of the fall harvest provides a poignant image of the
indestructibility of love. Sometimes a Biblical echo serves the
same purpose, as in the phrase "vessel of abscesses" (p. 100),
which describes the skull as the repository of horror.

An understanding and inevitably an appreciation of
Thomas's work must be premised, then, on an understanding
of the way he uses words—his propensity toward slang and
unusual or multiple meanings, his gnarled but usually deciph-
erable syntax, his rejuvenated clichés. But the reader must also
be aware of the voice, the persona, the particular identity
which Thomas assumes to advance the "narrative" of each
particular poem.

III
PERSONA

Thomas used the word "narrative" in a special sense. He
once defined poetry as "the rhythmic, inevitably narrative,
movement from an overclothed blindness to a naked vision." [21]
When asked in an early interview if he thought "there can
now be a use for narrative poetry," he replied, "Yes. Narrative
is essential. Much of the flat, abstract poetry of the present has
no narrative movement, no movement at all, and is consequently dead." [22]

The questioner, it would seem, meant by "narrative" something like the style of Tennyson or Masefield, the story in
verse. Thomas understood the word to mean simply a quality

[21] *Quite Early One Morning*, p. 188.   [22] *Ibid.*, p. 189.

of consistency, of direct expression. Treece says: "When we consider the normal connotation of the word 'narrative' and measure it against Dylan Thomas's poems, we see immediately that he meant something else—a mood, a *leit motif*, a series of images; but not a story, a continuous structure of event or characterisation." [23] "Narrative" to Thomas meant the "thread of action through a poem"; through narrative one achieves an "intellectual thing," a kind of ideational clarity or, in Thomas's words again, "lucidity."

The way Thomas eventually achieved "more meaning at first reading" was by becoming more narrative, both in the conventional sense and in his own sense of the term, for these senses are related. Thomas came to speak more directly to his reader, to put more connectives between images, to express his meaning in a "Ballad . . . ," to tell "A Winter's Tale," to address his reader without great concealment—as in "In Country Sleep"—and, finally, to write a work of almost nothing but direct speech—*Under Milk Wood.*

But even in his early poetry there is a strong narrative strain. It is didactic in that nearly every poem makes a statement about existence—in spite of the fact that impetuosity of diction, ambiguity of syntax, and a welter of imagery tend to obscure the statements. What these statements are we shall try to unravel in a later chapter. Here we shall confine ourselves to noting some of the personae Thomas assumes in making these statements.

The typical voice that speaks through the "narrative" of Thomas's poetry is that of the poet, who may be the fabled "spinner"—the weaver of magic tales, the singer, the bard, sometimes a prophet. Occasionally, it is the very autobiographical voice of Dylan Thomas himself as he writes to his dying father in "Do Not Go Gentle," or to his wife in "On a

[23] Treece (1956 edition), p. 13.

Wedding Anniversary" or "I Make This in a Warring Absence," or to his son in "This Side of the Truth." The poet and the man merge in the birthday poems, "Poem in October," "Poem on His Birthday," and "Twenty-four Years." And it is primarily the voice of the poet in "On No Work of Words," "In My Craft or Sullen Art," "I, in My Intricate Image," and "Especially When the October Wind."

It is customary, however, for the "narrative" line of the poems to be voiced by a kind of concrete universal, an Everyman who shifts character and point of view as the poem demands. This is the basic polyphonic voice of the Sonnets—the speaker is Poet, Christ, and Everyman. In "I Dreamed My Genesis," Thomas speaks through the unconscious mind; in " 'If My Head Hurt a Hair's Foot,' " he is first the unborn child and then the child's mother. In "When Once the Twilight Locks No Longer" and in "Before I Knocked," the voice is omniscient; it is that of a divinity.

The interesting thing to note, however, may be not so much *who* is speaking but rather *how* he speaks. Thomas much prefers to use the present tense, to describe an action taking place rather than a scene remembered. If the poem does involve remembrance of past events, as "From Love's First Fever to Her Plague," the remembering is often in the first person, by a particular character, at a particular point in time—the present. In this poem, for example, the poet "remembers" the process of his development from the moment of conception to maturity—the present:

> A million minds gave suck to such a bud
> As forks my eye.
>
> (p. 26)

In "Twenty-four Years" the method, much condensed, is the same—the poet remembers his prenatal existence but concludes in the present tense: "I advance for as long as forever is" (p. 110). Even in "The Tombstone Told When She Died," the poet has to be involved in the action—"I who saw in a hurried film" (p. 103)—and the crucial meaning of the poem is expressed in the first person, the voice of the dead woman: "I died before bedtime came."

In "Ceremony After a Fire Raid" (p. 143) Thomas conveys by ambiguity of voice, rather than image or statement alone, an age-old paradox—Hopkins's " 'Tis Margaret you mourn for"; Donne's "And therefore never send to know for whom the bell tolls; It tolls for thee."

> Myselves
> The grievers
> Grieve
> Among the street burned to tireless death
> A child of a few hours.

The poet sees himself a creature like Whitman, of many selves interrelated with all other creatures. He is both one of the grievers and one for whom they grieve. In the third stanza he is also one of the believers, all of whom also share in the guilt for the child's death:

> Forgive
> Us forgive
> Us your death that myselves the believers
> May hold it in a great flood.

Thomas said in regard to his projected "In Country Heaven" and the poems which would be included in it—"In Country Sleep," "Over Sir John's Hill," and "In the White Giant's Thigh":

The remembered tellings, which are the components of the poem, are not all told as though they are remembered; the poem will not be a series of poems in the past tense. The memory, in all tenses, can look towards the future, can caution and admonish. The rememberer may live himself back into active participation in the remembered scene, adventure, or spiritual condition.[24]

This particiation by the speaker, although clearly applied to the three poems in question, which were among his last poems, is a method which Thomas had used throughout his poetry. Even where it appears that he is writing a descriptive poem, he often suddenly inserts himself into the scene, as in "A Saint About to Fall." Here the poem opens with a description of the child falling out of heaven into life. Then for a few lines the newborn child speaks:

> O wake in me in my house in the mud
> Of the crotch of the squawking shores,
> Flicked from the carbolic city puzzle in a bed of sores
> The scudding base of the familiar sky,
> The lofty roots of the clouds.
>
> (p. 106)

Then the personal voice of the poet takes over, speaking directly to the child, and indirectly to the reader, throughout the rest of the poem.

In "Ballad of the Long-legged Bait," the narrative shifts for a few lines into the first person:

> Clash out the mounting dolphin's day,
> My mast is a bell-spire,
> Strike and smoothe, for my decks are drums.
>
> (p. 169)

"Poem on His Birthday" proceeds for more than eight stanzas in a third-person description of "the rhymer in the long tongued room,/Who tolls his birthday bell" (p. 190). But the last four stanzas of the poem are entirely first person:

[24] *Quite Early One Morning*, p. 180.

Oh, let me midlife mourn by the shrined
And druid herons' vows
The voyage to ruin I must run,
Dawn ships clouted aground,
Yet, though I cry with tumbledown tongue,
Count my blessings aloud.

The fact that Thomas is averse to the use of quotation marks, especially in his later poetry, may cause difficulty for the unsuspecting reader when he comes on lines like these from "Into Her Lying Down Head," Part III (p. 127):

A she bird sleeping brittle by
Her lover's wings that fold to-morrow's flight,
Within the nested treefork
Sings to the treading hawk
Carrion, paradise, chirrup my bright yolk.

Here the last line is the voice of the "she bird" to her lover. The absence of quotation marks is a problem even in the first poem in the book, "I See the Boys of Summer," and in several other places. It seems, however, to be rather arbitrary and perhaps even unintentional on Thomas's part, since numerous other poems *do* use such punctuation—"I Fellowed Sleep," "Find Meat on Bones," " 'If My Head Hurt a Hair's Foot.' "

The reader must *hear* the poem as well as see it on the paper. Only with the ear of the mind, for example, can we perceive that "To-day, This Insect" opens in the middle of a poetic meditation. The poet has been trying to think of a subject for a poem when he sees, and kills, an insect and suddenly becomes aware of its imagistic possibilities. "To-day, this insect, and the world I breathe/ [will be my symbols] Now that my symbols have outelbowed space" (p. 47). When we achieve this empathy with the mind of the poet, we can perceive the voices in his poetry much more easily.

IV

IMAGE

A good deal of the difficulty encountered in Thomas's imagery may be related to the multiplicity of devices he employed. There is the common practice of arbitrary association, derived principally from the Imagists and typified by Pound's "In a Station of the Metro." There is the juxtaposing of the personal and the private, the obvious and the occult, in the manner of the "heap of broken images" which opens *The Waste Land.* In Thomas there are also clear signs of the further dissociation and irrationality of the Surrealists, such as one finds in Gascoyne: "Butterflies burst from their skins and grow long tongues like plants,/ The plants play games with a suit of mail like a cloud" ("In Defence of Humanism"). There is sometimes the intellectual emphasis of the Metaphysicals, and in the later poetry a great deal of Romantic pictorialism with an occasional touch of Baroque flamboyance. And always there is the tendency to exploit verbal devices, puns, and homonyms, as a means for fashioning new images and for joining otherwise unrelated images.

Obviously no consideration of imagistic practices is going to produce wholesale lucidity, but an understanding of the practices of the poet is nevertheless a necessary step toward understanding. This is especially true in Thomas because a great many confusing and contradictory statements have been made about his imagery.[25]

[25] For example, Geoffrey Grigson, in "How Much Me Now Your Acrobatics Amaze," *A Casebook,* p. 119, called Thomas's poetry a "meaningless hot sprawl of mud." This same essay reveals a complete misunderstanding of Thomas's poetry and techniques; for example, Grigon's inability to perceive the formal pattern of "Lie Still, Sleep Becalmed" and his misreading of the lines "From every true or crater/

99

Many of the critical misconceptions concerning Thomas's imagery may be traced to his famous letter to Treece. That letter is extremely important because it not only sets forth what Thomas was trying to achieve, but also because, correctly understood, it provides basic insights into his working methods. Thomas began this letter by saying that his poems could not move concentrically around a central image. While holding that some poems by others need no more than one image, they move "around one idea, from one logical point to another, making a full circle," he went on:

A poem by myself *needs* a host of images, because its centre is a host of images. I make one image—though "make" is not the word; I let, perhaps, an image be "made" emotionally in me and then apply to it what intellectual and critical forces I possess—let it breed another, let that image contradict the first, make, of the third image bred out of the other two together, a fourth contradictory image, and let them all, within my imposed formal limits, conflict. Each image holds within it the seed of its own destruction, and my dialectal [sic] method . . . is a constant building up and breaking down of the images that come out of the central seed, which is itself destructive and constructive at the same time. . . .

The *life* in any poem of mine cannot move concentrically round a central image; the life must come out of the centre; an image must be born and die in another; and any sequence of my images must be a sequence of creations, recreations, destructions, contradictions. . . . I believe in the simple thread of action through a poem, but that is an intellectual thing aimed at lucidity through narrative. My object is, as you say, conventionally "to get things straight." Out of the inevitable conflict of images—inevitable, because of the creative, recreative, destruc-

---

Carrying cloud, Death strikes their house" (p. 120). (As opposed to a "true cloud," a "crater carrying cloud" probably carries bombers and bombs which will form craters—the poem was first published in 1941.)

tive and contradictory nature of the motivating centre . . . —I try to make that momentary peace which is a poem. . . . a poem of mine is, or should be, a water-tight section of the stream that is flowing all ways, all warring images within it should be reconciled for that small stop of time.[26]

Of Thomas's comments on his imagery the most curious is that which maintains that the images conflict. Strangely enough, this is the point most critics have accepted without question.[27]

The truth of the matter would seem to be that the images conflict and contradict in only the most general way, in the way that they are likely to clash in the work of many modern poets. Eliot's images of Sweeney, for example, conflict intensely with the nightingale and the Convent of the Sacred Heart. But this, since Eliot and Pound, is a relatively common practice. Furthermore, there is inherent in the very nature of metaphoric language a tendency toward conflict. This kind of conflict is sometimes characterized as "tension" and is suggested in Johnson's description of metaphysical images being "yoked by violence together." It is this tension, or violent yoking, or Coleridge's "reconciliation of opposites," that Thomas would seem to be describing. He put much the same idea in more practical terms in letters to Vernon Watkins. Once he explained that he described the newborn child as a "blazing" harsh head (in "The Tombstone Told When She Died") because it made the line "violent enough." [28] He voiced

[26] Treece (1956 edition), p. 37.

[27] Cf. C. Day Lewis, *The Poetic Image* (London, 1947), pp. 124–125. Tindall said that Thomas applied "Hegelian dialectic to imagery," in *Forces in Modern British Literature: 1885–1956* (Vintage, New York, 1956), p. 239; although more recently in his *Reader's Guide*, p. 18, he says, "We may be sure that the juxtaposition of incompatibles, whether of sound or pictures, is Thomas' method; but that the process is systematically 'dialectical' I cannot be sure."

[28] Watkins, p. 44.

the same idea also concerning "Unluckily for a Death," where, he explained to Watkins, a "sudden crudeness is . . . essential to the argument." [29] Whether metaphysical, surrealistic, or pictorial, most of Thomas's images have this harshness, this sense of struggle or intensity.

At the outset it is easier to see what Thomas did not want rather than to piece out precisely what he did want. Thomas, especially the earlier and more difficult Thomas, did not want a passive or reflective quality in his imagery, even though it was a quality found in some of the most sensitive poetry. He seems to have avoided poems that look back, recalling memories and expressing themselves in pictures or a series of obviously related pictorial images, such as George Barker's "To Any Member of My Generation":

> What was it you remember:—the summer mornings
> Down by the river at Richmond with a girl
> And as you kissed, clumsy in bathing costumes.

Successive occurrences of imagery like Eliot's "Preludes" likewise seem not to be sufficiently "destructive" for Thomas:

> You tossed a blanket from the bed;
> You lay upon your back, and waited;
> You dozed, and watched the night revealing
> The thousand sordid images
> Of which your soul was constituted.

In terms of a "dialectic" of imagery, however, there would seem to be more of a breeding, conflict, and new breeding here than in Thomas's work.

Thomas wrote a number of poems that recall the past and that use related "pictures." "Twenty-four Years" (p. 110) is a typical example. The first thing one notices about the imagery

[29] *Ibid.*, p. 63.

of this poem is that the "narrative"—in the sense we have just been discussing it, in the sense of the rational line, the "thread of action"—joins the imagery; and finally the meaning of the poem is the imagery. There is one inactive verb, "remind," in the first line, which sets up the memory frame. After it appears, everything either moves or is coiled ready to leap. The thought of the poem is carried by "bury," "walk," "crouched," "sewing," "dressed," "begun," "advance," and "is." Such a sense of action is one of the characteristics of a Thomas poem.

It is unprofitable, then, to emphasize the conflict-contradiction quality of Thomas's poetry as though the images actually formed a dialectic that led to an imagistic "synthesis." Though there are a few instances where this pattern might be found in a poem, the most profitable approach is to establish the "central seed." Regardless of what conflict Thomas felt in the process of writing, the feeling has little practical importance in understanding his metaphoric structures. The "central seed" is often buried, but, as with most difficult poetry, there is no better way of trying to untie the Gordian complexities than by determining precisely what the "central seed" is.

A demonstration from the prose might be appropriate here. Ineluctable events always engulf characters in Thomas's fiction—hardly less so in the later prose than in the earlier. But we understand the events that the characters of the later prose (1939 and after) experience much more readily than we understand those of the earlier characters. The main reason for this is very simple: we understand the "central seed" and the "thread of action" in the later stories, whereas we are greatly confused about them in the earlier stories. When the boy dreams in "A Visit to Grandpa's" (1940), Thomas tells us he is dreaming. When Thomas wants to describe the view of death from the other side of the sick bed in "The Visitor" (1935), he gives no hint of what he is about until late in the narrative, long after total confusion has overcome the reader.

Once Thomas was willing to give his reader a "central seed," all his fantastic associations assumed brilliant cohesion. *Adventures in the Skin Trade* (1939), for instance, inundates us with a series of inexplicable occurrences, but Thomas usually makes it quite clear under what *donnée* these events transpire. After Sam Bennet has unknowingly drained a bottle of eau de cologne and is blind drunk, Thomas accounts for his condition in these terms:

Then the birds flew down and kicked him on the head, carefully between the eyes, brutally on each temple, and he fell back into the bath.

That was all the birds singing under the water, and the sea was full of feathers that swam up his nostrils and into his mouth. A duck as big as a ship sailed up on a drop of water as big as a house and smelt his breath as it spurted out from broken, bleeding lips, like flames and water-spouts. Here came a wave of brandy and birds, and Mr. Allingham, naked as a baby, riding on the top with his birthmark like a rainbow, and George Ring swimming breaststroke through the open door, and three Mrs. Daceys gliding in yards above the flowing ground.

The darkness drowned in a bright ball of light, and the birds stopped.[30]

Imagine what this sequence of events would have meant to the reader if Thomas had decided not to mention the point that young Samuel had drunk eau de cologne.

Obviously, then, the "central seed" which Thomas recognized as the source of his images may be equated with the more common terms of central "mood," "feeling," or "idea" of the poem. Once we are able to posit the central emotion or idea, or

[30] *Adventures in the Skin Trade and Other Stories* (New York, 1956), p. 43.

both, of a poem, we are generally able to determine the meaning and relationship of images. In "The Force That through the Green Fuse" (p. 10), the destructive and creative forces of life are viewed from five different perspectives: the force in the fuse, the force driving the water, the hand that whirls, the lips that leech, and the "crooked worm." Yet all derive from the feeling, or perception, of decay in the very process of growth. All the images in the poem may be said to spring from this "seed."

The structure of imagery in "Twenty-four Years" (p. 110) is similarly related to a central perception: the embryo "crouched like a tailor/ Sewing a shroud for a journey." All the images in the poem are clearly related to this subsuming image. It is because the unborn child is "like a tailor" that he is "sewing" a shroud and that he is "dressed to die." It is because he is "sewing a shroud for a journey" that the sun is "meat-eating"—it will devour him when he emerges from the doorway—and that his "red veins" are "full of money"—his skin is his clothing, so his veins filled with lifeblood are his pockets filled with money for the trip. Maintaining the idea of the journey, the speaker advances forever toward the "elementary town," his life is a constant movement back into the elements.

The mixture of the surrealistic, imagistic, and metaphysical techniques one finds in the early Thomas is reminiscent of Hart Crane. But Crane, more influenced by Lawrence than by the metaphysical revival,[31] and more influenced by imagism than by its later surrealistic aberration, usually kept a more

---

[31] To judge from his correspondence, Crane was absorbed in Lawrence throughout his career. Crane once said that one of Lawrence's works meant more to him "than any book in the Bible." See *The Letters of Hart Crane*, ed. Brom Weber (New York, 1952), p. 395.

apparent connection between his images than did Thomas. Although one finds amazing similarities in phrasing and attitude, which Thomas himself admitted,[32] there is a quality of intellectual ingenuity, a hyperbolic quality, in Thomas which often makes his images more complex. Consider, for example, these respective handlings of the phonograph image. Crane writes in section VI of "The Bridge":

> The phonographs of hades in the brain
> Are tunnels that re-wind themselves.

In "I, in My Intricate Image" Thomas writes:

(Turn the sea-spindle lateral,
The grooved land rotating, that the stylus of lightning
Dazzle this face of voices on the moon-turned table,
Let the wax disk babble
Shames and the damp dishonours, the relic scraping.
These are your years' recorders. The circular world stands still.)

(pp. 42–43)

What is immediately noticeable in Thomas's image is its cohesion. It bears marked analogies with Donne's famous compass image. It has an intellectual extensiveness which Crane's lacks.

In this image, as in many of Thomas's other images, the key is verbal, the understanding turns on the word "sea-spindle," which means "a round pile or pipe placed on a rock or shoal as an aid to navigation." Once we understand this term, Thomas's image is almost as clear as Donne's compass. Thomas describes

---

[32] Treece (1956 edition), p. 43. Thomas told Treece that "a poet who had read some of my work told me that the most obvious modern influence in my poetry was Crane. And he was astonished . . . when I told him that I had never heard of Crane before. He showed me some of Crane's poems then, and I could certainly see what he meant; there were, indeed, two or three almost identical bits of phrasing, and much of the actual sound seemed similar."

the land rotating on a sea-spindle like a record turning around the spindle of a record player. Lightning will provide the arm of the record player dazzling "this face of voices" which is activated or turned by the moon. The "face of voices" is made up of the dead (who were drowned in the previous stanzas), and the "moon-turned table" is the sea, whose tides are governed by the moon. What does the record "babble"? "Shames and the damp dishonours," the poet says, "your years' recorders," the record of your lives. The final sentence, "The circular world stands still," is defined in its primary meaning by the conceit. The center part of this phonographic world, which is the sea (surrounded by the "grooved land"), like the center of any record, appears to stand still.

The "seed" of such images as the record player may be called spatial: the parts of one object (the record player) are seen in terms of another object (the earth). At the root of such images is a basic conceit, and when we grasp the conceit, or when Thomas does not become too hyperbolic, the image is fairly clear. (As, for example, in the cloud-woman analogy of "I Make This in a Warring Absence," p. 68) Thomas drew upon the cinema and language for some of the best images of this type.

"Our Eunuch Dreams" (p. 16) is concerned with appearance and reality, with the movies illustrating appearance:

> In this our age the gunman and his moll,
> Two one-dimensioned ghosts, love on a reel,
> Strange to our solid eye,
> And speak their midnight nothings as they swell;
> When cameras shut they hurry to their hole
> Down in the yard of day.

Day is reality. And when the film has ended, the reality of day is cast in doubt; the experience of the "dream" world has had

its effect. It has caused the viewer to wonder what is real and
what is unreal.

> They dance between their arclamps and our skull,
> Impose their shots, showing the nights away;
> We watch the show of shadows kiss or kill,
> Flavoured of celluloid give love the lie.

From this cinema figure Thomas takes a lesson as a poet. He
goes on to say (p. 17) that he "shall be a shouter like the cock,/
Blowing the old dead back." This cinematic world, this hypo-
critical and make-believe world which is generally believed to
be "true," will be exposed by the poet whose "shots shall
smack/ The image from the plates." His poetry will destroy
the false photographic world by its presentation of the true
reality.

In "The Tombstone Told When She Died," the speaker
comes upon a gravestone of a young woman who died in
childbirth. From this occurrence the speaker recalls particulars
of the woman's young marriage and mating. These thoughts
seem to him like a motion picture, and he says:

> I who saw in a hurried film
> Death and this mad heroine
> Meet once on a mortal wall
> Heard her speak through the chipped beak
> Of the stone bird guarding her.
>
> (p. 103)

On the last line, "And the dear floods of his hair," Thomas has
commented: "The word 'dear' fits in, I think, with 'though her
eyes smiled,' which comes earlier. I wanted the girl's *terrible*
reaction to orgastic [sic] death to be suddenly altered into a
kind of despairing love. . . . I wanted it slow & complicated,
the winding cinematic works of the womb." [33]

[33] Watkins, pp. 44, 45.

"Then Was My Neophyte" (p. 79) offers another example
of the cinema providing the cohesive elements for a series of
images. The poem sees God in terms of a movie director:

> He films my vanity.
>
> . . . . .
>
> His reels and mystery
> The winder of the clockwise scene
> Wound like a ball of lakes
> Then threw on that tide-hoisted screen
> Love's image till my heartbone breaks
> By a dramatic sea.

The overall sense of a motion picture helps us to determine
which of several possible meanings we should give to certain
words and phrases in this poem. For example, the description
of God as the "winder of the clockwise scene" might in
isolation appear to involve merely clocks and time, whereas
in this context it becomes clear that God is being pictured as
the operator of a projector which turns a roll of film clockwise
in order to throw the images onto the screen of life. What we
have is a movie of wind, sun, and stars—"the tilted arcs"—children (like the poet) making pictures with thumb and finger
and playing games, and, finally, God, the director, who has
wound the film of life and who has thrown on the sea an image
of love. The poem as a whole is spoken by a person watching a
film and recognizing himself in it: "Then was my neophyte."
(The Greek root of this word means "newly planted"—the
film shows the life story of the newly conceived child.)

The language images (discussed in Chapters One and Five)
present the same metaphysical quality, the same intellectual
relationship of part to part, as the cinema images. It is this type
of image, the extended conceit, the simple metaphoric
identification ingeniously developed, that most frequently
causes difficulty. When the intellectual pattern is firm enough,

as it is with the record player, the films, and most of the language analogies, the images are brilliantly successful. When, however, the metaphysical base is lacking, the image is likely to languish in hopeless opacity. The reason for this opacity, which in extreme forms must be regarded as a failure, may be due, to some degree, to surrealistic techniques. Here, from "How Shall My Animal," is an example of an imagistic passage which opens splendidly and clearly because based on a poet-fisherman conceit, but which trails off to a potpourri of images when the original conceit is left behind:

Fishermen of mermen
Creep and harp on the tide, sinking their charmed, bent pin
With bridebait of gold bread, I with a living skein,
Tongue and ear in the thread, angle the temple-bound
Curl-locked and animal cavepools of spells and bone,
Trace out a tentacle,
Nailed with an open eye, in the bowl of wounds and weed
To clasp my fury on ground
And clap its great blood down.

(p. 101)

The "fishermen of mermen" are poets who fish with "charmed, bent pin." Thomas, "I," a particular poet, not only fishes but is himself the line, "a living skein," and the bait, "tongue and ear in the thread." This poet is both fish and fisherman as he plumbs the sea of the imagination, as he "trace[s] out a tentacle." The imagery of the last lines seems to become fragmented. There is an apparent effort to link the fish-fisherman-poet to the goldfish, but all that seems definite is that the task of the poet is frightening and impossible. "Never shall beast be born," never shall a man be born who can map (like an atlas) the seas of the imagination, or who can sing the praises of a day—"Or poise the day on a horn."

When the generative idea or, as I have been calling it after

"The Churning Bulk"

Thomas, "the central seed" is strong enough, the device of the "imagistic potpourri" may be startlingly effective. This is the case with the notion of *time* which shapes and unifies the "quiet gentleman" and "ball" images of "Should Lanterns Shine":

> So fast I move defying time, the quiet gentleman
> Whose beard wags in Egyptian wind.
>
> I have heard many years of telling,
> And many years should see some change.
>
> The ball I threw while playing in the park
> Has not yet reached the ground.

(p. 72)

The images in these lines are no less disparate than those in some of the most difficult poems. Yet here the contrast—between time's overwhelming presence and youth which briefly defies time—welds the various images into an emotional-intellectual unity. The visual "quiet gentleman," the auditory "heard many years of telling," and the visual and tactile "ball I threw" all serve to convey the idea of a momentary stay in the inevitable process of change. (I recognize that the ball image is primarily an image of sight, but its chief effect here seems to be that of anticipation, and the anticipation seems to have as much the sense of feeling the ball again as of seeing it.)

It is, then, not so much a question of the disparity of the images as it is of the context into which they are placed. When there is neither the intellectual cohesiveness of the metaphysical, nor the more emotional cohesiveness of pervasive mood, as in the above lines, Thomas's early imagery tends to appear chaotic. The apparent chaos may be connected to some extent to the tradition of the surrealists—probably Breton, Gascoyne, and the very early Barker—although Thomas's poetry was itself an influence on some later surrealism, especially the Apocalyptics. The form of surrealistic imagery is not that of the intellectual design but rather that of depiction, of romantic description. Sometimes we can visualize Thomas's surrealistic imagery—but only as an abstract painting. The obscurity endemic in surrealistic imagery probably results from the frustration of our natural tendency to visualize, but it is also part of the very nature of visionary poetry. We can see such imagery in rudimentary form in Blake's "London":

> How the Chimney-sweeper's cry
> Every black'ning Church appalls;
> And the hapless Soldier's sigh
> Runs in blood down Palace walls.

It is difficult to see how anyone could visualize such an image before the surrealists. But when we cannot picture the soldier's sigh running down the palace wall in a stream of blood, we have to apprehend the image more immediately—we have to feel the impact of Blake's relating "sigh" and "blood." Either way, through surrealistic visualization or through physical apprehension, such imagery should have its effect.[34]

It is this feeling of a surrealistic gallery or of immediate physical presences that one gets so often in Thomas's early imagery. The last five lines of Sonnet V, for example, give us a Daliesque picture of a crucifixion:

[34] Giorgio Melchiori, *The Tightrope Walkers* (London, 1956), p. 238, says of this poem, "Here concrete images create, through compressed metaphors, composite mental pictures which cannot be visualized but preserve a character of actuality, are felt as physical presences rather than abstract conceits. And this is strikingly a feature of visions: they appeal directly to the senses as visible material objects, but at the same time cannot be visualized as pictorial compositions. Another characteristic is their directness: through the senses . . . only . . . images are conveyed to the mind. . . . In this way visionary poetry has, together with a certain indefiniteness, a strong physical impact."

"The Churning Bulk"

And Jonah's Moby snatched me by the hair,
Cross-stroked salt Adam to the frozen angel
Pin-legged on pole-hills with a black medusa
By waste seas where the white bear quoted Virgil
And sirens singing from our lady's sea-straw.

(p. 82)

In the preceding lines the poet has just recognized himself as a
Cain figure, and in that recognition he envisions himself un-
dergoing a Lawrentian crucifixion of the flesh (as opposed to
the spiritual crucifixion of Sonnet VIII). Jonah's Moby is the
spirit of evil, the Leviathan, the covering Cherub in Blake's
cosmography, who brings natural man, "salt Adam," an
awareness of spiritual or otherworldly value, "the frozen
angel." Adam is nailed, "stroked" in the sense of struck or
bound, perhaps even in the sense of cross-stitched, to this "frozen angel," who proves to be a cross. The cross is "pin-legged,"
and in view of the fact that others are also being crucified it is
"on pole-hills"; the "black medusa" may be a type of crown of
thorns or simply one of the horrible female figures that tor-
ment the central voice of the sonnets. This crucifixion takes
place in a nightmare of loneliness and in a mad world: "By
waste seas where the white bear quoted Virgil." And from the
waste seas all around natural man come the voices of the sirens,
tempting and tormenting.

One is liable, in the "Sonnets" especially, to feel that
Thomas is either playing a game or has led the reader into a
puzzling maze for which there is actually a simple but secret
exit. The alternatives are not exclusive. Sometimes Thomas is
playing with the reader, and the most fascinating part of the
game is that there is a simple answer. But in many instances of
impenetrable imagery Thomas must have been carried away
with the spirit of the poem (or the story, perhaps) and become
lost in the maze himself. In his correspondence with Miss

Johnson, Thomas cites a procedure for image-making which is in many ways a better explanation of his involved imagery than his much more famous letter to Treece. He gives an account of two people sitting in a room with just enough light to see each other. After they stare at each other continuously for some time, strange things begin to happen. Each sees the other change, one feature slips into the other, another feature becomes exaggerated, one disappears, the face itself vanishes in utter darkness. Then new features emerge—perhaps antlers or horns—indescribable shapes suggesting both heaven and hell. Daniel Jones recalls, "I remember one terrifying night when we stared at one another in the gathering darkness until our heads became griffin and wyvern heads." [35] Thomas called this procedure "invoking the devil." He invoked him often in the writing of both poems and stories.

What one derives, finally, from such imagery is a sense of immediate, physical strife—often of horror. This physical directness is at the center of Thomas's exploration of the dream world—"I Fellowed Sleep," "I Dreamed My Genesis" —and of his world of poetic creation—"I, in My Intricate Image." Of their kind, the poetry of dream, hallucination, intense states of unusual imagination, these poems are as good as we have in contemporary literature. They are clearly superior to what Thomas's contemporaries—the young Treece, Barker, and Gascoyne—were doing. All of these poets modified their apocalyptic mannerisms, and none more than Thomas. As has been said, Thomas, not content to work in this tradition, sought, in his own words, "more meaning at first reading." In striving for that greater clarity, he left behind the mannerisms of the surrealists and moved toward the romantic descriptiveness of the later poetry.

[35] Daniel Jones, "Dylan Thomas: Memories and Appreciations," in *A Casebook*, p. 279.

"The Churning Bulk"

This movement was slow, and we find in poems of 1938, 1939, 1940, and 1941 ("I Make This in a Warring Absence," "Because the Pleasure-bird Whistles," "Unluckily for a Death," and "Ballad of the Long-legged Bait," for example) a mixture of techniques. In such poems as these, Thomas's notion of the "central seed" again has particular relevance, because we usually are able to find the images most meaningful when we see the germinal mood or idea of the poem. "After the Funeral" is a typical poem of this transition period, and an examination of the images in that poem may well serve to illustrate the practices of Thomas in his movement from imagism and surrealism to romanticism.

All the major images in "After the Funeral" (p. 96) stem from a "central seed," and that seed is a boy grief-stricken by the death of an aunt and a poet who wants to memorialize that grief and the love that warranted it.[36] The first nine lines describe the grief of the boy, the next eleven the love remembered by the poet and the poet's desire to make that love immortal. The images in the first nine lines describe how the death of this aunt appeared to a small boy. Although somewhat staccato, these images are descriptive in a rather obvious and straightforward manner. They describe in succession the animals pulling the funeral wagon, the nailing down of the coffin,

[36] Thomas explains the source of this love in his description of a childhood visit to Ann Jones: "One minute I was small and cold, skulking dead-scared down a black passage in my stiff, best suit, with my hollow belly thumping and my heart like a time bomb, clutching my grammar school cap, unfamiliar to myself, a snub-nosed storyteller lost in his own adventures and longing to be home; the next I was a royal nephew in smart town clothes, embraced and welcomed, standing in the snug centre of my stories and listening to the clock announcing me. She hurried me to the seat in the side of the cavernous fireplace and took off my shoes. The bright lamps and the ceremonial gongs blazed and rang for me." "The Peaches," *Portrait of the Artist as a Young Dog* (Paperbook, New York, 1955), p. 13.

the appearance of the mourners, and the noise of the "spade that wakes up sleep." In the shadow of the coffin (figuratively), the boy was choked with grief; he could hardly breathe, thus he "sheds dry leaves." Line ten begins another "after." This "after" is similar to the first, the tears are still stuffed, but the boy has given way to the poet who is standing, remembering, "in a room with a stuffed fox and a stale fern." (Thomas took the fox and fern right from life: his story "The Peaches" describes Annie Jones's house and includes them among the furnishings.)

To say only that this poem springs out of the grief of a boy and the desire of the poet to memorialize the dead woman for whom the boy grieved, would be to make poetry into prose. The way Thomas made the "seed" into a poem was by expanding a metaphor. The metaphor he chose was a perennial one: water is life, dryness is death. "Ann was water to my life, her death is dryness to me. But I, the poet, will by this creation make a new fountain of life out of Ann's love." This fountain will pour forth forever, or at least until all the dryness of death is revivified and renourished with the water of existence; in other words, until

> The stuffed lung of the fox twitch and cry Love
> And the strutting fern lay seeds on the black sill.
>
> (p. 97)

Nearly everything in the poem depends on the central water metaphor, and nearly everything pertains to dryness and water, always with the life-death, fertile-infertile associations natural to the terms throughout Thomas's poetry. Grief, of course, is fruitless, and the eyes that weep (line 5) are "spittled" and the water is salted. The time of death is "tear-stuffed" (line 10) and is represented by the "stuffed fox and a stale fern." The time the poem remembers, "after the funeral,"

is a time of "snivelling hours" (line 13), but his memory of
Ann is that of a life-giving fountain:

> Whose hooded, fountain heart once fell in puddles
> Round the parched worlds of Wales.

Her death was like one quiet last drop of water "her death was
a still drop" (line 17). Her fame is a "holy flood," but her
body is broken. Therefore, he, the poet, will call all the life-
giving "seas to service that her wood-tongued virtue/ Babble
like a bellbuoy." The phrase "wood-tongued" means first that
her virtue is mute but also that her virtue is of the woods, it is
of nature. Her virtue is that of a kind and compassionate
existence, and the poet will make it also like the bellbuoy, a
guiding and lifesaving bell. The poet will also "bow down the
walls of the ferned and foxy woods" with his voice so that her
spirit of life and kindness may be known to all, may "sing and
swing through a brown chapel."

The poet must make out of this woman "meek as milk" a
"skyward statue," which is the poem, "carved from her in a
room with a wet window." The giant statue must be carved
because he knows that the real Ann is dead, her words "damp,"
her wits "hollow" (and dry), her face frozen in pain, her body
only "seventy years of stone." But his poem, his statue, will be
a "monumental/ Argument of the hewn voice, gesture and
psalm," like a fountain which will "storm [rain] me forever
over her grave," until the fox and the fern come back to life
and until all the dry and dead things have a new life.

The passage in which C. Day Lewis finds conflicting and
contradictory images begins "But I, Ann's bard." He says the
poem "shuttles backwards and forwards between the real
living Ann and the dead mythical Ann." He finds the framework of the poem "contrapuntal," turning on "an opposition
between the natural earthly woman and the religious object

she has become." Other images which appear to conflict are " 'hearth' or 'ferned and foxy woods' on one hand, and on the other the calling of 'the seas to service' 'over the hymning heads,' " and he finds these images resolved in such a phrase as "wood-tongued virtue." Day Lewis concludes, "At the end of the poem these wood-symbols are merged into each other; by the dialectical method Mr. Thomas described, each has in a sense turned into its opposite; the fox has become something like a fern ('The *stuffed lung* of the fox twitch and cry Love'), the fern moves like a fox ('And the strutting fern lay seeds on the black sill')." [37]

One would not be tempted to dispute the notion that the dead figure of Ann Jones contradicts the poetic figure the poem makes of her, if it were not that such a reading leads finally to a wrenching and forcing in which the poem is misconstrued. Inevitably, the dead and the image we make of the dead are disproportionate. Such contradictions are so general, however, that they do not in any way show us what the poem means or how Thomas used imagery. There is a natural and unavoidable disparity, but it is in no way a particular feature of Thomas's poetry.

Naturally, not all of Thomas's poems can be expected to confine themselves to so clear a metaphor as the water-life base of "After the Funeral." But the imagistic variations which Thomas develops on the idea of water—from spittle to seas to fountains—typify his practices in a mixture of imagism, surrealism, and romanticism, typify more significantly the conjunction of craftsmanship and imagination in shaping a fully realized poem.

The well-developed romantic or descriptive imagery of Thomas's postwar poems does not present the obstacle to

[37] C. Day Lewis, *The Poetic Image*, pp. 124, 125.

understanding that the imagery in his earlier poems does, and as a result the later poems have been often and deservedly praised. There is no obscurity or esthetic failure, for example, in "A Winter's Tale" when Thomas describes the lonely protagonist

>   ringed by the winged snow
> And the dung hills white as wool and the hen
> Roosts sleeping chill till the flame of the cock crow
> Combs through the mantled yards and the morning men
>
>   Stumble out with their spades,
> The cattle stirring, the mousing cat stepping shy,
> The puffed birds hopping and hunting, the milkmaids
> Gentle in their clogs over the fallen sky,
> And all the woken farm at its white trades.
>
> (pp. 131–132)

There is, of course, a problem of interpretation here, of just what the relationship is between the description and the whole poem. But the images per se, the pictures they present and the senses they richly invoke, the spatial canvaslike relationship the individual images bear to the overall scene—all these things are present in the perfection of poetry. Nowhere in the language is such a scene more finely given—from the paragram of "ringed" and "winged" to the tactile delicacy of "milkmaids/ Gentle in their clogs over the fallen sky."

Thomas's rhetorical "paraphernalia" (to use his term) is, finally, not as unusual as it at first appears. Obsessed with intensity, Thomas dredged the deeps of dream and the unconscious for images, played poetic billiards with words, and often lost himself and his reader in syntactical labyrinths. But always he knew what he wanted and even in his most obscure period he could sound like a latter-day Dr. Johnson: "There is more than poetry in poems, in that much of even the most considerable poem is unpoetical or antipoetical, is dependent upon the wit that discovers occult resemblances in things apparently unlike" (*New Verse*, December, 1935). Thomas's imagination and verbal wit never flag, they shine through metaphysical and surrealistic obscurities, and in his best work they add that indefinable degree of texture that spells genius.

CHAPTER THREE

"The Hewn Voice":
Auditory Techniques

> this monumental
> Argument of the hewn voice, gesture and psalm,
> Storm me forever over her grave.
> "After the Funeral"

> Ah, so. You speak in riddles but
> I read the rhyme.
>> Clytaemnestra: *Libation Bearers*
>> (trans. Richmond Lattimore)

THERE is little doubt that Dylan Thomas was deeply influenced by the Welsh bardic tradition, little doubt that although he was relatively unfamiliar with the metric formulations of *cynghanedd* he was nevertheless affected by them. John Ackerman, who deals extensively with Thomas's Welsh backgrounds, cites at one point Parry's *History of Welsh Literature* to draw an appropriate parallel between Thomas and traditional Welsh concepts of poetic form:

It is important here to recall the critical standpoint which determined Welsh poetry down to the end of the eighteenth century.

Craft and Art of Dylan Thomas

. . . That standpoint is that sound is as important as sense; that metre and cynghanedd, *the whole framework of verse, are as much a part of the aesthetic effect as what is said. . . .* The tendency of modern criticism has been to consider primarily the thought expressed in a poem; as for the rhythm, the rhymes, the alliteration, they are desirable no doubt but are regarded as an adornment of the verse.[1]

There is the suspicion that Parry does not here go far enough in evaluating sound in Welsh poetry, nor does Ackerman in considering sound in Thomas. For it is often a case of the sound being *more* important than the thought, of sound taking precedence over sense.

While the perspective of Thomas as a "Welsh bard" is useful in placing Thomas in a tradition, it is of little help in understanding his actual auditory structures. These follow no traditional Welsh patterns; they are determined solely by his own very general principles, by his own indefinable intuitions, and by the context of the individual poems.

In a letter to Vernon Watkins, for instance, after explaining that he wanted to achieve more than rhythmic effect, Thomas wrote:

I think you are liable, in your criticisms of me, to underrate the value—or, rather, the integrity, the wholeness—of what I am saying . . . and often to suggest alterations or amendments for purely musical motives. For instance, "Caught in a somersault of tumbled mantime" may (and I doubt it) sound more agreeable— we'll leave out any suggestion of it sounding inevitable because it is, however good the implied criticism, a group of words *outside* the poem—to the "prophesying ear" than "In an imagining of tumbled mantime," a line I worked out *for* its sounds & not in

---

[1] Thomas Parry, *A History of Welsh Literature*, trans. H. Idris Bell (London, 1955), p. 48, cited in John Ackerman, *Dylan Thomas: His Life and Work* (London, 1964), p. 8. The italics are Parry's.

spite of them. [The remarks concern "Unluckily for a Death," and the lines referred to have been dropped from the version of the poem in *Collected Poems.*] [2]

Thomas here makes three points: One, even if the suggested change were a rhythmic improvement (which he doubts), rhythmic improvement is not the major purpose of his auditory organization. Two, sound exists in a whole, in a body of related sounds; it has *integrity* in the root meaning of the term. Finally, sound within this whole, within this body of interrelated sounds, is formed on the level of the phrase and line—"for its sounds and not in spite of them."

In conversation with Brinnin, Thomas further commented on his idea of interrelatedness. Brinnin recounts the conversation:

He began almost every poem merely with some phrase he had carried about in his head. If this phrase was right . . . it would suggest another phrase. In this way a poem would "accumulate." Once given a word or phrase or a line . . . he could often envision it or "locate" it within a pattern of other words or phrases or lines that . . . had yet to be discovered.[3]

Having spent considerable time (in the preceding chapter) discussing the meaning of "After the Funeral," I shall now consider that poem briefly as an illustration of Thomas's practice of "accumulation." A very early version of this poem

[2] *Dylan Thomas: Letters to Vernon Watkins*, ed. Vernon Watkins (London, 1957), p. 66. Thomas goes on to say that Watkins's criticism was often concerned with the "aural betterment . . . of details, without regard for their significance in a worked-out, if not a premeditated-*in-detail*, whole."

[3] John Malcolm Brinnin, *Dylan Thomas in America* (Compass, Boston, 1955), p. 126.

exists in Thomas's 1933 Notebook,[4] and it reveals two striking features. The wording of the finished version is the same as the first only in the first line; every other word has been changed. And the sounds of that opening line are unimportant in the early version but all-important in the later poem. In the first instance, the heavily stressed rhythm of the opening line is not maintained; while in the second the five-stress pattern runs throughout. (The syllables vary irregularly in the first and the grammatical segments are longer, whereas in the second each line has exactly ten syllables—the number in the opening line—and the grammatical segments are shorter.) The increased segmentation results in an increased number of primary stresses. In the early version, there is no apparent relationship between the sounds of the opening line and those of subsequent lines; the carry-over of word sounds from any given line is minimal. In the finished poem, the first line initiates a series of related *a* sounds that follow in subsequent lines; furthermore, there are subtle relationships between word groups—note, for example, the emphasis on the *l* sounds, particularly the *s-l* variations. I shall have a good deal more to say about these practices shortly, but for now I trust the point about accumulation of sounds is clear.

This chapter has two overall objects: to demonstrate the range of Thomas's auditory imagination and to give some idea of how his craftsmanship changed and developed.[5] It will

[4] Numbered poem "Six" in the Notebook begun February 1, 1933. The Notebook, from which I am not permitted to quote, is at the Lockwood Memorial Library in Buffalo.

[5] This chapter is limited to outlining the range and citing specific instances of Thomas's auditory practices. For fuller and more scientific accounts of Thomas's prosody, the reader should consult Katharine T. Loesch's *Prosodic Patterns in the Poetry of Dylan Thomas* (University Microfilms, Ann Arbor, 1961), and for further examples of metrical and auditory characteristics the reader should examine Thelma L. B. Murdy's *Sound and Meaning in Dylan Thomas's Poetry* (University Microfilms, Ann Arbor, 1962).

attempt to do these things by examining successively the three most important ways word sounds are interrelated: intonation, phonemic arrangements, and affinitive patterning. Intonation includes meter, rhythm, pitch, and stress; the phonemic is concerned with syllable manipulation, consonant clusters, and vocalic augmentation and diminution; the affinitive covers the principle of repetitive design, whether by rhyme and assonance or by syntactical repetitions.

I
INTONATION

The direction of Thomas's intonational development is from a poetry of strong metrical stress to a poetry of flowing, rhapsodic cadence. Accompanying this shift, and an important part of it, is a change from a highly complicated, metaphysical, and involved imagery to a more general, pictorial, and simple imagery. The relationship between imagery and rhythm is both complex and nebulous, but it has long been apparent to critics that the more compressed the image, as in Thomas's earlier work, the more one-dimensional the auditory stress. The more fully developed, the more room given the image, the more range and variation the auditory elements are able to attain.

In the early poetry, the intonational patterns are usually strong and regular. "Intensity seems to be the chief value of his style, an effect is brilliantly achieved . . . under the impulse of a steady rhythmic pulse and a taut, heavily end-stopped line. . . . He used language percussively like a pianist playing with his forearms." [6] Consider this relatively early example:

[6] Robert Martin Adams, "Taste and Bad Taste in Metaphysical Poetry: Richard Crashaw and Dylan Thomas," *Hudson Review*, VIII (Spring, 1955), 55.

Light breaks where no sun shines;
Where no sea runs, the waters of the heart
Push in their tides;
And, broken ghosts with glow-worms in their heads,
The things of light
File through the flesh where no flesh decks the bones.

(p. 29)

This stanza typifies not only the "steady rhythmic pulse" of Thomas's early poetry (roughly 1934–1938) but also suggests a number of those intonational features which Thomas subtly varied in subsequent years—the preponderance of primary and secondary stresses to the almost total exclusion of intervening weaker stresses, syllabic regularity, and repetitive devices.

With few exceptions, Thomas's verse is accentual syllabic. Its stress pattern generally sounds as though it is iambic, but this very justifiable assumption cannot always be borne out by traditional scansion.[7] Thomas may, in fact, have depended on an iambic expectancy, as he varied his rhythm beyond any customary iambic formulation and then—by completely unprecedented innovations—created his own rhythm, which is very close to iambic.

These points can be demonstrated from the opening line of "Light Breaks." First, what readers felt as a "steady rhythmic pulse" is explicable when we realize that this line (and, gen-

---

[7] Where the poem seems to justify using traditional metrical terms such as iambic or spondaic, I try to use them. Where it strikes me that Thomas has taken great liberties with traditional metrics, I resort to the Smith-Trager classification of stresses and junctures. See George L. Trager and Henry Lee Smith, *Outline of English Structure* (Washington, D.C., 1957). Also of interest in this regard is Seymour Chatman, "Comparing Metrical Styles," in *Style in Language*, ed. Thomas A. Sebeok (Cambridge, Mass., 1960), pp. 149–172.

erally, the whole poem) is practically without tertiary stresses (in the Smith-Trager scheme). Thomas seems to read the opening line in this fashion: $/_2\text{Light}_2 \rightarrow {}^3\text{bréaks}_2 \rightarrow {}_2\text{where}_2$ ño ${}^3\text{sûn}_1\ {}^3\text{shínes}_1$ /. There are two intonational characteristics that tend to give this line iambic qualities: the primary-secondary alternation and the repeated pitch drops. It is the pitch characteristic which makes the reading sound like an iambic line—which the scansion could not support. But, finally, it is the metrical strength of the line, and of the poem, which is its dominant feature. The absence of weak stresses, the relative absence of enjambment, the overpowering press of emphatic monosyllables—these are the marks of the early intonation.

The syllabic regularity of "Light Breaks" is more pronounced than most of the early poems and, in this sense, is clearer evidence of Thomas's consistent interest in syllable counting. With but one exception, the same relative line in each stanza has the same number of syllables. The first line in each stanza has six syllables; the second, ten; the third, four; the fourth, ten; the fifth, four; the sixth, ten. The only exception is the final stanza, where the fifth line has six instead of four syllables. That such syllable regularity was consciously worked out is clear from worksheet notations.

"Light Breaks" is so typical of Thomas's syntactical repetitions that it might be worth anticipating his syntactical methods with one observation at this time. On the literal level of the poem, the repetitions in "Light Breaks" set up a series of correspondences. Thus, the literal action of the poem is a description of human generation, but implied in this action is the generation of the world—perhaps, as some commentators have felt, even the generation of thought, although the imagery does not support this correspondence very strongly. The repetitive phrases not only make it easier to speak the poem but, at the same time, convey the very notion of one action with multiple facets. (Eliot does much the same thing in "Sweeney Among the Nightingales," where Sweeney's actions in the barroom have parallels in both history and nature. At one point, for example, Sweeney and the nightingales act analogously: "Sweeney spreads his knees/*Letting* his arms hang down," while the nightingales sing and "*let* their liquid siftings fall"—Italics added.) In Thomas's poem, the first line in each stanza is a subject-verb-object construction, the "where no" of the first line is repeated four times, the word order and stresses of the third and fifth lines are repeated in each stanza.

Throughout *Collected Poems* there is a relative increase in the use of polysyllabic words, in the use of prepositional phrases, adverbial compounds, and even in the use of articles. Thus, as enjambment, metric and rhythmic variations, and phrasing alternations become more common, the emphatic beat diminishes and the poetry seems to flow ever more easily. By 1938, the intonational features epitomized by "Light Breaks" had undergone startling modification.

Thomas knew how "to reason by the pulse,/And, when it quickens, alter the actions' pace" (p. 72). Quite often he achieved this rhythmical effect in conjunction with a manipulation of vowel and consonant sounds, so that it is impossible to differentiate the source of that effect. For example, in the last two lines of "There Was a Saviour,"

Exiled in us we arouse the soft,
Unclenched, armless, silk and rough love that breaks all rocks,
(p. 140)

we find an apparently purposeful contrast of *s*'s, *l*'s and *k*'s as well as an unexpected rhythm which combines in one line iambic, trochaic, and spondaic feet, so that the sound of the words seems to reinforce the literal meaning, the paradox of a "silk and rough love that breaks all rocks."

"Hewn Voice"

In "Love in the Asylum" (p. 119), Thomas chose a form peculiarly appropriate to the meaning. The alternation of two-stress lines and five-stress lines within the stanzas, and even the alternation of the stanza form so that the first and fourth stanzas contain two short lines and one long one while the two stanzas which follow each of these have two long lines and one short one, suggests the unpredictable "madness" of the girl.

One of Thomas's most popular and most effective poems, "Poem on His Birthday" (p. 190), is also one of the finest examples of his mastery of intonational manipulation. The poem is actually built in a strict stanzaic pattern. Each stanza contains nine lines of alternating three- and four-stress patterns. This pattern, however, is loose enough and so full of run-on lines that the shorter lines often contain only two stresses (including the first three short lines in the poem) without upsetting the dominant meter. There is also a consistent rhyme scheme in each stanza—*ababcdcdc*—based on the vowel sounds of the words involved. This too is consistent enough so that it can be found in every stanza but variable enough so that the poet can "rhyme" words like "birds," "spurns" and "spear" without upsetting the pattern or the ear of the reader.

The poem opens with slow insistency, full of spondees (or, from another metrical perspective, primary and secondary stresses), *k*'s and other stopped consonants, and plosives,

> In the mustardseed sun,
> By full tilt river and switchback sea
> Where the cormorants scud,
> In his house on stilts high among beaks
> And palavers of birds
> This sandgrain day in the bent bay's grave
> He celebrates and spurns
> His driftwood thirty-fifth wind turned age;
> Herons spire and spear.

The last lines of each of the first three stanzas epitomize this movement—or, rather, lack of movement: "Herons spire and spear," "Herons, steeple stemmed, bless," "Herons walk in their shroud." This, of course, supports the literal description of the "toil" and "anguish" of life and approaching death. But by the sixth stanza the rhythm has become imperceptibly smoother and more flowing, as the poet thinks of the possible purpose in his toil and anguish.

> And freely he goes lost
> In the unknown, famous light of great
> And fabulous, dear God.
> Dark is a way and light is a place,
> Heaven that never was
> Nor will be ever is always true,
> And, in that brambled void,
> Plenty as blackberries in the woods
> The dead grow for His joy.
>
> (p. 191)

The increasingly flowing cadence is accompanied, and partly caused, by the longer phrases and sentences. In fact, the last five stanzas of the poem are parts of one sentence. The words are put together more euphoniously. The meter becomes more consistently iambic, so that trochaic and spondaic feet serve only to slow down the movement momentarily instead of halting it altogether as they did at first. The continuents—*m*'s, *n*'s and *l*'s—now predominate:

> Yet, though I cry with tumbledown tongue,
> Count my blessings aloud:
>
> Four elements and five
> Senses, and man a spirit in love
> Tangling through this spun slime
> To his nimbus bell cool kingdom come
> And the lost, moonshine domes,

"Hewn Voice"

And the sea that hides his secret selves
Deep in its black, base bones,
Lulling of spheres in the seashell flesh,
And this last blessing most.

(pp. 192–193)

(This domination can be attributed in part to the different emphasis which results from a more flowing rhythm. Nevertheless, we do feel the presence of these consonants as part of the total effect.) In this particular quotation there is also the echo of the *bl* sound in the word "blessings." It appears in the words "bell" and "black," is repeated in another "blessing," and reaches its climax in "blooms," thus carrying the idea of "blessings" throughout this passage. The word is a crucial one in the poem, somewhat like the dominant note in a piece of music (as opposed to the tonic, which in this poem might be the words "die" and "death"). The word "bless" appears at the end of the second stanza, giving the first indication of the poetic affirmation of the goodness and beauty of nature and life which is central to this poem. There is a definite echo of the word by phonemic augmentation in the adjective "fabulous" applied to God halfway through the poem and then a repetition of it in "blessed, unborn God and His Ghost."

An interesting aspect of Thomas's intonational development is the role of his nominal and adjectival compounds. Thomas's addiction to hyphenated expressions like "sea-stuck towers," "five-fathomed Hamlet," or "tom-thumb vision" was noted by his earliest critics. But the most significant element in this regard is that his early compounds and hyphenations are generally strong, monosyllabic, adjective-noun combinations. And because these combinations almost always contain strong and secondary stresses, they thus add to the rhythmic emphasis of the poetry. Compound words appear no less frequently in the later poetry, but here, as in the poem just examined, they are most frequently polysyllabic compounds—"tumbledown tongue," or "thunderclap spring," for instance.

An even clearer instance of this change and of its effect is "Fern Hill."

> Now as I was young and easy under the apple boughs
> About the lilting house and happy as the grass was green,
>   The night above the dingle starry,
>   Time let me hail and climb
>   Golden in the heydays of his eyes.
>
>   (p. 178)

structure

The "apple boughs," "the lilting house," and the "dingle starry" contribute to the rhythmic pattern in a way early compounds rarely did. They add to the sense of ease and smoothness—the disappearance of what earlier was called percussive forearms. Of course, these compounds are but a small part of the variety and subtlety of "Fern Hill." The basic alternating, up-and-down, back-and-forth intonation is further reinforced by a slowing down at the end of most of the stanzas. The quickly moving first two lines of the above stanza tell of youth amid the apple trees. But the third line introduces the first of many antinomies—night. The feeling is already provided—by, among other things, that perfect play on "heyday"—that youth and apples belong to day and to the past. The next two lines begin by supplanting anapestic and iambic feet with trochaic, and it becomes natural to read these lines more slowly—as Thomas does in his recordings. This rhythmic alternation is emphasized by the combination of long and short lines, as well as strong and weak stresses, stopped and continuant consonants, and is finally brought home by that splendid rolling last line of the poem: "Though I sang in my chains like the sea."

"Fern Hill," with its rhythmic variations, with its numerous short prepositionals ("over," "under," "about"), with its polysyllabic compounds ("windfall light," "spellbound horses"), with its tantalizing folk-tale approximations ("once below a time," "all the sun long"), and, finally, with its carefully contrived repetitions (of spatial terms and colors, as well as assonance and alliteration)—on these grounds the poem culminates Thomas's intonational development.

Thomas usually has a theory behind his practice, and the theory borne out by his shifting intonational practices is his peculiar synesthetic conviction, which we discussed in Chapter One, that sound has a shape and shape has a sound. What the "shapes" of his early poems were perhaps only Thomas could have explained, but the syllabic count of "Light Breaks" should suggest one possible answer.

To have each line possess exactly the correct number of syllables was an urge that grew with Thomas, and, the more complicated and longer his poems became, the more prodigious became his syllable blocks. His thinking on this matter is curiously close to that of a sculptor. Paul Becker, who translated Thomas into German, remembers him commenting shortly before his death: "The only way to lure a poem from one language into the other without draining its magic would be to understand that the words of a poem are material, similar to stone, before it is made into a sculpture. If a poem is written in English . . . that is like a torso made out of marble. Translating now from English into another language, would be like copying the marble torso in red sandstone." [8]

Thomas's ideas of poetic shape are best demonstrated in his "Vision and Prayer" (pp. 154–165). The two shapes of this poem are determined by syllable control; it is a rather mechanical, almost a sculptural process. Thomas obviously thought that the printed shape of a poem had an emotional effect.—In "Vision and Prayer" there are two designs: the Vision poems

[8] Quoted by Constantine FitzGibbon in a letter to me.

are diamond-shaped; the Prayer poems are in the form of a double pyramid. To hazard a completely subjective reaction: the first suggests a movement from nothingness to nothingness yet, because it is diamond-shaped, simultaneously conveys the feeling of richness and value. The double pyramid may conceivably be seen as springing from an immeasurable ground of hopefulness, passing through dryness, finally coming to an expansive point of exultation and acceptance.

Regardless of the emotional effect of these shape poems, the syllable control they demonstrate is typical of all the later poems. As the rhythm of Thomas's poems loosened, the "shape" of the poems became compensatingly richer. "Poem on His Birthday," for example, follows a speech-stress pattern that varies from a low of two to a high of seven stresses per line, but the number of syllables in each line follows an almost perfect pattern. The poem has twelve nine-lined stanzas, and the syllable pattern is as follows:

Stanza	Syllables per Line
I	6 9 6 9 6 9 6 9 5
II	6 9 6 9 6 9 6 9 6
III	6 9 6 9 6 9 6 9 6
IV	6 9 6 9 6 9 6 9 6
V	6 9 6 9 6 9 6 9 6
VI	6 9 6 9 6 9 6 9 6
VII	6 9 6 9 6 9 6 9 6
VIII	6 9 6 9 6 9 6 9 6
IX	6 9 6 9 6 9 6 9 6
X	6 9 6 9 6 9 6 9 6
XI	6 9 6 9 7 9 6 9 6
XII	6 9 6 9 6 9 6 9 6

While the reading of these poems "flows," their appearance on the page reveals how precisely they were "hewn."

II
PHONEMIC SYMBOLISM

Phonemic suggestiveness is one of the most ancient devices of the poet, but a device upon which recent psycholinguistic research has cast some new light, giving a partial empirical basis to what poets have always felt instinctively—that certain vowels and consonants *within a context* may have a meaningful symbolic value.[9] By constant attention to manipulation of long and short vowels, vocalic diminution and augmentation, patterning of plosives, stops, and liquids, phonemic chiasmus, Thomas created an esthetic of sound. His persistent concern was to fashion an "auditory correlative" to the literal sense of each poem, and his effort was so deliberate and energetic that virtually every auditory device available to English poetry finds expression in his work.

Thomas's vocalic and consonantal symbolism is cumulative only in the sense that the further his work progressed the more complete became his "esthetic of sound." But even in his earliest poems he both asserted and demonstrated his absorption with auditory techniques. In "Especially When the October Wind," first published in October, 1934, Thomas wrote:

> Some let me make you of the vowelled beeches,
> Some of the oaken voices, from the roots
> Of many a thorny shire tell you notes,
> Some let me make you of the water's speeches.
>
> (p. 19)

[9] R. Brown, A. Black, and A. Horowitz, "Phonetic Symbolism in Natural Languages," *Journal of Abnormal and Social Psychology*, L (May, 1955), 388–393. For a further discussion of this subject, see my article "The Auditory Correlative," *Journal of Aesthetics and Art Criticism* (September, 1958), 93–102.

And, as a kind of proof that he at least instinctively believed in phonemic suggestiveness, he concluded, "By the sea's side hear the dark-vowelled birds." His mastery of such suggestiveness can be seen throughout his poetry. One of the clearest and simplest examples of this is in "Lament." Here the high front vowels which predominate in the opening lines dealing with youth,

> When I was a windy boy and a bit
> And the black spit of the chapel fold,
> > (p. 194)

shift gradually backward, as the poem progresses, to the long *or* where the poet describes age in the last stanza,

> Now I am a man no more no more
> And a black reward for a roaring life.
> > (p. 196)

Consciously or unconsciously Thomas has associated the short vowels with youth and the long vowels with age and has emphasized his association by rhythmic stresses on the appropriate syllables.

He establishes in most of his poems a value for vowel sounds by a literal context, then expands that value by repeating and stressing the vowel sound. In this manner, "dark" back vowels dominate "Altarwise by Owl-light" (p. 80) and in the context of the poem are associated with the idea of death and night ("owl-light"). In the same poem, the feeling of evil and horror is established in the third line, "Abaddon in the hangnail cracked from Adam," by the repetition of the sharp *a* sound /æ/, and then intensified by its further repetition in "atlas-eater," "mandrake," "hatched," "salvage," "Capricorn and Cancer." This same sharp *a* continues to dominate all the sonnets until we reach the last lines of Sonnet X in which there is a subtle shift to stressed *ar* and *er* sounds as the poet speaks of merciful peace:

> Green as beginning, let the ga*r*den diving
> S*oar*, with its two b*ar*k tow*er*s, to that Day
> When the w*or*m builds with the gold straws of venom
> My nest of m*er*cies in the rude, red tree.
>
> (p. 85)

The use of the short, front vowels to suggest harshness is frequent in Thomas, as in "The Hunchback in the Park":

> Eating bread from a newspaper
> Drinking water from the chained cup
> That the children filled with gravel,
>
> (p. 123)

and in "There Was a Saviour":

> Two proud, blacked brothers cry,
> Winter-locked side by side,
> To this inhospitable hollow year.
>
> (p. 140)

In the latter example, the stopped consonants and velars are also utilized with the short vowels. This usage appears also in "And Death Shall Have No Dominion," accentuating the images of twisting and cracking:

> Under the windings of the sea
> They lying long shall not die windily;
> Twisting on racks when sinews give way,
> Strapped to a wheel, yet they shall not break;
> Faith in their hands shall snap in two,
> And the unicorn evils run them through;
> Split all ends up they shan't crack.
>
> (p. 77)

The refrain "And death shall have no dominion" is, in contrast, smooth and flowing, in rhythmic stress as well as phonenically. Similar vowels and consonants, reinforced by the intricate intonational pattern, have an onomatopoeic effect in "Over Sir John's Hill":

> Flash, and the plumes crack,
> And a black cap of jack-
> Daws Sir John's just hill dons.
>
> (p. 187)

The numerous stopped consonants add to the effect of the heavily stressed rhythm and compound words to choke one's speech as the poet mourns near the beginning of "After the Funeral,"

> Windshake of sailshaped ears, muffle-toed tap
> Tap happily of one peg in the thick
> Grave's foot, blinds down the lids, the teeth in black.
>
> (p. 96)

The poet's voice cries rhapsodically without impeding consonants as the poem progresses:

> monumental
> Argument of the hewn voice, gesture and psalm,
> Storm me forever over her grave.
>
> (p. 97)

Thomas contrasts the front and back vowels to parallel the literal meaning in these lines from "Poem in October":

> My birthday began with the water-
> Birds and the birds of the winged trees flying my name
> Above the farms and the white horses
> And I rose
> In rainy autumn
> And walked abroad in a shower of all my days.
>
> (p. 113)

The phonemic "symbolism" moves from the *i*'s of the birthday's beginning to the pivotal line, "And I rose," where these sounds yield to the broader vowels which dominate the last line. This pattern suggests a movement or, more exactly, an expansion which conforms to the literal meaning and with the syllabic expansion of the lines.

Thomas was striving for an effective use of sound symbolism from the very beginning. "If I Were Tickled by the Rub of Love," which appeared in his first book of poems, is a fine example of his assonant and alliterative use of the small, sharp vowels and the velar consonants. And Thomas's own reading of a stanza like

> If I were tickled by the lovers' rub
> That wipes away not crow's-foot nor the lock
> Of sick old manhood on the fallen jaws,
> Time and the crabs and the sweethearting crib
> Would leave me cold as butter for the flies,
> The sea of scums could drown me as it broke
> Dead on the sweethearts' toes
>
> (p. 14)

shows how much he savored the bitterness of the sound as well as the thought.

As he progressed, Thomas repeatedly tried to develop intonational and phonemic elements to a truly pantomimic correlation with meaning. Consider these lines from his very late poem (1950) "In the White Giant's Thigh":

> Or rippling soft in the spinney moon as the silk
> And ducked and draked white lake that harps to a hail stone.
>
> (p. 198)

Only one word could be considered truly onomatopoeic—"rippling." But these two lines illustrate the use of sound correlating with sense. The section that the lines come from is one dealing with the past loves of dead women, specifically with the sexual act. These two lines describe the quivering of human flesh in the act of love. The flesh ripples as the surface of a lake—a lake dotted with ducks and drakes— vibrates to a hailstone. There is a contrast here between the smooth flesh and the jagged hailstone. Thomas, with his concept of intercourse as the starting point of death, tried to get both life and death, love and destruction, into these lines. The liquid consonants of the first line contrast with the stopped consonants of the second. The stress pattern of the first is gentle; in the second it stomps, light-heavy, light-heavy. Also, the vowel sounds in the first are shorter; the vowels in the second are generally more open. In brief, the sound of these lines correlates with the literal meaning to suggest sexual activity and destruction. The stress, the vowel sounds, the consonant arrangement, and the literal context are all indispensable elements in achieving this effect.

It becomes even more evident in the later poems that the dominant vowels or consonants, or both, are intimately related to the overall mood and atmosphere of the particular poem. For example, in Part III of "Ceremony After a Fire Raid" (p. 145), we find not only the syntactical repetition of "into" and "over" phrases, and the compulsive movement of a chanting rhythm, but also the ponderous "organpipe" eloquence of the long *o* and *u*—"luminous," "golden," "glory"—and their back-vowel cognates—"*or*ganpipes," "b*ur*ning," "wh*i*rling," "s*u*n's h*o*vel," "sl*u*m," "*u*nder—all culminating in the rolling, awe-inspiring last three lines:

> Er*u*pt, fo*u*ntain, and *e*nter to *u*tter *f*or *e*ver
> Gl*o*ry gl*o*ry gl*o*ry
> The s*u*ndering *u*ltimate K*i*ngd*o*m of genesis' th*u*nder.

Frequently Thomas's fascination with word sounds is revealed in his correspondence. In one 1934 letter to Pamela Hansford Johnson, for example, Thomas says that the word "drome" gives him a vision of the gates of heaven, and he suggests that the long *m* is the cause of this celestial association. He says further that the movement of God is conveyed in the long *o*.

It is no wonder that Thomas's poetry, starting from such an emotional bias, is a great compendium of almost all the possible devices of phonemic symbolism available to the poet. There would seem to be little advantage in further multiplying examples that the reader should, by now, readily be able to find for himself.

III
AFFINITIVE PATTERNS

W. K. Wimsatt has pointed out in Milton's poetry "agnomination . . . a kind of play or echo of a sound or set of sounds . . . a kind of extenuated pun, a fleeting shadow of pun, an extension of the ideas" [10] by means of similar sounds. Agnomination is one type of affinitive patterning. "In the Beginning" (p. 27) is an early poem showing the rudiments of such a structure. There is, of course, syntactical repetition throughout. But the initial phrase, "in the beginning," also provides the *b* which is echoed throughout the poem, first in "bough of bone" and subsequently in bilabial *b*'s and *p*'s, labial *v*'s and *f*'s, culminating in "brain," "blood," and the "ribbed original of love." The poem is about creation, the "bough of bone" being God, the "rib" from which all creation was formed, as was mankind from Adam's rib. The last lines return to the same metaphor, the central image of the poem. It is

[10] William K. Wimsatt, Jr., *The Verbal Icon* (Lexington, Ky., 1954), pp. 209–210.

inevitable that the emphatically repeated *b* and its cognates should form an oblique association in the mind between sound and meaning.

The prodigiously involved vowel and consonant arrangements in Thomas's later poems always complement the literal meaning. (Kenneth Burke has described forms such as these in Coleridge, under the term "musicality." [11]) Alliteration, cognate alliteration (*p-b, f-v, ch-j*, etc.), and assonance are present in almost all his poems, as well as examples of phonemic augmentation, diminution, and chiasmus. [12] But in the later poems, especially the most successful ones, the meaning, the imagery, and the form are all significantly affected by auditory affinities.

Thomas's affinitive patterns may differentiate sections or a group of lines from the rest of the poem, thereby clarifying or enhancing the literal meaning. In these lines from "It Is the Sinner's Dust-Tongued Bell,"

Time's *c*oral *s*aint and the *s*alt grief drown a foul *s*epul*ch*re
And a *wh*irlpool drives the *p*rayer*wh*eel,

(p. 92)

the two reversals in sound (consonantal chiasmus) reinforce the reversal in thought, the paradox. ("Sepulchre" merely

[11] Kenneth Burke, *The Philosophy of Literary Form* (Vintage, New York, 1957), pp. 296–304. My debt to Burke's terms and his insights is considerable.

[12] Burke defines "cognate" letters as letters which are related to one another by the position of the mouth in pronouncing them. Thus *m, b*, and *p* are cognates of one another but not of *z* or *k*. "Augmentation" and "diminution" are terms which Burke has borrowed from music where a theme in quarter notes may, by augmentation, be repeated in half notes or, by diminution, in eighth notes. "Chiasmus," borrowed from the terminology of rhetoric, "designates an a-b-b-a arrangement." When applied to poetic sound it may be discovered in a reversal of vowels or of consonants, or sometimes both. See Burke, pp. 296–299.

repeats the *s-k* complex.) The idea of barrenness is reinforced in these lines from "In the White Giant's Thigh,"

> But nothing bore, no mouthing babe to the veined hives
> Hugged, and barren and bare on Mother Goose's ground,
>
> (p. 199)

where "bore, no," "barren," and "bare on" all echo each other, by augmentation or diminution. Two examples of phonemic chiasmus from "In Country Sleep"—"*Illu*mination of *music*" reversed four lines later as "*music* of *elem*ents," and "*l*u*ll*ed bl*ack*-ba*ck*ed/ Gu*ll*" (p. 185)—suggest by their innate musicality the beauty and harmony which the poet is here trying to evoke.

In "Why East Wind Chills," the *w* (and perhaps the *l*) takes on the gestural connotation of wind:

> Why east wind chills and south wind cools
> Shall not be known till windwell dries
> And west's no longer drowned
> In winds that bring the fruit and rind
> Of many a hundred falls;
>
> (p. 62)

while in these lines from the "Ballad of the Long-legged Bait" the repeated *s* certainly strengthens the implied connection between women and sin:

> Sussanah's drowned in the bearded stream
> And no-one stirs at Sheba's side
>
> But the hungry kings of the tides;
> Sin who had a woman's shape
> Sleeps till Silence blows on a cloud
> And all the lifted waters walk and leap.
>
> (p. 171)

In an early poem, "To-day, This Insect," Thomas supplements his verbal meaning—the similarity between Adam and madmen, and the contrast between the endless love and the lover's certain end—by the sound manipulation:

> Adam I love, my madmen's love is endless,
> No tell-tale lover has an end more certain.
>
> (p. 48)

The third stanza of "I, in My Intricate Image" patterns its *m*'s:

Beginning with doom in the ghost, and the springing marvels,
Image of images, my metal phantom
Forcing forth through the harebell,
My man of leaves and the bronze root, mortal, unmortal,
I, in my fusion of rose and male motion,
Create this twin miracle.

(p. 40)

The alliteration of the *m*'s accentuates the connection in meaning Thomas wished to convey in the words "marvels," "images," "mortal," "unmortal," "male motion," and "miracle." He is saying that his "images," his poems, are a kind of miracle created out of both physical and nonphysical resources. In "Out of the Sighs," the augmentation of the sound from "*a little*" to "*all*" points up the contrast in meaning and the change of stress in

> A little comes, is tasted and found good;
> All could not disappoint.
>
> (p. 56)

The musicality of "A Winter's Tale" is so intricate and so pervasive that only tedious analysis could do it justice. We can, however, point out the cognate alliteration of *f*, *v*, and *w* together with the long *o* which, in taking on the meaning of the words with which they are associated in the poem—sn*o*w, *w*ind, *f*alling, *v*oice—help to establish a haunting sensation of

144

falling snow in the first few stanzas and throughout the poem. In the central section the short vowels, stopped consonants, and sibilants, here closely associated with the word *listen* itself, certainly intensify the idea of listening to the whispering voice of the past:

> Listen. The minstrels sing
> In the departed villages. The nightingale,
> Dust in the buried wood, flies on the grains of her wings
> And spells on the winds of the dead his winter's tale.
> The voice of the dust of water from the withered spring
>
> Is telling. The wizened
> Stream with bells and baying water bounds. The dew rings
> On the gristed leaves and the long gone glistening
> Parish of snow. The carved mouths in the rock are wind swept
> strings.
> Time sings through the intricately dead snow drop. Listen.
>
> (pp. 133–134)

We may also point out the specific contrast between the stopped *d*'s, which Paget and Johannesson tell us is the gestural speech movement signifying the end, destruction, or death in Indo-European languages,[13] and the repeated *ing* which tends to imply a continuation of condition because of its present-participial usage. The sounds in this part of the poem are a

---

[13] Sir Richard Paget and Alexander Johannesson have correlated gestural sounds in many languages according to a theory that language originated in mimetic action by the speech organs. For a discussion of the significance of stopped *d*'s as well as other sounds according to this theory, see Paget, *Human Speech* (London, 1930), Chaps. VII, VIII, and IX, and *This English* (London, 1935); Johannesson, "Gesture Origin of Indo-European Languages," *Nature*, CLIII (February 5, 1944), 171–172; "Gesture Origin of Semitic Languages," *Nature*, CLIV (October 7, 1944), 466; "Origin of Language," *Nature*, CLVII (June 22, 1946), 847–848; "Origin of Language," *Nature*, CLXII (December 4, 1948), 902; "The Gestural Origin of Language," *Nature*, CLXVI (July 8, 1950), 60–61.

correlative to the poet's exhortation to "listen" to the living voice of the past, the dead.

Thomas's "Lie Still, Sleep Becalmed" (p. 153) provides an excellent example of affinitive patterning. The sounds of these first four refrainlike words are carried throughout the poem in an involved type of configuration, basically like Wimsatt's "agnomination."[14]

The most obvious repetition of the sound in this key phrase is the echo of the *s* and *l* which appears in most of the syntactically important words: "silent sea," "salt sheet," "slow sad sail." But it is significant that the long *i* of "lie" is also echoed in "night," "silent," "mile." The *ee* of "sleep" is repeated not only in "sea" but also three times in the phrase "salt sheet," each time with a kind of jarring effect to accentuate the idea of the harshness of the breaking wave. And "becalmed" finds its repetition in "sound" and "drowned." In the line "We heard the sea sound sing, we saw the salt sheet tell," there is a parallel vowel progression ("sea sound sing—salt sheet tell) and an imperfect chiasmus (*sea sou*nd . . . *sa*lt sh*eet*) which helps to underscore the balanced thought. Diminution ("silent" to "salt") and alliteration are factors linking "silent sea" and "salt sheet" to each other, and the phrase "*sl*ee*p b*eca*l*med" has a chiasmus (*p* and *b* being cognates). The quantitative difference between the words "lie" and "still," "sleep" and "becalmed," forms a kind of "emotional semantic" [15] that is also present throughout the poem. The combination of numerous anapests, spondees, and caesuras within a relatively strict sonnet form (with slant

<hr/>

[14] A more detailed analysis of this type was carried out by James T. Lynch on a Keats sonnet. See "The Tonality of Lyric Poetry: An Experiment in Method," *Word*, IX (December, 1953), 211–224.

[15] Victor M. Hamm, "Meter and Meaning," *Publications of the Modern Language Association*, LXIX (September, 1954), 700.

rhymes in an *ababcdcdefgefg* pattern) provides an echo of the irregular rhythm of breaking waves in the sea.

A development of an affinitive pattern based on the sounds of certain key words is also present in the first half of "In Country Sleep" (p. 181). Here the crucial words are "spelled asleep," which appear at the end of the second line. "Sleep" is used four times in the first three stanzas and "spell" three times in the first four. Rhyme and assonance emphasize the effect with such words as "leap," "deep," "weep," "dell," "well," "cell." The vowel sounds of the two words are often repeated, and other words echo the opening consonants, *sp* or *sl:* "slow," "spinney," "spike," "spume." The phrase "slow and deep" in the second stanza is an augmentation of "sleep," directly followed by "spelled" to make the connection even more obvious. And, of course, there are other *s* and *l* sounds which echo the two dominant words. The direct repetition of the "spelled asleep" sounds of the first four stanzas is followed by subtle variations. "Knelling" changes to "kneel" four words later, and then "wheeling" is found further on, with other *ee* sounds between. The phrase reversed, "sleep spelled," then appears, is rhymed with other words, and gradually shifts into "falls," which dominates the last lines of the first section to suggest by its constant repetition the act of falling.

By the emphasis on the sounds of "spelled asleep," Thomas extends the literal meaning associated with the words throughout the poem. The affinitive pattern forms an auditory correlative to the meaning. Essentially, the poem is a plea to the child to sleep peacefully, shielded by her own innocence and that of nature. She lies "spelled asleep" now by the words of fairy tales, whose magic she is admonished never to fear because it does not really exist. She is warned to fear only the spirit of evil (the Thief) which is everywhere in the world and will cast another kind of spell on her if she leaves the innocence of her childhood existence, of nature and "country sleep." Her sleep is itself the symbol of her innocence. But it also refers to death, "until tolled to sleep by the stern/ Bell." The poem concludes with the thought that if this child always believes in and fears evil, she will never succumb to its spell and the lawless world without God which it implies.

"It is not at all the meaning the words had that counts," says Blackmur, "but the meaning that repetition, in a given situation, makes them take on." He cites pun as one form of repetition, rhyme a terminal, alliteration an initial form. Of the refrain, he says, it is a "means of emphatic ordering; . . . it modifies meaning itself by giving to gesture a conventional form . . . . [It] is the emphatic measure of all those gestures that have to do with the declaration of recurrence, return, rebirth and new birth, of motion in stillness and stillness in motion, of permanence in change and change in permanence." [16]

Thomas's use of the pun as a form of repetition is so obvious that it needs little discussion. Its significance, however, is usually not so much auditory as it is semantic. For example, in "If I Were Tickled by the Rub of Love," one could say that the constant use of the words "rub" and "tickle" do provide a cohesive factor in the auditory effect of the poem. But it would be more accurate to say that the whole literal meaning of the poem turns upon the changing meaning of these words, and the auditory effect is only incidental. Thomas's refrains, however, certainly do have an auditory as well as a semantic effect, as in "Do Not Go Gentle into That Good Night" or in "And Death Shall Have No Dominion."

Syntactical repetition, the repetition of whole phrase or sentence structures, may be considered as a somewhat less

[16] R. Blackmur, "Language as Gesture," *Accent Anthology* (New York, 1946), p. 485.

obvious refrain. Thomas employs this device in numerous ways throughout his poetry. Some form of it, as has already been suggested, may be found in every poem in Thomas's *Eighteen Poems*, "The Force That through the Green Fuse" (p. 10) being the best example. In each of this poem's four stanzas, the first line makes a declarative statement, the second develops the statement in terms of the narrator, the third concludes the statement, the fourth contains the refrain "And I am dumb to . . . ," and the fifth line deals with what the poet is dumb to tell. This repetitive syntax conditions the mind in a more effective way than the reader realizes, imparting some of the omnipresent emotion of rising and falling, of cyclic inevitability.

In "All All and All the Dry Worlds Lever" (p. 38), the phrase "all all and all" serves as a musical motif. It comes both first and last in the poem. It forms the explicit theme of Part I and Part III by the repetition of the whole phrase and also of the word "all." In the third line, "All from the oil, the pound of lava," the word "oil" (which also appears in the third line from the end) is certainly phonemically similar, and even "lava" repeats the sounds in reverse. "Fellow" and "fallow" in the second stanza also echo the "all" sound. Part II provides a variation of the theme in which the syntax is somewhat different from the first and third parts and in which the "all" sound is muted but still present in the words "mortal," "metal," "bridal," and "mauling." The sound also appears in the first stanza of Part III in "couple," "caul," and "mechanical," for example, as the poet gradually returns to the repetition of the entire motif.

This poem also has a perfectly regular rhyme scheme—*abacbc*—which is not immediately noticeable because it is based on consonantal repetition and vowel change. In the first stanza, for example, "lever" rhymes with "lava," "ocean" with "ashen," and "flower" with "fire." It is interesting to note that Thomas thus pairs "lover" and "lever" twice. In fact, almost all of the rhymes reveal or strengthen the implied connection between the worlds of inanimate matter and of life—"ocean" and "ashen," "fellow" and "fallow," "morrow" and "marrow," "mortal" and "metal," "blood" and "blade," "milling" and "mauling," "vice" and "voice," "suckle" and "circle," "bud" and "blood," "oil" and "all." This connection in meaning is also the basic metaphor upon which the whole poem is built.

"The Seed-at-Zero" (p. 49) is a poem built on stanzaic repetition. The eight stanzas are actually four pairs, and each stanza in the pair is identical to the other except for a change in certain key words. In the first two stanzas, the "trodden womb" becomes the "manwaged womb," the line "Dumbly and divinely stumbling" becomes "Dumbly and divinely leaping," and "manwaging" becomes "warbearing." In the second two stanzas, the "rumbling ground" becomes "guarded ground," "riddled sea" becomes "virgin sea," "virgin stronghold" becomes "riddled stronghold," and the "keeper of the key" becomes the "loser of the key." Similar changes occur in the last two pairs of stanzas, and, of course, the repetition combined with those changes provides an almost perfect corollary to the act of seduction which the poet is describing. In "Lament," one of Thomas's last poems, he uses this same device along with phonemic symbolism to tell the life story of the "old ram rod" from childhood to old age.

"In the White Giant's Thigh" (pp. 197–199) has two significant syntactical patterns. In the first part of the poem, the repetition of the phrase "Through throats where many rivers meet" clarifies the poet's perception that the women are praying through the same medium as the curlews, that is, through the throats of nature with which they have become one. The scene then shifts to the past lives of these dead women, and this second section is delineated by the syntactical motif "Who once . . . ." The parallel arrangement of the sentences in the form "Who once" is grammatically extended five more times by *or* constructions. We read: "Who once . . . loved . . . , or twined . . . , or . . . lay . . . , now clasp me . . . "; "Who once were . . . brides . . . , or . . . goose-girls . . . now" call by means of the curlews. There is an echo of this syntax in the final section, where "they . . . who heard . . . [now] teach" the poet about "the love that is evergreen," the love that is still fertile in the vegetation that rises from their dust.

One of the most interesting examples of Thomas's effective use of repetitive techniques is "The Conversation of Prayer" (p. 111). This poem, concerned with two attitudes of prayer and the profound implications of the different attitudes, is describing a paradox. The idea of the pure innocence of youth is upended in favor of the caring, loving adult. And the contradiction and contrast of the thought is mirrored in the sound and form of the poem. First, there is an internal rhyme in the middle of every line, so that the rhyme scheme for *each* stanza is actually *abbacddcab*—a rhyme that is constantly turning back upon itself. Then lines 8 and 9 are an almost exact reversal of the phrases in lines 1 and 2. Lines 13 and 14 revert again to the original order of lines 1 and 2, retaining the rhyme but changing one phrase. The phrases in lines 3 and 4 are echoed in lines 10 and 11 in an intricate rearrangement and development. This pattern of statement followed by inversion, development, and restatement provides an auditory counterpart to the hope in sorrow, age in youth, youth in age, warmth in death, cold in life, love in suffering, grief in not suffering—all the ideas that underline the poem. The attitude of the man is selfless and loving; that of the boy is selfish. The man is "full of tears that she [his love] will be dead," while the boy doesn't care "to whom in his sleep he will move." Both prayers express "the same grief," the elemental human desires and hopes, says the poet, but the answers depend not on the sound but on the substance of the prayers. In the intentionally ambiguous phrase "the quick and the dead," the poet is saying not only that the prayers concern the living and the dead, but also that one prayer is alive and the other dead. And the man will find life "in the fire of his care," while the child who cares deeply for no one "shall drown in a grief as deep as his made grave." The aging process, even in the child's sleep, will carry him toward the same stairs where the man prayed, toward the experience of love and grief and death.

As a matter of fact, Thomas was devising unusual rhyme schemes from the very beginning, rhymes which he called the "warp" of his poetry. These earlier schemes especially were made out of slant rhymes such as we have already pointed out in "All All and All the Dry Words Lever." The second poem in his first book, "Before I Knocked" (p. 8), for example, has a clear *ababab* pattern using such rhymes as "womb," "home," "worm," and "ghost," "last," "christ." Such slant rhymes are sometimes very subtle, as in "Where Once the Waters of Your Face" (p. 12). In this poem the pattern *abcabc,* which is explicit in the fourth and last stanza—the climax of the poem—is limited to the consonantal endings in the other stanzas (except for the third line in the second stanza). Thus we find that Thomas has paired words with opposite connotations such as life and death or sea and land to enhance his basic metaphor—"face" and "ice," "splice" and "loose," "tides" and "shades," "weeds" and "voids." This type of rhyme allows for endless variations and includes all types of cognate alliteration and assonance. It also allows the poet to deviate from it when necessary without jolting the reader. In "My World Is Pyramid" (p. 35), an *ababcc* pattern

"Hewn Voice"

is present in every stanza, sometimes as obvious as "doubles" and "dabbles" or "sleep" and "deep" and occasionally as oblique as "scudded" and "cyanide" or "drill" and "angel."

Once we become aware of Thomas's use of slant rhymes, we can find them in at least half of the poems that appeared in his first two books. Apparently he also intended to use such a pattern in his "Altarwise by Owl-light" sonnet sequence (pp. 80–85). We can trace it quite clearly in the first few poems, but it becomes less and less exact and finally disappears altogether in the last three sonnets (which were originally published separately). The pattern is clearest in the first five sonnets—*abcbacdedefgfg*. And this accords perfectly with the syntactical pattern of all ten poems, a pattern which reverses the traditional sonnet form by placing the sestet first, followed by two quatrains. This pattern thereby provides one key to Thomas's intention in this sequence—to reverse the meaning of various traditional images and ideas.

In Thomas's later poems the rhyme schemes become either more exact, as in "A Winter's Tale," "In Country Sleep," "A Refusal to Mourn . . . ," and many others, or more whimsical. That is, Thomas may use a rhyme or slant rhyme without too close a concern with a specific pattern. In several poems he has long, complicated stanzas with rhyme patterns that are almost identical, but not quite. Among these are "A Saint About to Fall" and "Into Her Lying Down Head." These poems are often distinguished by unusual arrangement of lines or by long and difficult syntax, or both. "Over Sir John's Hill" (pp. 187–189) actually has an almost perfect rhyme scheme—*aabccbdeaed₁d₂*—along with the rhythmic pattern, which is repeated in all five difficult stanzas.

Thomas, by his intricate manipulation of intonational, phonemic, and affinitive sound patterns, achieves in his later poems what Craig La Drière would call "pure poetry," in which "the aesthetic principle is so prominent as to over-shadow the others [grammatical, logical, and rhetorical], . . . raising the elements of sound to a status roughly coordinate with those of meaning." [17] Thomas became so completely the craftsman of verbal sounds that he exposed himself to one of the perennial complaints made against his poetry—that his work sounds beautiful but means nothing. Thus has arisen that paradoxical critical consensus which holds that the later poetry is Thomas's best while at the same time the poems of this period reveal a decline in poetic powers. Derek Stanford finds in the final period "a felicity of diction . . . covering monotony of perception." [18] Elder Olson says the late Thomas became "a bit too consciously the bard, overwhelming us with his copiousness of language, his eloquence, booming at us, working on us too obviously, even exciting himself unnecessarily." [19]

Such judgments may be akin to those of Shaw's phonetician (Higgins) who hears "native woodnotes wild" in the speech of Doolittle and says, "Sentimental rhetoric! that's the Welsh strain in him." The later Thomas is the almost inevitable outcome of a constant concern with auditory effects, and his final poems result in a distinct achievement in that tradition of English poetry stretching from the Old English through Crashaw, Keats, and Hopkins—not in sentimental rhetoric.

There is no question that the exploitation of auditory elements is a legitimate practice for the poet, but there is some question whether we have "Swinburnian incantation" or that "strong strain in British poetry which shouts a sheer delight in words." [20] The most succinct solution to the problem is Pope's:

[17] Craig La Drière, "Structure, Sound, and Meaning," *Sound and Poetry* (New York, 1957), p. 91.
[18] Derek Stanford, *Dylan Thomas* (New York, 1954), p. 130.
[19] Elder Olson, *The Poetry of Dylan Thomas* (Chicago, 1954), p. 22.
[20] Geoffrey Moore, "Dylan Thomas: Significance of His Genius," *Kenyon Review*, XVII (Spring, 1955), 273–274.

"Hewn Voice"

True ease in writing comes from art, not chance,
As those move easiest who have learn'd to dance.
'T is not enough no harshness gives offence;
The sound must seem an Echo to the sense.[21]

The important word is *echo*, for the sound must echo something; it cannot stand alone. When the verse has little or nothing to say, the extensive use of auditory devices is justly called "felicitous" or "copious," as it is in a jingle, doggerel, or TV commercial. But I do not believe this is the case with Thomas, except for parts of *Under Milk Wood*. The problem is essentially one of discerning just how the sound supports or "echoes" the sense. Sound alone does not indicate distinctive achievement; it must be coupled with imagination and intellectual daring. Thus judgments of Thomas's auditory correlatives—beyond the technical judgment that they demonstrate a superb mastery of language—are dependent on the fullest possible understanding of the poetry. For such an understanding we must examine in detail the themes and the vision of the work.

[21] Alexander Pope, "An Essay on Criticism," II, lines 362–365. Pope's whole section dealing with sound and sense does in miniature and in general what this chapter attempts in detail and in particular.

CHAPTER FOUR

"Dark Is a Way":
Theme and Encounter

And freely he goes lost
In the unknown, famous light of great
And fabulous, dear God.
Dark is a way and light is a place,
Heaven that never was
Nor will be ever is always true.
                                   "Poem on His Birthday"

THOMAS'S rhetorical and auditory complexities tend to obscure the fact that his poetry and also, in a more general way, his prose comprise a body of significant statements. These statements passionately exclaim about things the poet has seen or done, about happenings in the world of which we would have no knowledge if he did not tell us. He exhorts, he begs, he explains, he curses, he blesses; above all, he tells us what he accepts and what he rejects. And when one examines the work specifically in terms of its statements, a comprehensive argument emerges.[1]

[1] I am using the word *argument* in this chapter in its literary sense of main idea, plot, or theme, not in its logical sense of reasoned disputa-

"Dark Is a Way"

With prophetic clarity, Thomas suggested the direction and nature of his argument in his earliest public comments on his work. "My poetry is," he replied to an inquiry in 1934, "or should be, useful to me for one reason: it is the record of my individual struggle from darkness towards some measure of light . . . . My poetry is, or should be, useful to others for its individual recording of that same struggle with which they are necessarily acquainted." [2] Thomas's journey through darkness toward light is the clear direction of the argument of all his work. This is not to say, however, that his themes and subject matter hold an exhaustive or logical brief for any precisely defined position. The impetus and continuing character of the argument is emotional: "I hold," he wrote in an early letter to Treece, "a beast, an angel, and a madman in me, and my enquiry is as to their working, and my problem is their subjugation and victory, down-throw and upheaval, and my effort is their self-expression." [3] The conclusion of the argument is likewise emotional in that its final expression is symbolic, its final form is mythic. But within these emotional boundaries there are certain ideas and lines of thought which were of serious intellectual concern to Thomas and should also be explored by his readers.

Thomas's journey from darkness to light, put in more discursive language, is the continuous endeavor to find beauty, love, and purpose not only in the senses but even when the senses fail. Put another way, it is an attempt to find a position,

---

tion. I am in complete agreement with I. A. Richards's statement that "many, if not most, of the statements in poetry are there *as a means* to the manipulation and expression of feelings and attitudes, not as contributions to any body of doctrine of any type whatever." *Practical Criticism* (Harvest, New York, 1929), p. 180.

[2] From *Quite Early One Morning* (New York, 1954), p. 188, quoted in *A Casebook*, p. 102.

[3] *Dylan Thomas: The Legend and the Poet*, ed. E. W. Tedlock (London, 1960), p. 14.

or an attitude, from which painful existence, and ultimately death itself, may be tolerable.[4] This search is both chronological and dialectical, i.e., it transcribes a chronological course from youth to age (best seen in the four birthday poems), and within this course it continually examines new situations and positions in a loosely Hegelian fashion. Thomas's Hegelianism —probably all he knew of Hegel—consisted of the conviction that thought and belief were matters of thesis, antithesis, and synthesis. The synthesis was never final or lasting, it simply yielded a new thesis. (Thomas ascribed this dialectic to his image-making, too vaguely I believe, but it is applicable to his whole intellectual framework.) [5] It is this dialectical frame which explains, finally, his peculiar mixture of relativism and absolutism. For example, Thomas was continually making contradictory remarks which ended in universal positive affirmations. One of his most intriguing series of contradictions leading to affirmation is in the stanza quoted as the epigraph for this chapter:

[4] Lawrence Durrell sums up the impulse toward artistic creation from the awareness of mortality: "Man . . . as soon as he noticed the irreversibility of process in the natural world, became afraid and decided to invent a way of circumventing death. . . . So far we have found no way of halting this process in nature—the stream of time flows always one way, towards dissolution and death." *A Key to Modern British Poetry* (Norman, Okla., 1952), p. 14.

[5] Thus we see, as already observed in Chapter Two, that Thomas's famous remark about conflicting images has more relevance in terms of how he felt, or of how he thought, than it does as a method of explaining his images. I am drawing these distinctions between life and work, image and theme, in order to find more precise terms for understanding Thomas and his work. Contradictory complementarity seems a better concept to apply to Thomas's life, the idea of imaginative accumulations evolving from a central seed seems a more accurate description of his imagery, while Thomas's idea of the dialectic seems the best way to speak in general terms about his themes.

"Dark Is a Way"

And freely he goes lost
In the unknown, famous light of great
And fabulous, dear God.
Dark is a way and light is a place,
Heaven that never was
Nor will be ever is always true.

(p. 191)

Consider just the last two lines. There is a very logical reason why "Heaven that never was/ Nor will be" is true. Heaven, almost by definition, is a state of awareness or experience outside of time. Thus it could never be associated with *was*, or *will be*, but only with *is*. But regardless of the logic of this statement, there is a dialectical tenor to this declaration, to the whole stanza, and at the center of all of Thomas's most serious argument. What it amounts to is this: within the constant building up, the contradiction and destruction of the dialectic, there remains the unchanging nature of the dialectic itself; above all the relativities of the process from thesis to synthesis, there abides the absolutism of the dialectic itself. And it is this permanence within constant flux, perhaps a faith in reason although all reasons finally falter, that characterizes the dialectical core of Thomas's argument.

Fortunately, the chronology of Thomas's argument is lyrically simple: the early work is principally concerned with themes of revolt, the middle work with themes and situations of reflection and debate, the late work with themes of praise and consent. At one extreme he rejects life's conventions, at the other he accepts the inevitable; at one he cries out in revulsion against dying, at the other he exults in the experience of life and even of death. His beginning is full of rage, shock, confusion, and horror; his end is full of calm, a spirit of acceptance, and a singing praise of the world. Within this very neat movement of revolt, debate, and consent occur numerous impassioned and involved dialectics. Each theme introduced is capable of being contradicted, and usually is, as the argument of the poetry moves through antithesis after antithesis toward its final synthesis of affirmation.

I
REBELLION

There are two contesting impulses in Thomas's rebellion. One is destructive, antisocial, adolescent. The other is constructive, a persistent striking through the mask of illusion to come to the truth, or at least to what he could feel was a true encounter. One is the rebellion of banality; the other that of the great artist, the reformer, the mystic. The two emphases are never completely separated in Thomas: his revolt never becomes entirely banal, never truly mystical. Camus, as might be expected, defines these tendencies with trenchant suggestiveness. Writing of Lautréamont, Camus says, he "makes us understand that rebellion is adolescent. Our most effective terrorists, whether they are armed with bombs or with poetry, hardly escape from infancy." There is in this rebellion, Camus goes on, the "pathos" of "a child's mind ranged against creation and against itself . . . beating against the confines of the world." On the other hand, there is in rebellion, even in adolescent rebellion, a craving for a more satisfying existence, even for an ideal world. Camus's observations on the metaphysical value of rebellion are singularly applicable to Thomas's work:

It can . . . well be said of the poets who rushed to assault the heavens, with the intent of turning everything upside down, that by so doing they affirmed their desperate nostalgia for order. As an ultimate contradiction, they wanted to extract reason from unreason and to systematize the irrational. These heirs of romanticism claimed to make poetry exemplary and to find, in its most harrowing aspects, the real way of life. They deified blasphemy and transformed poetry into experience and into a means of action. Until their time those who claimed to influence men and events, at least in the Occident, did so in the name of rational rules. On the contrary, surrealism, after Rimbaud, wanted to find constructive rules in insanity and destruction. Rimbaud, through his work . . . , pointed out the path, but with the blinding, momentary illumination of a flash of lightning.[6]

Thomas's obsession with physical conditions and actions, his early exaltation of word over idea, his emotionalism, often brought his work close to banality. Even in his best work he sometimes tries unnecessarily to excite us [7]—"Heigh ho the blood and berry,/ And nail the merry squires to the trees" (p. 3)—without due regard to the overall direction of the poem. Larger examples of such superficiality are contained in poems Thomas wisely left out of his collected volume—although *Collected Poems* is not entirely free of superficial poems (see "Now," pp. 60–61). The most detrimental banality in Thomas is found in his prose treatment of the nether world and witchcraft. This theme is effectively treated only in one early story, "The Enemies" (*Adventures in the Skin Trade* . . .). Here Mrs. Owen, the witch, and her husband, the devotee of the copulating earth, are pitted against the hapless Reverend Mr. Davies in a scene of overwhelming strength. The witch theme, however, mars "The Holy Six," is unsuccessfully treated in "The School for Witches," and encourages Thomas to concentrate on atmosphere, to the detriment of character, in *The Doctor and the Devils.*

This tendency toward the trivial Thomas can exploit, however, with great effectiveness in his comic work. What is

[6] Albert Camus, *The Rebel*, trans. Anthony Bower (Vintage, New York, 1956), pp. 82, 81–82.

[7] Elder Olson, *The Poetry of Dylan Thomas* (Chicago, 1954), p. 22.

destructive to the poetry, harmful to the symbolic prose, is the very condition of his comic prose. The reason is clear: the comic prose contains a satiric corrective lacking in the other work. The stories of *Portrait of the Artist as a Young Dog* all implicitly contain the ironic viewpoint of the adult telling about his youth. A description which sees aunts at Christmas as the "eternal aunts" conveys a satiric judgment to the reader, for only with age does one come to realize such relatives are "eternal."

The finest exploitation of the trivial occurs in his "Adventures in the Skin Trade," the longest of the prose pieces and a work he once hoped to make into a novel. If Thomas had possessed the staying power to have completed this undertaking, the finished work might very well have been a major contribution to comic literature. "Adventures" is an incomparable exercise in the humor of the absurd. At times reminiscent of Joyce and Beckett, it maintains a much clearer narrative line than either *Ulysses* or *Molloy* and is thus much more easily approached and enjoyed. The comic touch which Thomas so superbly illustrated in this 1941 work, he approximated in his dramatic *Under Milk Wood* ten years later. But the comedy of the latter work, coming as it does from a time of consent rather than of revolt, lacks some of the sharpness of the early work. It loses in directness what it gains in felicity.

The themes of rebellion in the "Adventures" are at once banal and nihilistic. The protagonist, appropriately called Samuel Bennet, recounts a revolt against family and convention which reminds one of an episode from a court delinquency report. A teen-age boy, getting up early on the day he is to leave his home and go to the city to work, systematically sets about destroying those things most meaningful to the other members of his family. He breaks his mother's china, he writes crude comments on a batch of papers his father was correcting (Dylan's father was a teacher), and he burns some of his sister's prized needlework. There is a clear strain throughout Thomas's poetry of such disdain for values commonly held by others, although he is never as childishly antisocial as in his prose.

An important aspect of Thomas's rejection of convention is his elemental emphasis on the Keatsian maxim that truth should be proved in the pulse. His appeal for a full life is for a fully physical life. And his persistent lust for sensation invariably brings his observation on the absurd to a physical rather than a metaphysical level. He is forever reminding us, as in "A Grief Ago," that we shall but shortly rejoin the matter from which we have so lately sprung and that the only sensible thing to do is to experience fully our present state of existence, to realize and share in the primal forces of nature:

> Let her inhale her dead, through seed and solid
> Draw in their seas.
>
> (p. 64)

He urges us to make the most of light and of the conceiving ("manshaped") moon and to avoid whatever is not deep as a pulse beat:

> Foster the light nor veil the manshaped moon,
> Nor weather winds that blow not down the bone.
>
> (p. 69)

Strip life to its essence, he goes on:

> But strip the twelve-winded marrow from his circle;
> Master the night nor serve the snowman's brain
> That shapes each bushy item of the air
> Into a polestar pointed on an icicle.

(The snowman's brain here, as snow in general in Thomas, is an image of death, and we are told not to serve him who turns "each bushy item" into a pointer toward death.) Experience everything, without hypocrisy and without inhibition.

That convention with which the work is most frequently concerned is religion, Christianity in particular. The short story "The Tree" is a virtual syndrome of the ideas and emotions involved in Thomas's revolt against religion and is well worth examining in some detail. Revolt perhaps is not the perfect term, for something like Camus's idea of a "nostalgia for order" eventually builds a new religion out of the ashes of the old. In the very instant of rebellion against the establishment, the seeds of a new establishment are planted.

"The Tree" (*Adventures in the Skin Trade* . . .) deals with innocence and evil, with the perpetuation of evil and the destruction of innocence. Like all of Thomas's symbolic short stories, "The Tree" is concerned with a few simple actions. The story involves an old gardener, a boy, and an idiot. The time of the action is just before and on Christmas Day. The gardener is a mysterious but bungling figure; he knows all the stories in the world but cannot repair a rake. The idiot is equally mysterious; he has been wandering the countryside, the Jarvis valley, and has been cared for by the people. Like Myshkin and Benjy, he is a type of Christ: "And asking for water, he was given milk." A mysterious inner voice tells him to go to the home of the boy and gardener. "As he bent with a rake over the dung and the trodden grain, he heard a voice rise in his heart." He goes to this place, to the place of the gardener and the boy and to an enigmatic elder tree which the boy worships. There the boy fastens the idiot to the tree with wire the gardener was unable to repair the rake with. (I suspect the wire is rusty and dirties the hands of both the gardener and the boy. Thomas, however, does not make this apparent—he simply uses the wire to connect the old man and the boy.) The story ends: "The idiot felt the wire that had not mended the rake close round his wrists. It cut into the flesh, and the blood from the cuts fell shining on to the tree.

"Brother, he said. He saw that the child held silver nails in the palm of his hand."

The story, in brief, recounts the crucifixion of an idiot by a child. The idiot does not want to be crucified, but he submits, an *agnus Dei*. The action takes place in the symbolic world of Thomas's early work, which, in turn, is derived from the intellectual and emotional *Weltschmerz* of the young Thomas. When we ask why the boy crucifies the idiot, we ask in effect why evil exists. The answer to this question is inferred in the particular circumstances and characters of the tale: a boy, a gardener, a tree, a tower, Christmas Day, the Jarvis valley, and a crucifixion.

Thomas begins with the tower, and we might be wise to follow his lead. "Rising from the house that faced the Jarvis hills in the long distance, there was a tower for the day-birds to build in and for the owls to fly around at night." In the first published version of the story, Thomas had begun with a description of the Jarvis hills and the Jarvis valley. But in rewriting the story he eliminated this and emphasized the tower. The second paragraph of the story reads: "The child knew the house from roof to cellar; he knew the irregular lawns and the gardener's shed where flowers burst out of their jars; he could not find the key that opened the door of the tower."

The door of the tower is opened on Christmas Eve by the gardener. But the boy discovers that there is nothing in the tower, the tower is empty. "The child began to cry because there were no secrets. Over and over again he explored the empty room, kicking up the dust to look for a colourless trap-door, tapping the unpanelled walls for the hollow voice of a room beyond the tower." There is nothing in the tower for the boy. But he learns from his vantage point there of the existence of the hills he could never see before. "They are the Jarvis hills, said the gardener, which have been from the beginning."

The gardener's emphasis on the key which will unlock the tower is misleading, because the tower itself is empty. Likewise the boy is misled by the gardener's emphasis on "the tree." "The gardener loved the Bible. . . . But the death of Christ on a tree he loved most." But the child does not love the tree of Calvary, he loves the tree in his own garden, he worships and venerates it; and the gardener tacitly supports this tree worship.

> I prayed to the tree, said the child.
> Always pray to a tree, said the gardener, thinking of Calvary and Eden.
> I pray to the tree every night.
> Pray to a tree.
> The wire slid over the teeth.
> I pray to that tree.
> The wire snapped.
> The child was pointing over the glasshouse flowers to the tree that, alone of all the trees in the garden, had no sign of snow.
> An elder, said the gardener, but the child stood up from his box and shouted so loud that the unmended rake fell with a clatter on the floor.
> The first tree. The first tree you told me of. In the beginning was the tree, you said. I heard you, the child shouted.
> The elder is as good as another, said the gardener, lowering his voice to humour the child.

The boy exists in a world where there is no secret in the tower save the awesome Jarvis hills, which have existed from the beginning, so he finds mystery in his garden, in the elder tree. The copulating earth of the witch Owens is the lasting force of the world, the pagan elder tree is accepted as the rood of Christ, Christmas is turned into Good Friday. The boy seeking truth ends in madness. The gardener's wire, which could not fix a rake, in the hands of the child kills a man. Innocence is still sent to Golgotha; only the indifferent supernality of the Jarvis hills remains the same. What this story tells us about the early work and world of Dylan Thomas is perhaps best summed up in the insight of Raja Rao: "When the world is not the self, it becomes real, and becomes a nightmare: confusion is its very nature." [8]

"The Tree" is not only significant in its own right, it is also significant because it typifies the methods and themes of the prose up to 1939. What actually happens in these stories is always of bare simplicity: a circus fat man and a homeless mother and child ride a merry-go-round all night to comfort the hungry infant. A writer watches his friends about his death bed—after he has died. A clergyman cremates the child of his incestuous union with his daughter. A madman who has deformed his wife falls asleep in the lap of a girl who wears a beautifully flowered dress. "The Mouse and the Woman," "The Map of Love," "Prologue to an Adventure," and "A Prospect of the Sea" are all related by male-female, boy-meets-girl themes of sexual initiation. More often than not what Thomas expresses is revulsion. The writer of "The Mouse and the Woman," for example, has killed the woman he loved. He killed because he could not stand the female form:

They were . . . naked. . . . Eve could not have been as beautiful. They ate with the devil, and saw they that they were naked, and covered up their nakedness. In their good bodies they saw evil for the first time.

[8] Raja Rao, "André Malraux among the Gods of India," *Texas Quarterly* (Winter, 1961), 109.

Then you saw evil in me, she said, when I was naked. I would as soon be naked as be clothed. Why did you cover up my nakedness?

It was not good to look upon.

If the early prose reveals anything, it reveals a world in which the old mislead the young, in which the young aggravate the error to madness; it reveals a world, as we shall see in more detail later, in which sex cannot be withstood, in which sex is the source of the greatest wonder. But it is a world in which sex cannot be enjoyed, in which sex initiates one into madness and murder.

This world of the prose is thematically identical with that of the poetry. When the girl in "A Prospect of the Sea" lifts her dress to provoke the boy (who thinks "They're calling me in for tea"), she is performing the function of almost all the female figures in the poetry—save the melodramatic figure who dies in childbirth ("The Tombstone Told When She Died"). Several incidents in the prose are, in fact, identical with those in the poetry. In "A Prospect of the Sea," for example, the boy says, "If she loves me until I die, . . . she will carry me away inside her. . . . This is the story of a boy being stolen. She has put a knife in my belly and turned my stomach round." This is a variation of that puzzling expression "a rooking girl . . . stole me for her side," in "If I Were Tickled by the Rub of Love" (p. 13). The female who steals is the mother who takes the seed. The verbal phrases and symbols which are shared by the prose and the poetry are too numerous to mention; there is, however, only one explicit narrative sequence which is repeated in both poetry and prose. "An Adventure from a Work in Progress" and "Ballad of the Long-legged Bait" were begun within a short period of each other, and, judging from early "Ballad" drafts, the "Adventure" comes very close to being a prose statement of "the deadly female" theme which is so ingeniously treated in the "Ballad."

Sin was one of the orthodox terms, noted in Chapter One, which Thomas never rejected—he simply redefined it, and one of its equations was sex. Sex is sinful in a peculiar way for Thomas. There are some Apocalyptic overtones: the redeemed are those "not defiled with women," and, rightly understood, the lost are those who commit fornication with the whore of Babylon. But such associations seem more a part of some cultural veneer than a central conviction for Thomas. Sex is evil because it brings forth life into suffering and, quite inconsistently, because this new life makes the living expendable. As early as 1931, Thomas had accused those who brought him into life. He wrote in October of that year, in his Notebook, a poem entitled, "Written for A Personal Epitaph," in which he asked, who is to blame? His answer is mother, whose "crime" of love shaped his being in her womb.

It seems inevitable that Thomas should have followed Milton and interpreted the "Fall" in sexual terms. The apple of Genesis is, for Thomas, a "bearded apple" (p. 46), and sexual desire is "the devil in the loin" (p. 13). This is why Thomas has Christ say (in Sonnet VIII, p. 84)

> I by the tree of thieves, all glory's sawbones,
> Unsex the skeleton this mountain minute,
> And by this blowclock witness of the sun
> Suffer the heaven's children through my heartbeat.

Christ, whose death on the "tree of thieves" redeemed mankind, is the heavenly surgeon who amputates man's sin (sex) and henceforth brings souls to heaven by His love.

Utilizing a preponderantly puritanical definition of sin, Thomas's rebellion can be seen as perfectly logical. Since sex is obviously one of the deepest of man's needs and also essential to the continuation of the human race, God is manifestly unjust, and for man there is no way out. Thus, in the prose and poetry of revolt, life itself is often seen as evil. Life must by its very nature reproduce itself, and such reproduction only leads to death. Not only is conception a theft, but sin itself can be said to have "a woman's shape" (p. 171). In "In the White Giant's Thigh," Thomas compares women, among other things, to whores by his pun "Who once were a bloom of wayside brides in the hawed house" (p. 198). The comparison is intended in a benevolent way, since sex can also be seen as an escape from the universal sinfulness of life. Sex is therefore illicit, and all women, wives or not, are "brides in the hawed house." In this regard it is interesting to note the comment of one of the characters in his story "Where Tawe Flows": " 'Marriage [is] . . . legal monogamous prostitution.' " [9]

At least partly because of the connection in Thomas's mind between sin and sex, one of the controlling views in his poetry is that of sex as a trap, a "long-legged bait." Although some poems call for a full physical life and others reject conventional mores, sex in still other poems is, nevertheless, presented as a snare, a source of pain and anguish:

> This world is half the devil's and my own,
> Daft with the drug that's smoking in a girl
> And curling round the bud that forks her eye.
> (p. 14)

And again:

[9] *Portrait of the Artist as a Young Dog* (New York, 1940), p. 94.
Cf. Northrop Frye, *Fearful Symmetry* (Princeton, 1947), p. 73, where he points out a similar attitude: "Of course the legal and ecclesiastical idea of marriage as a trap baited with the sex act and snapped at consummation Blake, like Milton, thought obscene."

"Dark Is a Way"

Joy is the knock of dust, Cadaver's shoot
Of bud of Adam through his boxy shift,
Love's twilit nation and the skull of state,
Sir, is your doom.

(p. 22)

Sex is something convention rigidly controls, so convention is
attacked. But after convention has been abolished and we stand
face to face with the fact of sex (as we shall shortly see even
more clearly when we discuss the marriage poems), the mask is
ripped off and we are staring into the face of death—"The
mummy cloths expose an ancient breast" (p. 72). In "I Make
This in a Warring Absence," Thomas says:

"See," drummed the taut masks, "how the dead ascend:
In the groin's endless coil a man is tangled."

(p. 89)

In a passage from "My World Is Pyramid," which I take to be
a description of human genesis, he reveals an almost pathologi-
cal sense of disgust with human generation:

The patchwork halves were cloven as they scudded
The wild pigs' wood, and slime upon the trees,
Sucking the dark, kissed on the cyanide,
And loosed the braiding adders from their hairs;
Rotating halves are horning as they drill
The arterial angel.

(p. 35)

The "patchwork halves" of the human creature were evil even
before and during conception, are already cuckolding in the
womb.

Thomas's rebellion against the paradoxical attraction and
revulsion of sex is closely related to his reaction against much
of traditional Christianity, a point already touched on but one
that could use further elaboration. For Thomas's whole rebel-

171

lion and revulsion, like Camus's rebellion, "is born of the spectacle of irrationality," the conviction that man exists in "an unjust and incomprehensible condition." [10]

This is the antithesis of the Christian view, and, almost inevitably, Thomas's iconoclasm early turns against the Christian attitude because of its apparent inability to deal fully and convincingly with the realities of life. In the mystery of the Incarnation, for example, Thomas finds cause for pitying Christ and, implicitly, all involved in the event. Using Christ as a representative of humanity, he has mankind say:

> Remember me and pity Him
> Who took my flesh and bone for armour
> And doublecrossed my mother's womb.
>
> (p. 9)

Christ is to be pitied for taking on human flesh, and in this form He "doublecrossed" his mother's womb not only by being born to die but also because he brought her suffering twice, by dying on the cross as well as by being born in the first place. If Thomas had the virgin birth in mind, he could also be invoking the conceit of Christ entering the womb to take flesh and leaving it in the form of a child: literally, he crossed the womb twice.

Thomas's revolt against religion takes several forms. He mocks, denies, defies the practices and beliefs of the Christianity that he knows, and, somewhat paradoxically, at the same time builds with Biblical and religious symbols his personal mythology. We shall concentrate on the first of these practices now and on the second in the next chapter.

One of the simplest and clearest expressions of the early attitude, Thomas's denial of divine mercy, can be seen in "The Hand That Signed the Paper" (p. 71). After describing evils

[10] Camus, *The Rebel*, p. 10.

and sorrows that can result from a single signature on a piece of paper, he concludes:

> A hand rules pity as a hand rules heaven;
> Hands have no tears to flow.

But, although the "hand" has "no tears," it does indeed exist. There is always, for Thomas, some inscrutable *force* which controls the destiny of the earth and its creatures:

> The hand that whirls the water in the pool
> Stirs the quicksand; that ropes the blowing wind
> Hauls my shroud sail.
>
> (p. 10)

This force is viewed, in the early poetry, as First Cause rather than as a personal being. "In the Beginning" (p. 27) is a description of creation based on metaphors for this First Cause: "the three-pointed star," "the pale signature," the "three-eyed, red-eyed spark," "the word," "the brain." This poem, however, concludes by describing Him as "the ribbed original of love," an early indication of Thomas's final affirmation of "great/ And fabulous, dear God" (p. 191) and the weeping God of "In Country Heaven." [11]

While Thomas rejects organized religion, he does not deny the kindness of some religious people, as in "After the Funeral":

> I know her scrubbed and sour humble hands
> Lie with religion in their cramp.
>
> (p. 97)

The ironic humor of "Lament" is an indirect attack on religion, as it describes the whistling wickedness of the "black spit of the chapel fold" (p. 194) who is "dying of women" among the angelic harpies and "deadly virtues." But it also

[11] See Chapter Five.

humorously judges the "old ram rod" whose unhappy dotage
and death are scarcely to be envied:

> Now I am a man no more no more
> And a black reward for a roaring life,
> (Sighed the old ram rod, dying of strangers),
> Tidy and cursed in my dove cooed room
> I lie down thin and hear the good bells jaw.
>
> (p. 196)

A more specific attack on conventional religion can be seen
in Sonnet V (p. 82):

> And from the windy West came two-gunned Gabriel,
> From Jesu's sleeve trumped up the king of spots,
> The sheath-decked jacks, queen with a shuffled heart;
> Said the fake gentleman in suit of spades,
> Black-tongued and tipsy from salvation's bottle.

These lines are obviously a parody of Christian Scripture and
of the apocalyptic preaching of the Welsh Chapel. In this
parody, on one level at least, the Book of Revelation becomes a
western novel in which Gabriel is the "two-gunned" marshal.
(He is presumably on the side of the law because of his
connection with "Jesu's sleeve." It may also be relevant that St.
John wrote his book from the island of Patmos in the Medi-
terranean and sent it east to the seven churches of Asia. Not
only was John in the West, but Gabriel's voice came to him
from behind—even further West.) This western marshal
"trumped up" (as with the trumpet of Apocalypse, as a
fabricator, and, finally, as a western cardplayer) the angel of
death, the hosts of the sinners, and the Whore of Babylon. The
preachers of religion are "fake" gentlemen, hypocrites, liars. It
is from this vision of salvation and damnation that young
Thomas, the "Byzantine Adam," revolted to become an outcast like Ishmael, a runaway like Jonah.

"Dark Is a Way"

Sonnet IX represents a rejection of Christianity from a different angle. After describing the mummification and burial of the crucified Christ-poet, Thomas gives an ironic picture of what the resurrection has meant in the "desert," the wasteland of this world:

> This was the resurrection in the desert,
> Death from a bandage, rants the mask of scholars
> Gold on such features, and the linen spirit
> Weds my long gentleman to dusts and furies;
> With priest and pharaoh bed my gentle wound,
> World in the sand, on the triangle landscape,
> With stones of odyssey for ash and garland
> And rivers of the dead around my neck.
>
> (p. 85)

The scholars and the "linen spirit" (the death impulse as well as the spirit of respectability) have consigned Christ "to dusts and furies." They have relegated him to the past of pharoah and pyramid, mourned and praised him with stones ("With stones of odyssey for ash and garland"), and drowned him (and his true meaning) by tying "rivers of the dead" (rules of conduct?) around his neck. The resurrected Christ of life and love has been used by Christians to preach "death from a bandage"—evidently the fear of death and sin. And this is why the "tale's sailor from a Christian voyage" will "hold half-way off the dummy bay" in Sonnet X. He does not wholly reject Christ, "the blown word," but he does reject the "dummy bay" of conventional Christianity.

A related description of Christ is to be found in "Do You Not Father Me" (p. 54). In that poem, Christ is imaged as a tower who is both God and man. He is related to all human beings as brother, sister, father by His human nature. Yet, because He is also God, He is "the lovers' house," the source of life and love (sex and sin). And he was "razed" like Isaac by

175

his own people ("they were mine"), who "hacked" down his tower in compliance with the will of God, of whom Abraham is a figure. But, for different reasons, both his human murderers and God who was also responsible now stand "aghast" at the results. For, rising out of the destruction, as if out of seaweeds cast up on the sand, are "The salt sucked dam and darlings of the land/ Who play the proper gentleman and lady." Forgetting their humble origin, the offspring of Christ (and of the evolutionary sea) are self-sufficient hypocrites. To Christ who still asks to be "love's house," the embodiment of God's love, in spite of the "masons" who try to seal up his tomb, they reply that love and death, womb and tomb, have nothing to do with the "grave sin-eater," the savior who "assumes the sins" of the dead.[12] For them, love is still sinful and death inevitable. (Christ is also a figure of the poet, of course, in this poem as elsewhere, but the denial of Christianity remains a significant aspect of the poem.)

Simpler evidence of Thomas's disregard for the elements of traditional Christianity can be seen in "This Bread I Break" (p. 45). The central image in this poem is, of course, the Eucharist, the bread and wine of the Christian communion service. The poem reveals Thomas's thought process clearly. In the first stanza he describes the bread and wine in purely natural terms, their origin in growing oats and grapes. In the second stanza he adds to the description the metaphor "blood" in the "flesh" of the grapes. Furthermore, "the oat was merry in the wind"—these things of nature are seen as virtually human in their experience of life. Man, he says in both stanzas, has killed the life of these plants. In the third stanza we see what this

[12] William York Tindall, *A Reader's Guide to Dylan Thomas* (New York, 1962), p. 96. The play on the word "tower" which is involved in this poem is discussed in my Chapter Two. Frye, in *Fearful Symmetry*, p. 387, points out that "Blake identifies the dead body of Jesus with the body of Antichrist, the form which the social hatred of Jesus creates out of Jesus."

metaphor has been driving at. This bread and wine ("flesh" and "blood") are products of the creative force behind all life, "born of the sensual root and sap." Therefore, since the poet too is a product of that creative force, is alive just as the oat and the grape were alive, "My wine you drink, my bread you snap." The Christian communion represents for Thomas not the love of God but rather the cruelty and destructiveness of man. Even the use of the irreverent word "snap" conveys iconoclastic motivation. Thomas's reinterpretation of Christian symbols and of the meaning of Christ is an important aspect of his rejection of orthodox belief and will be discussed more fully in the next chapter.

Thomas is one with Lawrence in his rejection of orthodox restrictions of sexuality. Thomas inverts one traditional attitude when he makes continence an evil and sexual activity an unqualified spiritual good. The former he describes as: "the choir and cloister/ Of the wintry nunnery of the order of lust." Of the latter, the physical love of man and woman, he says:

> and the ceremony of souls
> Is celebrated there, and communion between suns.
> Never shall my self chant
> About the saint in shades while the endless breviary
> Turns of your prayed flesh.
>
> (pp. 120–121)

Thomas seems even closer to Lawrence when he describes Christianity as the "carcass shape" and mourns the loss of a divine blood consciousness.

> I sent my own ambassador to light;
> By trick or chance he fell asleep
> And conjured up a carcass shape
> To rob me of my fluids in his heart.
>
> (p. 5)

One of Thomas's strongest attacks on organized religion has been mistakenly understood as a tribute to Christianity and Christ. In "There Was a Saviour" (p. 139), he actually contends that Christians live in an unreal, self-indulgent world, completely unmindful of the needs of their fellow human beings. The poem begins:

> There was a saviour
> Rarer than radium,
> Commoner than water, crueller than truth;
> Children kept from the sun
> Assembled at his tongue
> To hear the golden note turn in a groove,
> Prisoners of wishes locked their eyes
> In the jails and studies of his keyless smiles.

Note here that the "children kept from the sun" are the ones who assembled to hear Him. Sun, with Thomas, in a truly pagan and primitive sense, is a symbol of the life force. And these children listened to "the golden note turn in a groove," pretty sounds on a record—fine words removed from reality. Those kept from the sun are "prisoners of wishes," that is, wishful thinkers. These are the ones, then, who are the followers of the rare savior. And what did they do? They "locked their eyes/ In the jails and studies of his keyless smiles." The result of their locked eyes is made more clear in the third stanza, where Thomas says that the believers were comfortable, complacent, and sentimental in their religion:

> There was glory to hear
> In the churches of his tears,
> Under his downy arm you sighed as he struck.

But there was no real brotherhood, no real humanity there:

"Dark Is a Way"

O you who could not cry
On to the ground when a man died
Put a tear for joy in the unearthly flood
And laid your cheek against a cloud-formed shell.

Divorced from reality, Thomas says, the churchgoer was unmindful of real suffering and wept self-indulgently about "unearthly" sorrows, taking comfort in an empty shell of belief with no more substance than a cloud. The poem goes on to tell how the war has changed this indifference, and how the poet and the believer have now been forced to share the agony of mankind. And thus there is aroused in them "the soft,/ Unclenched, armless, silk and rough love that breaks all rocks." This is a form of impassioned humanism to which Thomas's revolt turned at this point, but it is not a faith in, nor even a praise of the faith of, the savior "rarer than radium."

In "Shall Gods Be Said to Thump the Clouds" (p. 52), Thomas proclaims his Job-like revolt against anthropomorphic explanations of natural phenomena: [13]

> Shall gods be said to thump the clouds
> When clouds are cursed by thunder,
> Be said to weep when weather howls?
> Shall rainbows be their tunics' colour?

No, says Thomas, "It shall be said that gods are stone." He concludes, "Let the stones speak/ With tongues that talk all tongues." Here we can catch an ironic parody of a New

---

[13] See for example, Jeremiah 51:16: "When he uttereth his voice, there is a multitude of waters in the heavens; and he causeth the vapours to ascend from the ends of the earth: he maketh lightnings with rain, and bringeth forth the wind out of his treasures." And Job 37:20 provides one of many Biblical parallels to Thomas's poetic cadence and grammatical structure: "Shall it be told him that I speak? if a man speak, surely he shall be swallowed up."

Testament passage as well. Christ told the Pharisees that if His disciples did not cheer Him upon His entrance into Jerusalem on Palm Sunday even the stones of the streets would have spoken to greet Him (Luke 19:40).

But Thomas recognized that the mere flouting of convention was not a sufficient *modus vivendi*. Although he would perhaps have liked to be a rebel without a cause, and though he often acted this way in his lifetime, his poetry reflects his realization of the limitations of such an attitude:

> I have longed to move away but am afraid;
> Some life, yet unspent, might explode
> Out of the old lie burning on the ground,
> And, crackling into the air, leave me half-blind.

> (p. 73)

In "Once Below a Time" (pp. 147–149), he describes his own unconventional behavior, caricatures himself as a kind of merman in the midst of "the tailors," the rest of conventional mankind:

> Then swift from a bursting sea with bottlecork boats
> And out-of-perspective sailors,
> In common clay clothes disguised as scales,
> As a he-god's paddling water skirts,
> I astounded the sitting tailors,
> I set back the clock faced tailors.

But, he says, though he managed to deceive and astonish his fellow men, he could not deceive "my maker,/ The cloud perched tailors' master with nerves for cotton." This maker who sews with nerves instead of cotton thread, this "idol" (and "idol tailor" because this is only one representation of God—anthropomorphically similar to the tailors),[14] sees through his pretensions and his mask:

[14] A further account of the tailor imagery appears in Chapter Five.

"Dark Is a Way"

On the old seas from stories, thrashing my wings,
Combing with antlers, Columbus on fire,
I was pierced by the idol tailor's eyes.

God forces him to see himself as he really is—

> the boy of common thread,
> The bright pretender, the ridiculous sea dandy
> With dry flesh and earth for adorning and bed.

After such an unmasking, although he will never "regret the bugle I wore/ On my cleaving arm as I blasted in a wave," the poet is ready to give up, to live as other men do, to abandon a hopeless fight:

> Now shown and mostly bare I would lie down,
> Lie down, lie down and live
> As quiet as a bone.

The refurbished cliché here, "live" instead of "die," helps to convey the totality of his defeat and surrender. The poet is not even going to die a martyr's death—he is simply going to give up.

Rebellion and revulsion constitute one of the major concerns of Thomas's poetry, reveal a serious and unconventional pessimism, but also lead to insight and enlightenment. In "If I Were Tickled by the Rub of Love" (p. 13), he says in several ways that if he were urged by the desire to love he would fear neither religious restraint, "I would not fear the apple nor the flood," nor "the gallows nor the axe" (stanza 2), nor even the grave (stanza 3). But, he says, there is something that moves him more than the "rub of love" and that is:

> the worm beneath my nail
> Wearing the quick away.

The poem concludes that mortality, death, is "the rub, the only rub that tickles," and thus *man*, the present, living, actuality, must be the measure of all things. "Man," Thomas both states and prays, "be my metaphor." "My symbols," he comes to say elsewhere, "have outelbowed space" (p. 47). And, more memorable (p. 40), "I, in my intricate image, stride on two levels." What is revealed on one level implies meaning on another, the natural informs us of the supernatural, out of the struggle comes the miracle of vision:

Beginning with doom in the ghost, and the springing marvels,
Image of images, my metal phantom
Forcing forth through the harebell,
My man of leaves and the bronze root, mortal, unmortal,
I, in my fusion of rose and male motion,
Create this twin miracle.

It is from the struggle, the revulsion, the revolution that the process of growth begins, that knowledge is derived. Thomas early expressed this idea in a social context, and the expression summarizes the direction and intention of his rebellion. He wrote that the poets of his generation must pray and work for a revolution, though not necessarily a bloody one. He hoped that the chaotic outdated machinery of society would be destroyed so that the postwar generation could enjoy and fulfill its genius and glory before the world.[15]

II
ENCOUNTER

Thomas's rebellion and iconoclasm were aimed at what he hoped would be a fruitful examination of the human predicament. Thus what he rejects in one poem, or even in part of one poem, he comes to re-examine in another, or even in the latter part of a single poem, in order to find the new knowledge or the new value he sought. It is this quest and attainment, quest

[15] P.H.J. correspondence.

and failure, encounter and awareness, encounter and doubt that mark what I call the themes and situations of "debate." The tone of these themes and situations was well established as early as 1930, when Thomas wrote (in his Notebook): [16]

> If God is praised in poem one
> Show no surprise when in the next
> I worship wood or sun or none.

More often than not it is God and sun who are praised by Thomas or whose merits, at least, are weighed and considered. Rejecting the God of tradition created for Thomas the need for finding, or at least positing, a new God. This new God in his most common manifestation—and his manifestations are many and confusing—is a spirit, the unknowable spirit of mystery, part human, part divine. The God-spirit appears in Thomas's work under the aegis of constructive iconoclasm coupled with what amounts to a deep nostalgia for belief. Perhaps the clearest statement of Thomas's attitude is found in a poem published in *Adelphi*, September, 1933.

> No man believes who cries not, God is not,
> Who feels not coldness in the heat,
> In the breasted summer longs not for spring,
> No breasted girl, no man who, young
> And green, sneers not at the old sky.
> No man believes who does not wonder why.

His main correspondent of these years, Pamela Hansford Johnson, complained that the sentiment of this poem was puzzling. Although Thomas did not directly explicate the stanza for her, he nevertheless did in a subsequent letter offer a comment which is a nearly perfect gloss on the quoted lines. Stressing the need for every man, but especially for the poet,

---

[16] Quoted by Maud, *Entrances to Dylan Thomas' Poetry*, p. 95.

to be a critic, he described Jesus as a critic, whose subject for understanding and appreciation was God and who fulfilled his critical calling by explicating God to His fellow human beings. Thomas was talking about himself here as much as about Jesus, and his poetry attempts to explain the meaning of God, or life, to both himself and his reader. In the same letter he went on to describe God as our spiritual country which we must all explore and by exploring discover the laws that we ought to obey. He called criticism an aspect of appreciation and claimed that both love and hatred include more appreciation of God and the world than mere uncritical or lukewarm acceptance.

One of the ways Thomas finds his little holding in the country of the spirit is by exploring various encounters, those of youth-age, father-son, father-daughter, husband-wife, as well as man-God. The first of these encounters is dramatized in the opening of *Collected Poems*—"I See the Boys of Summer." There are three groups, or voices, involved in this confrontation: The first voice is that of an old man, the critic, a father figure. The second voice is that of the young men, those who want to experience a full sensual life. One is the voice of restraint, the other the voice of revolt. The third voice is a choric voice which appears briefly in the third part of the poem. This part, consisting of only six lines, finds each of the voices speaking alternately. Each of the lines is a sentence; each makes a statement. The opening line repeats the charge of the critic, "I see you boys of summer in your ruin." The next line repeats the defense of the boys, "Man in his maggot's barren." This is followed by the mollifying statement—a compromise between the two previous ones—that "boys are full and foreign in the pouch," which I take to mean that the problems of youth are those of sexual exigency. The speakers each speak once again. First, the critic, "I am the man your father was," which is evidently an appeal to traditional authority. The boys counter with a derogatory claim to be "the sons of flint and pitch." Then comes the poet's final ironic comment which seems to say that both points of view, views that appear to be poles apart, are actually in agreement, are saying the same thing finally—"O see the poles are kissing as they cross."

The fiercest encounter of the poetry is a debate between a father and son, and, again like the "boys of summer," the poem is concerned with the conduct of life. The situation, however, is the reverse of that in the earlier poem. In "Find Meat on Bones" (pp. 74–75), it is the older man who counsels revolt and the younger man who, apparently after he had tried to follow his father's advice, cannot accept the Promethean role. The father tells the son to enjoy himself before "the ladies' breasts are hags/ And the limbs are torn." When old age comes there will be time enough to speak of true love, of which the rose is a symbol. Now, he tells him:

> "Rebel against the binding moon
> And the parliament of sky,
> The kingcrafts of the wicked sea,
> Autocracy of night and day,
> Dictatorship of sun.
> Rebel against the flesh and bone,
> The word of the blood, the wily skin,
> And the maggot no man can slay."

The son, in passion having spent his love, is now haggard and withered. Furthermore, he has fallen in love and now sees the foolishness of his father's advice:

> I cannot murder, like a fool,
> Season and sunshine, grace and girl,
> Nor can I smother the sweet waking.

Revolt is vain, he says; man must consent. "Light and dark are no enemies/ But one companion." Yet the father cannot accept the conditions of nature:

"War on the spider and the wren!
War on the destiny of man!
Doom on the sun!"

And the poem closes with the son's plea, a very peculiar plea in Thomas's poetry, "Before death takes you, O take back this." This poem bears comparison with Thomas's other two poems to his father, "Do Not Go Gentle into That Good Night" (p. 128) and "Elegy" (p. 200 in the 1957 edition of *Collected Poems*). Fifteen years or so after "Find Meat on Bones" (first published in 1936), Thomas still finds his father "too proud to die." Although he grew gentle in his old age (see Chapter One), he was still disdainful of God (p. 202) and he still refused to cry, either from pain or from sorrow. In "Do Not Go Gentle . . . ," Thomas says that "wise men," "good men," "wild men," and "grave men" all find reason for sorrow or repentance at the coming of death. They have either loved life too much or not enough. Thomas's father has been the epitome of the critic—the man of passionate resistance, he is *the* critic. It is in this sense that we should understand "Rage, rage against the dying of the light." Thomas is still exhorting his father to reject, to criticize, to express the value of life by raging against death. Whether his tears constitute a curse or a blessing on his son, they would be better than this gentle and terrible silence. The son's petition climaxes in outright prayer:

> you, my father, there on the sad height,
> Curse, bless, me now with your fierce tears, I pray.

The father's silence threatens to refute a way of life and to reject that critical iconoclasm which was for Thomas the only means, whether expressed in love or hate, by which value could be found by man.

"Do Not Go Gentle . . ." does not deal with the implications of this silence—these implications, one suspects, were uncongenial to Thomas's mind. It is profitable to note, however, that the one literary echo in this poem is from Byron's *Childe Harold's Pilgrimage* (Canto 3, stanzas 92–97). Byron's phrase describes the splendor of the storms rolling through the mountains: "The brightest through these parted hills hath forked/ His lightnings." Thomas wrote: "Because their words had forked no lightning they/ Do not go gentle into that good night." If we tried to imagine the father in Thomas's villanelle replying to his son, one of the most appropriate replies possible would be from Childe Harold (Canto 3, stanza 97):

> Could I embody and unbosom now
> That which is most within me,—could I wreak
> My thoughts upon expression, and thus throw
> Soul, heart, mind, passions, feelings, strong or weak,
> All that I would have sought, and all I seek,
> Bear, know, feel, and yet breathe—into one word,
> And that word were Lightning, I would speak;
> But as it is, I live and die unheard,
> With a most voiceless thought, sheathing it as a sword.

These lines are appropriate not because they add anything to the poem itself; the poem is a model of perfection. But Byron's lines suggest the natural course of the argument of Thomas's poetry—a course Thomas chose not to follow. What he urges on his father, he declines to follow in his own work. Thomas's thought becomes more and more sheathed in the beautiful sounds of his auditory correlative. Revolt moves toward faith; debate moves toward inexplicable symbol.

Thomas once described his poetry as "two sides of an unresolved argument." His statement is capable of badly misleading us. The argument of the poetry is, after all, whether life is worth living or not worth living. If worth living, on what terms? If not, why not? In numerous ways, the argument is early and repeatedly decided in favor of life. The terms of the argument, the conditions of what constitute the valuable life, are, however, never fully articulated. The clearest expression of these conditions is to be found in the dramatic encounters—such as "Do Not Go Gentle . . . ," where the value of rebellion is praised. But fully as important as these encounters (more of which we shall see shortly) is the persistent theme of silence, of the incapacity of man ever to know what is best. One of the strongest themes in Thomas's earlier work is the futility of knowledge. Generally, this is limited to intellectual comprehension; Thomas is usually willing to listen to nature to find an understanding of life. Occasionally, however, he laments the insufficiency of both intellect and intuition: "I have been told to reason by the heart/ But heart, like head, leads helplessly" (p. 72). It is this sense of rational helplessness that found famous voice in the refrain of "The Force That through the Green Fuse" (p. 10)—"and I am dumb to tell."

The inability "to tell," to solve the riddle of the endless debate, creates the desire to lie always "by seasand, watching yellow/ And the grave sea," to "mock who deride." Time after time it creates the central pathos of the human condition—not the inability of the mind to comprehend but the frailty of the heart before the "rock" of the world and the breaking of the golden weather (p. 91).

It is interesting to note that, although Thomas's emphasis on his inability becomes a kind of personal rhetorical device, the conclusion in the later poetry is not the same. In "Ceremony After a Fire Raid," for example, he writes:

> I know not whether
> Adam or Eve, the adorned holy bullock
> Or the white ewe lamb
> Or the chosen virgin
> Was the first to die.
>
> (p. 144)

But these are not meant to indicate his inability to understand; they are rather a list of details about which no man can be certain. Thomas hastens to assure the reader that he knows what he knows, and the poem builds toward a symbolic, even a sacramental, acceptance. (An important part of the imagery of the last stanza, pp. 145–146, is bread and wine: "Into the bread in a wheatfield of flames,/ Into the wine burning like brandy.")

The mind before the impenetrable magnitude of existence flounders in questions; questions which, like Blake's about the maker of the lamb and tiger, or like Yeats's about Leda and the knowledge and power of Zeus, leave the mind in a perpetual state of wonder and suspension. They are not so much meant to be answered as they are to provoke a state of wonder, to suggest the finiteness of man's knowledge. As a young man, Thomas pondered about the perception possible to an illiterate boatman with one eye. Would such a man see and hear poetry in the movement of the water and the fish, or would he be a ghostly creature in a stony world? But, Thomas decided, such questions required merely a reinterpretation of old metaphysical answers. Other questions he found too frightening for answers.[17]

Presumably one of the dreadful questions is that which Thomas asks in "How Shall My Animal" (p. 100). He wonders how man's flesh, his creative and sentient elements, can endure the iron embrace of clay. The poem voices a cry of animal pain, a lonely, fearful looking toward death through the lidless eye of instinct. How shall man the animal endure burial? Thomas gives no answer except to tell his animal to

Lie dry, rest robbed, my beast.
You have kicked from a dark den, leaped up the whinnying light,
And dug your grave in my breast.

(p. 101)

[17] P.H.J. correspondence.

There is no answer, only the facts of animal existence; born out of the "dark den" of the womb, we leap in the sun, and the grave is already implicit in the very fact of our being alive.

Rhetorical questions play a prominent part in conveying this sense of inability to solve, finally, anything to do with life. Thomas uses them in Sonnet IV to mock mankind's inability to find answers. He asks:

> What is the metre of the dictionary?
> The size of genesis? the short spark's gender?
> Shade without shape? The shape of Pharaoh's echo?
>
> (p. 81)

And then, in parentheses, he remarks, "(Questions are hunchbacks to the poker marrow)." These questions by the adolescent about the meaning of life are deformities, hindrances, to the natural inclinations of the "poker marrow," the life force, the newly discovered sexual drive. Once again he is torn between reasoning by the head and by the pulse.

Some of Thomas's questions are slightly less rhetorical in that he entertains sane answers, and in that the absence of any final answer becomes in effect the most pessimistic of all possible answers. This is the drift of the questions in "Why East Wind Chills" (p. 62):

> Why east wind chills and south wind cools
> Shall not be known till windwell dries.
>
> . . . . .
>
> Why silk is soft and the stone wounds
> The child shall question all his days,
> Why night-time rain and the breast's blood
> Both quench his thirst he'll have a black reply.

But man will continue to question and search, the children will continue to ask "When cometh Jack Frost?"—although not until the "long-last sleep" of the children "shall a white answer echo from the rooftops." But, Thomas says, there is an answer, known at least to the stars:

> All things are known: . . .
>
> . . . . .
>
> Though what the stars ask as they round
> Time upon time the towers of the skies
> Is heard but little till the stars go out.

And man ought to be content despite the pain of his ignorance:

> I hear content, and 'Be content'
> Ring like a handbell through the corridors,
> And 'Know no answer,' and I know
> No answer to the children's cry.

One of the few ways of coming to terms with this lack of knowledge is seen in "Was There a Time" (p. 59):

> What's never known is safest in this life.
> Under the skysigns they who have no arms
> Have cleanest hands, and, as the heartless ghost
> Alone's unhurt, so the blind man sees best.

Those who ask no questions, who do and see as little as possible, are least likely to get hurt.

The questioning continues in "Ears in the Turrets Hear." This poem, based on the image of the human being as an island, may be understood on at least two levels. It may be read as a meditation by a woman on whether or not to receive man (the imagery is similar in many ways to that of "The Seed-at-Zero," p. 49) or as a meditation by any human being as to whether or not to trust other human beings and life itself. In either case, the question is:

> Hands of the stranger and holds of the ships,
> Hold you poison or grapes?
>
> (p. 68)

Is life evil or good, is sexual passion and its result bitter or sweet?

Despite the overwhelming epistemological pessimism and the inescapable conclusion that man is incapable of ever knowing the meaning or the worth of life, the poems of dramatic encounter describe unceasing efforts to come to terms with life. Regarding marital sex, for example, his poetry provides an almost continuous argument against more traditional views of romance and monogamy. How much of this is owing to his stormy marital life it is impossible to say, but there is an obvious relation. Thomas's several poems dealing with man and wife chronicle a relationship in which sex generally causes unhappiness. He refers to "the plagued groom and bride/ Who have brought forth the urchin grief" (p. 93) and says, "Too late in the wrong rain/ They come together whom their love parted" (p. 138).

"I Make This in a Warring Absence" (pp. 87–89), as we saw earlier, is an extended treatment of marital love, presenting it as continuous warfare. "She," in disdain and haughtiness, has refused his advances, left him weak and desirous ("And this weak house to marrow-columned heaven,/ Is corner-cast, breath's rag, scrawled weed"), broken his self-respect ("pride is last"), and made him into a child ("By magnet winds to her blind mother drawn,/ Bread and milk mansion in a toothless town"). She has made cruelty innocent and innocence guilty, has made even the rocks and trees around him become images of sex because of his need:

> She makes for me a nettle's innocence
> And a silk pigeon's guilt in her proud absence,
> In the molested rocks the shell of virgins.

Her refusal brings about his lustful conquest,

"Dark Is a Way"

Destruction, picked by birds, brays through the jaw-bone,
And, for that murder's sake, dark with contagion
Like an approaching wave I sprawl to ruin,

and temporary truce,

And though my love pulls the pale, nippled air,
Prides of to-morrow suckling in her eyes,
Yet this I make in a forgiving presence.

Occasionally sex does yield some sort of visionary joy, as in "Love in the Asylum" (p. 119):

And taken by light in her arms at long and dear last
I may without fail
Suffer the first vision that set fire to the stars.

But it is only a brief respite from sorrow:

She sleeps in the narrow trough yet she walks the dust
Yet raves at her will
On the madhouse boards worn thin by my walking tears.

"Into Her Lying Down Head" (p. 125) is a compendium of Thomas's attitudes toward life and sex. The poem argues one of Thomas's central convictions: sexual intercourse is a cruel, necessary, and inevitable part of existence. Thomas called it "a poem about modern love" and gave a brief statement about its meaning to Watkins: "All over the world love is being betrayed as always, and a million years have not calmed the uncalculated ferocity of each betrayal or the terrible loneliness afterwards." [18] The crucial lines in the poem are found in Part III, p. 127:

[18] *Dylan Thomas: Letters to Vernon Watkins*, ed. Vernon Watkins (London, 1957), p. 92.

And out of every domed and soil-based shell
One voice in chains declaims
The female, deadly, and male
Libidinous betrayal,
Golden dissolving under the water veil.

Every element of creation cries out with one voice—in chains because there is no alternative, because it is part of the nature of creation—for copulation and procreation. This copulation is a purely physical act, an uncontrollable instinct. Like gold it seems beautiful, but it is meaningless, swallowed up and dissolved by the sea of life.

This vision of life is the source of most of the images in the poem. For the male, the sperm cells are his enemies because they cause the uncontrollable sexual drive (second line and next to the last line), and the female is a deadly temptation. For the female, the male is a necessary evil, an "always anonymous beast," whose trespassing she must endure for the sake of reproduction.

The word "head" is short for "maidenhead." As such it is analogous to an eyelid or the membrane covering a drum. And the womb itself is like a hidden eye or a "hair-buried ear." (There is a similar idea involved in "On the Marriage of a Virgin," p. 141, "Her heart all ears and eyes, lips catching the avalanche/ Of the golden ghost who ringed with his streams her mercury bone.") And the phallus, flying like Noah's dove because it is in search of life, rekindled because it is like a candle (as in "Light Breaks . . . "), but unkind because its demand is so overpowering, is "man-bearing" because it carries the cells of new life.

The sexual act is next seen as a "raping wave" (which may include a pun on the name "Dylan" meaning "wave," as it does in "Warring Absence"—"Like an approaching wave I sprawl to ruin," p. 88). The ocean in this sense is symbolic of chaos, or at least of freedom, especially sexual freedom, as in "Ballad of the Long-legged Bait." New life is created out of the sea in the "casting tides" (p. 37) of sexual intercourse. And whales, the symbolic kings of the sea, are the synecdochic figures of sexual passion. (In "Warring Absence" the anticipation of sex is an "omen" of "whalebed and bulldance," p. 87, and in the "Ballad," p. 168,

> Whales in the wake like capes and Alps
> Quaked the sick sea and snouted deep,
> Deep the great bushed bait with raining lips
> Slipped the fins of those humpbacked tons
>
> And fled their love in a weaving dip. . . .

The sperm cells in the "fountains of origin" are seen as potential human beings, unknown and unknowable like passing strangers or ghosts. And the namesakes of these potential beings—Don Juan, King Lear, Queen Catherine, or Samson—are alike in that they were all betrayed or brought low by the force of passion. (Queen Catherine is Henry the Eighth's first wife.) In the sixteenth line the "dark blade and wanton" is a refurbishing of "gay young blade." The image is now of a hayfield in which the male is the mower and the female the hay to be mown. The phonetic similarity between "sighing" and "scythes" intentionally accentuates the idea of scything (and also calls to mind the scythe of death). The impersonality of the description of the mower who "Rode and whistled a hundred times/ Before the crowing morning climbed" is also worth noting. The final image of Part I is of man as an island, specifically England (that "green and pleasant land," Blake's *Albion*), where the woman is sleepwalking because she is no longer fully conscious. Her body has been blinded, spellbound by that "enamouring island," sung to sleep like a baby in the swaddling clothes of the man's loins, and like a beloved runaway child she has been caught and "laid" in the "acorned" (from which oaks grow) sand.

Whereas Part I leaves a relatively pleasurable impression of satisfied desire, Part II shifts suddenly to Thomas's idea of the woman's view of sex as a necessary evil. The woman is a captive in the darkness of their room, full of fear and horror. She hears the "male moan" from a "numberless tongue," a faithless creature. The walls seem to be covered with snakes (symbols of the satanic serpent as well as of fear), and the man seems like a monster, "furnace-nostrilled" with passion and "column-membered" (the phallus). The whole process of love-making reminds her of her lost innocence. From her point of view, sex itself, or sexual awareness, is the thief that stole away her innocence (which completes the picture of Thomas's totally thieving world). The theft of her innocence coinciding with adolescence, first came in the form of an imaginary "oceanic" (as all-pervasive as the ocean) lover, and now comes again as this particular man. The Calvinistic attitude is always at least residually present in Thomas, making sex evil, and intercourse inevitably implies that the man makes "his bad bed in her good/ Night, and enjoyed as he would." (Even her jealousy, used in the dialectal sense of devotion to her husband, cannot erase her fear and horror of sex.)[19] Woman is always bewailing "the theft of the heart/ In the taken body at many ages"—the evil necessity and cruelty of sex. The sexual act is always another celebration of the defilement of woman, although the man remains unaware and unable to share this feeling because of his own pride. The darkness of the night is the "solemnizing nightpriest" celebrating the black mass of

[19] Frye, *Fearful Symmetry*, pp. 72–73, points out that for Blake, too, "The natural man who attempts the state of Beulah or love is in a state of 'jealousy.' . . . The Selfhood . . . can regard the [beloved] only as a possession."

sexual intercourse, and the woman endures "her holy unholy hours with the always anonymous beast."

Part III universalizes the particulars of I and II. What is true of the man and woman is also true of all the elements of nature. The she bird sleeps "brittle"—that is, in fear—beside her lover, the hawk, a bird of prey. And, like all females, she sings of death, heaven, and reproduction—"Carrion, paradise, chirrup my bright yolk." The eternal female lies "open as to the air" like a window "to the naked shadow" (another description of the "anonymous beast"). She "lies alone and still" while the man also "mourns in the sole night"; both are always alone in a cruel world. And she is "innocent between two wars"—torn between the horror of sex, "the incestuous secret brother," and the necessity of reproduction, "in the seconds to perpetuate the stars." The final victors in the whole drama are the sperm cells, "the second comers." They are "severers" because their coming signifies the end of sexual pleasure, and, having achieved their objective, they "rest their pulse and bury their dead" in her womb. Their "dead" are either the "waste allotments" (p. 30) or the newly conceived embryos, or both.

Thomas's marriage poems constitute one long argument against marriage, in which any poetic treatment of a more satisfying form of sexual expression is missing. For him marriage ends rather with that pathetic Rabelaisian "old ram rod" of "Lament."

> Now I am a man no more no more
> And a black reward for a roaring life.
>
> (p. 196)

If there is any sexual fulfillment, it occurs only in the realm of myth, only in the past, with the dead women of "In the White Giant's Thigh." And this is where Thomas's argument will finally lead us—not into new mores, or into actual fulfillment, but into imaginative fulfillment, into myth.

All of this confirms again the hopelessness of raging against the night, the absence of any logical, rational line of thought in Thomas's scheme of things. Arguing simultaneously that man is incapable of ever knowing right from wrong and that man must believe, must have faith, was no paradox to Thomas. These very themes—the determined amorality of existence and the need for faith—are in fact the substance of Thomas's two poems addressed to his children.

Everything is decided, Thomas tells his son Llewelyn in "This Side of the Truth," everything is determined before man has any chance to act, or to change:

> all is undone,
> Under the unminding skies,
> Of innocence and guilt
> Before you move to make
> One gesture of the heart or head.
>
> (p. 116)

"Good and bad," Thomas explains to his six-year-old son, are simply "two ways/ Of moving about your death."

Does this mean that life is meaningless? Certainly not. Man is absolutely limited in terms of logical understanding, or moral certainty, but the universe is ultimately a place of life, not death. The void may be meaningless to the mind of man, but as a cauldron of love, not of hate (p. 117).

The themes and encounters of revolt and consent deal, then, with these concerns: they argue for a fully physical life, yet deny sex, marital sex in particular, any possibility of providing happiness. They stress repeatedly the inability of the rational mind to know either right or wrong. They reject all traditional Christianity, yet invoke Christian archetypes to call for an indefinable religious spirit. In a kind of inverse Calvinism, they present a determined universe: not determined to damnation but to love. Given this premise, consent is not only logical but inevitable.

There is no better summary of both the rationale and the direction of Thomas's debate than his "Out of the Sighs" (pp. 56–57). Man's struggle, he tells us, is full of agony and grief. If "out of the sighs" anything comes, it is not much, only the certainty that we have either temporarily succeeded—or again failed. In the course of the struggle

> the spirit grows,
> Forgets, and cries;
> A little comes, is tasted and found good.

But Thomas says of struggle, and of this growth, that thought and sex and the trivial pleasures of life are not enough to cure man's unhappiness:

> Were that enough, bone, blood, and sinew,
> The twisted brain, the fair-formed loin,
> Groping for matter under the dog's plate,
> Man should be cured of distemper.
> For all there is to give I offer:
> Crumbs, barn, and halter.

All there is to living, Thomas says, is: crumbs—a minimum of food; barn—the least kind of shelter; and halter—the burden of labor and the noose of death. All he can see is that it is a dog's life, but the implication throughout the poem is that this is not enough. The poet is not satisfied with this answer.

In the poems and stories of revolt, the emphasis is on the sighs, the grief, the "crumbs, barn, and halter." In poems and stories of the later period, the emphasis is on the little that comes, on the growth of the spirit, on what is "tasted and found good." It is on Rilke's *dennoch prisen:* praise still, praise in spite of everything.

III
CONSENT

The themes and situations involving consent have two sources: dreams and nature. Neither of these sources is capable of close logical scrutiny; both are centers out of which various emotional attitudes and prejudices arise. But Thomas's attention to these two subjects does eventually reveal a sufficient shift in attitude toward such traditional values as faith and love to enable us to trace his ever-increasing commitment to an "everlasting Yea."

Thomas's dream poems, like his prose works utilizing dream techniques, defy paraphrase precisely because they deal with a realm of experience beyond rational language. In our own attempts to recount even the clear highlights of a dream we inevitably resort to such phrases as: "It was the strangest thing," "I felt as though," "I was running but not running." Such phrases might equally well preface any interpretation of Thomas's dream work.

The young Thomas felt that the dream world was as important as the waking world. He examined, exploited, encouraged his dreams, finding in them whole new realms of existence. Repeatedly in his letters he refers to abolishing the distinction between the waking and sleeping mind, to the fact that a particular episode finds its source in a dream. In discussing Thomas's obscurity we noted that much of his imagery and symbolic organization was involved with dreams and that he questioned which world, the waking or the sleeping, was the more real. There is also another relation between dream and poetry: just as the poet is threatened by dryness, so the dreamer is threatened by nightmare.

But the point to stress regarding the thematic statements of consent is that dreams, again much like poetry itself, promise another dimension of existence. There are three explicit dream poems, "Our Eunuch Dreams," "I Fellowed Sleep," and "I Dreamed My Genesis." (The same methods and techniques which are used in these poems are used in most of the first eighteen poems and, more instructively, in the "Altarwise" sonnets.) These three all find cause for optimism beyond the confines of the material world. "Our Eunuch Dreams" concludes that the world is a "lying likeness," it is "The dream that kicks the buried from their sack/ And lets their trash be honoured as the quick" (p. 17). In the midst of this world all that one can do is to "Have faith." And from this faith will come a new life: "we shall be fit fellows for a life,/ And who remain shall flower as they love."

"I Fellowed Sleep" revolves on that old mother-father antagonism. When the sleeping poet flees the earth, he finds a second reality "far from the stars" and there he weeps with another self, with another child of his mother. Then there seems to occur an encounter between the mother and the poet in which the mother warns against the dreaming flights: "These are but dreaming men. Breathe, and they fade," she says. He breathes and fade they do. But the world will not return to its drab reality. All the living air now speaks to him. The dreamer and the poet are inseparable, and the poet cannot unlearn the ways of the dreamer:

> I spelt my vision with a hand and hair,
> How light the sleeping on this soily star,
> How deep the waking in the worlded clouds.
>
> (p. 32)

"I Fellowed Sleep" concludes with the images of Jacob and the ladder—images used elsewhere by Thomas to indicate the ceaseless striving of man. In the final line of the poem there is the enigmatic picture of the "fathers' ghost . . . climbing in the rain"; not so enigmatic, however, when we realize that Thomas associated his father with the questing, affirmative spirit.

𝒞 "I Dreamed My Genesis" (pp. 33–34) is closest of the three to the dead end of nightmare, telling as it does of the "sweat of sleep." It is an account of the poet's painful evolutionary origins and of his awareness, as representative of Man, of the continued pain of modern life. But there is the rising of the skeleton, the "rerobing of the naked ghost," the persistence of mankind. With this vision of man's quenchless search for life and for vision, Thomas can say at the end of the poem: "vision/ Of new man strength, I seek the sun." 𝟕

The thematic import of dreams is usually a renewed conviction of the worth of life, a renewed effort to climb upward. The logical connection between the dream poems and the major statements of Thomas's affirmation or consent—the nature poems—is faith, which in turn is intimately associated with love. There is little attention to the matter of faith and dreams in Thomas, I suppose because he presumed that the state of dream was a state of faith. The one clear reference to these terms is in "When Once the Twilight Locks No Longer." Here, in a reversal of Milton's Adam, who dreamed of Eve and awoke to find her true, Thomas's man "drowned his father's magics in a dream" and awoke to find death: "All issue armoured, of the grave,/ The redhaired cancer still alive" (p. 4). That dream became reality, and, ever since that first dreamer, man has lived in nightmare. Thus can Thomas's God say:

> By trick or chance he fell asleep
> And conjured up a carcass shape
> To rob me of my fluids in his heart.
>
> (p. 5)

"The dream," Thomas says even more clearly in a later poem, "has sucked the sleeper of his faith" (p. 17).

There is little or nothing of faith or creativity in the references to nature in the earliest poems. Nature is usually a mirror of man's own death-destined existence:

> A worm tells summer better than the clock,
> The slug's a living calendar of days;
> What shall it tell me if a timeless insect
> Says the world wears away?
>
> (p. 53)

or:

> A process in the weather of the world
> Turns ghost to ghost; each mothered child
> Sits in their double shade.
>
> (p. 7)

One of the few suggestions of nature's prodigal creativity finds voice in a poem, "Where Once the Waters of Your Face," addressed to a sea channel. Thomas describes the locale of this poem very clearly in his letters to Pamela Hansford Johnson, and Watkins also gives a description of the place. The channel runs between Worm's Head and Gower Peninsula off the coast of Rhossilli, Wales.[20] Thomas explains how the water in this channel empties at low tide, leaving a dry sea bed, and at full tide the channel is filled with the sea and makes Worm's Head an island.

With this very literal *compositio loci* we can now examine this early harbinger of Thomas's mature attitude toward nature. The poem (p. 12) plays on three factors: the irrepressible fertility of the sea rhythm, the opening verses of Genesis, Thomas's own procreative activities on the sands of Rhossilli (real or imagined it is impossible to say). The first of these is

[20] Watkins, p. 91.

what holds the poem together, making it, essentially, a hymn to the channel and, by extension, to the sea and to life. The "green knots," for example, are the swift-flowing waters of the channel which are spliced into the "tided cord" of the sea at high tide and are cut off by low tide (seen as "the green unraveller/ His scissors oiled, his knife hung loose," because low tide is a figure of death). But the water that had been in the channel is now one with the "clocking tides" in the deep sea where the seaweed grows, and the dry seaweed remains. Children, too, shadows in the distance, play among the uncovered rocks. And the poem concludes with a testament of faith in life:

> Dry as a tomb, your coloured lids
> Shall not be latched while magic glides
> Sage on the earth and sky;
> There shall be corals in your beds,
> There shall be serpents in your tides,
> Till all our sea-faiths die.

The sea, with both corals and serpents, will last as long as creation and mankind's faith in life.

Throughout his poetry, Thomas associates "magic" with both creative activity of all types and with faith, because it has to do with the unknowable, the intuitional, the inexplicable. And this magic is something which has been lost by contemporary humanity. Man has "drowned his father's magics in a dream" (p. 4), and "The dream has sucked the sleeper of his faith" (p. 17). In the early poetry, Thomas's emphasis is on the

> cock-on-a-dunghill
> Crowing to Lazarus the morning is vanity,
> Dust be your savior under the conjured soil.
>
> (p. 42)

But even though "the morning is vanity" and he denies a
supernatural rebirth, "the conjured soil" implies creativity, a
new birth of some sort out of the dust.

This is the kind of affirmation implied in "And Death Shall
Have No Dominion." And it also involves an implicit denial of
the terrifying judgment of the dead in Revelation. Thomas, as
always, adapts Christian scripture and symbol for his own
purpose, and that purpose is far different from traditional
Christian purpose. In St. Paul (Romans 6:9), the phrase "death
hath no more dominion" refers to the eternal life of a spiritual
aspect of man called the soul. Thomas's poem has nothing to
do with a soul, nor with resurrection, nor with any kind of
personal afterlife. His poem is simply and absolutely a highly
imaginative statement of the scientific fact that matter cannot
be destroyed. It is hard, I suppose, to prove this when Thomas
drums St. Paul into us by using his phrase six times in twenty-
seven lines. But the point of the poem is clear at the end:

> Though they be mad and dead as nails,
> Heads of the characters hammer through daisies;
> Break in the sun till the sun breaks down,
> And death shall have no dominion.

(p. 77)

Though a man be dead as a doornail, his flesh will go on living,
will be hammered "through daisies," and will break forth
beneath the sun—until "the sun breaks down." This is the life
over which "death shall have no dominion," as far as Dylan
Thomas is concerned.

Thomas has a similar thought in mind in the last lines of
Sonnet X when he speaks of

> that Day
> My nest of mercies in the rude, red tree.
> When the worm builds with the gold straws of venom

(p. 85)

"That Day" is an ironic reference to the Day of Judgment, which for Thomas is the time when his body will have been decomposed by the worm and formed into new life—in this case a tree. The tree is "rude" because it is both common and rugged, and it is "red" because it is a living thing. The worm builds with "venom" because it is the worm of death, but the venom is made up of "gold straws" because it contains the elements of new life.

It might well be pointed out that Thomas's use of colors here is consistent with his use throughout his poetry. Green is youth and happiness; red is—by association with blood—life and passion; black is disaster, evil, death. Gold is fertility, happiness, success. White is used generally in its traditional sense of innocence and spirituality, or occasionally in its more Blakean, and Lawrentian, sense of infertility and sexual moribundity.

The themes of acceptance appear with increasing frequency in the forties. Acceptance covers many things—primarily acceptance of death—but also acceptance of all the smaller deaths that eventuate in that final death. Thomas speaks of a child's death in a London fire raid (p. 112) as majestic and refuses to mourn because she is now one with the creating earth. He will not mourn until "the still hour/ Is come of the sea tumbling in harness," until all the creating life of the earth is stilled. He now sees the child "robed in the long friends," all the generations of mankind who have preceded her. With the death of the first man, the cycle of human and organic life was formed so that no further death occurs. The one dying partakes in the cycle of living nature, "After the first death, there is no other." This expression, by the way, approximates a Biblical statement, based on Revelation 20:14. In the context of this poem, it could be taken to mean simply that she died before she could sin, so she cannot be subject to the second death, which is the consignment of the unbelieving dead to hell. But its wording indicates as more likely Thomas's general contention that there is *no* second death for anyone.

For Thomas, as for Blake, the universe turned on faith. (Blake says in "Auguries of Innocence": "If the sun and moon should doubt,/ They'd immediately go out.") This faith was not in any doctrine, but in the value of being alive, in the inherent life force that makes both man and nature continue to reproduce:

> All all and all the dry worlds couple,
> Ghost with her ghost, contagious man
> With the womb of his shapeless people.

And in this reproduction, life achieves the true and only perfection:

> All that shapes from the caul and suckle,
> Stroke of mechanical flesh on mine,
> Square in these worlds the mortal circle.
>
> (p. 39)

Faith for Thomas is also an aspect of innocence. This is clear in "In Country Sleep," for example. But even those who lose this innocence shall not be destroyed. In "And Death Shall Have No Dominion," Thomas says that although

> Faith in their hands shall snap in two,
> And the unicorn evils run them through;
> . . . they shan't crack.
>
> (p. 77)

Faith is something that is lost through the experience of evil (and evil would, in this sense, have to be construed as belief in death rather than in life). This concept of the meaning of "faith" explains the "faithless sleep" (p. 127) of "Into Her Lying Down Head." The girl is "faithless" because she lost her innocence; it has been stolen by "the thief of adolescence" (p. 126) who made her aware of her mortality.

The war years gave Thomas a different perspective on faith—a perspective from which he realized his own need. In "Holy Spring" he writes:

I climb to greet the war in which I have no heart but only
    That one dark I owe my light,
Call for confessor and wiser mirror but there is none
    To glow after the god stoning night
And I am struck as lonely as a holy maker by the sun.

(p. 177)

Here is an instance of something we see more and more in the later Thomas—a reliance on obsessive images rather than on a development of themes or even of "encounters." The sun becomes the ultimate expression of faith, of hope, of some sort of immortality. This is why it is the sun which christens him in "Vision and Prayer" (p. 165). This is why he tells his daughter that without faith the sun appears "lawless" (p. 186), whereas if she keeps her faith it will be "as deathless as the outcry of the *ruled* sun" (italics mine). And though Thomas on his thirty-fifth birthday only "prays . . . / Faithlessly unto Him" (p. 192), he finally opens his *Collected Poems* with the statement that his poems "are written for the love of Man and in praise of God" (xiii). Faith finally becomes virtually synonymous with love.

Like faith, love undergoes subtle alterations of meaning. At the outset, it is associated primarily with the physical. Thomas speaks of frustration as "frozen loves" (p. 1). In a phallic reference, love is described as dripping and gathering (p. 10). Love is a "rub" (p. 13), a "fever," and the end of love (children) is a "plague" (p. 24). The body is "love's house . . . and the tower death" (p. 55).

Beyond the description of love in terms of its creative

function—"the ribbed original of love" in "In the Beginning" (p. 28)—the clearest early indication of Thomas's broadening or spiritualizing of love comes in "And Death Shall Have No Dominion." Here he speaks of love continuing after the lovers are dead: "Though lovers be lost, love shall not" (p. 77). Throughout the marriage poems there is an antagonism between love as sin "all love's sinners . . . kneel to a hyleg image" (p. 93) and the feeling that physical love is the only love proper to man:

> All love but for the full assemblage in flower
> Of the living flesh is monstrous or immortal,
> And the grave its daughters.
>
> (p. 121)

But the middle period of his poetry certainly develops significantly the regenerative notions of other than physical love. There is the cry of "Love" in "After the Funeral"; there is the love of a mother for her child in "The Tombstone Told When She Died" and " 'If My Head Hurt a Hair's Foot.' " It is the unknown stranger, the one "loved least," who is depicted in "Deaths and Entrances" as the saviour, the one who dies in our stead, "the last Samson of your zodiac" (p. 130). In the same vein he describes, in "There Was a Saviour," those who had been selfish and self-sufficient and who

> Now break a giant tear for the little known fall,
>   For the drooping of homes
>   That did not nurse our bones,
> Brave deaths of only ones but never found,
>   Now see, alone in us,
>   Our own true strangers' dust
>   Ride through the doors of our unentered house.
> Exiled in us we arouse the soft,
> Unclenched, armless, silk and rough love that breaks all rocks.
>
> (p. 140)

To his son Llewelyn he says—reflecting his own inverted kind of Calvinism—that all of creation is determined but that both good and bad are subsumed in an all-embracing love:

> And all your deeds and words,
> Each truth, each lie,
> Die in unjudging love.
>
> (p. 117)

In "The Conversation of Prayer" (p. 111), the love of the adult for another human being is stronger and more alive ("quick") than the child's natural selfishness and lack of awareness.

A beneficent spirit as divine as life comes finally to be involved with human love. Thus man, in "A Winter's Tale," is delivered from his need by losing himself "all in love" (p. 133), and this all-embracing love is to be found, as we shall see, in death. In the final poem of the book, "In the White Giant's Thigh," he prays that the dead may teach him this unending love, the love that outlasts death and time:

Teach me the love that is evergreen after the fall leaved
Grave, after Belovéd on the grass gulfed across is scrubbed
Off by the sun and Daughters no longer grieved
Save by their long desirers in the fox cubbed
Streets.

> (p. 199)

Thomas's four birthday poems provide cumulative evidence of his developing concepts of love and faith. "Especially When the October Wind" (p. 19), may be considered the first, since his birthday was October twenty-second. It was originally known as "Poem in October," now the title of his poem on his thirtieth birthday.

"Especially When the October Wind," written when Thomas was twenty, reflects the melancholy of the poet who sees everything around him in terms of words, vowels, voices, notes, and speeches. As he walks near the sea the wind is cold, an ill-tempered sun is implied in "crabbing," and his own shadow looks crablike. Even the birds are harbingers of death—"Hearing the raven cough in winter sticks"—and the poet walks "on fire" with the desire to create poetry out of the frosty scene. In the third stanza the clock, the weathercock, and the grass all signal the coming of winter.

The cock, derived from the weathercocks on the roofs of barns and the tops of steeples in Wales, not only watches and reveals the world of time and weather, it also reveals man's own weak nature, as did the cock whose crow was a reminder of Peter's denial of Christ. This is the sense of the "cock-on-a-dunghill/ Crowing to Lazarus the morning is vanity" (p. 42). The poet too is "a shouter like the cock,/ Blowing the old dead back" (p. 17); he is the "Old cock from nowheres and the heaven's egg" (Sonnet I, p. 80), who plucked the "sea eye" of medusa and the "minstrel tongue" of the "pin-hilled nettle" (Sonnet VI, p. 83) to reveal the true horror of life.

At the end of this birthday poem (p. 20), the poet sees that his "heart is drained that, spelling in the scurry/ Of chemic blood, warned of the coming fury." And "by the sea's side . . . the dark-vowelled birds" continue to sing. The whole world is moving toward the destruction of the "coming fury" of winter.

"Twenty-four Years" (p. 110) reveals a similar gloom. The poem (already discussed in Chapter Two) has to do with Thomas the man, rather than Thomas the poet. But this man, though "dressed to die," is nevertheless advancing "In the final direction of the elementary town/ . . . for as long as forever is." Death is the end of the individual but not of life.

"Poem in October" (pp. 113–115), written on the occasion of the poet's "thirtieth year to heaven," 1944, reveals a completely changed attitude. For one thing, we notice immediately that Thomas now sees himself as either on his way to heaven or in the sight of heaven:

> It was my thirtieth year to heaven
> Woke to my hearing from harbour and neighbour wood
> And the mussel pooled and the heron
> Priested shore
> The morning beckon
> With water praying and call of seagull and rook.

The wood is his neighbor, the herons are priests, the morning beckons, the water prays, and the sea birds call. Thomas, the man and the poet, moves in harmony with nature (ironically) like one of the justified Old Testament patriarchs who "walked with God."

> And I rose
> In rainy autumn
> And walked abroad in a shower of all my days.

At the "high tide" of his life he leaves the "still sleeping town" and climbs a hill overlooking the town and the harbor, where he finds "a springful of larks in a rolling/ Cloud"

> and the sun of October
> Summery
> On the hill's shoulder.

From this vantage point, the town and the "rain wringing/ Wind" are "faraway under me" and

> all the gardens
> Of spring and summer were blooming in the tall tales
> Beyond the border and under the lark full cloud.

This joyous vision of "blithe" spring and summer to follow the "rainy autumn" would have been sufficient for him to

"marvel/ My birthday/ Away," if it were not for another
vision, which suddenly appears, of the innocence and the
"true/ Joy" of Thomas "the long dead child." With his vision
he realizes his age, comprehends that he "stood there then in
the summer noon" of his life, and that autumn is not far
away—"though the town below lay leaved with October
blood." And he prays for one more year of life and poetic
creation, one more year of singing his "heart's truth" "on this
high hill."

The contrast between the sacramental quality of nature in
this October poem and in the earlier October poem is inescapable. Here is the hilltop vision in which both future and past
appear as summer, and a love which makes the poet look
beyond the "October blood" in the hope of continuing life. At
the age of twenty, Thomas's heart was "drained." But at the
age of thirty, his heart was apparently full:

> O may my heart's truth
> Still be sung
> On this high hill in a year's turning.

For his thirty-fifth birthday, Thomas wrote one of his last
testaments to the acceptance of life, "Poem on His Birthday"
(pp. 190–193). Here, the poet is in his "house on stilts" *high* on
a cliff *overlooking* the sea. This "slant, racking house," from
which he can see so much of the world around him, especially
the birds and fishes "on their cold, dying trails," is like a bell
tower or steeple in which "the rhymer in the long tongued
room/ . . . tolls his birthday bell." The bells of Wales, as
elsewhere, ring out for joy on special occasions, for sorrow at
death, and for passing time on their clocks. And this "birthday
bell" has the same purpose. The poet both "celebrates and
spurns/ His driftwood thirty-fifth wind turned age." And the
herons, who appeared as priests in "Poem in October" and as

saints in "Over Sir John's Hill," here parallel the poet. (Their sacerdotal significance for Thomas may be partly derived from their relationship to the sacred ibis of Egypt but probably more directly from their stance and their black-and-white coloring when seen from a distance.) The herons represent the world of nature in its correspondence with the world of man. The poet "celebrates and spurns"; the herons "spire and spear." The poet in a metaphorical steeple "tolls his . . . bell"; the herons, "steeple stemmed, bless." The poet wound in the "hewn coils of his trade perceives/ Herons walk in their shroud."

But despite this prolonged perception of the whole world moving toward an anguished death, the poet hears, "In a cavernous, swung/ Wave's silence," the knelling of the angelus. From the place of death (the cave and the sea) comes the commemoration of the announcement of the Incarnation and of acceptance of God's will. Thomas then hears his own bells tolling for the scars and disappointments, the wrecked loves of his life "Steered by the falling stars." And he fears "tomorrow . . . in a blind cage" before he is finally released from the chains of life,

> And love unbolts the dark
>
> And freely he goes lost
> In the unknown, famous light of great
> And fabulous, dear God.

The dichotomy of dark and light set up in these lines is developed in the rest of the poem. "Dark is a way and light is a place," Thomas says. He goes on to say that the place of light is Heaven, an inexplicably true "brambled void" in which

> Plenty as blackberries in the woods
> The dead grow for His joy.

In this place he too might be happy, though "gulled" (deluded), a "chanter in young Heaven's fold/ . . . at cloud quaking peace,/ But dark is a long way." And so he remains "on the earth of the night," knowing that there will come the Day of Judgment, when the sea shall give up its dead and all unbelievers shall be cast into the lake of fire (Revelation 20: 12–15). Though he prays, he prays without traditional religious faith:

> Faithlessly unto Him
>
> Who is the light of old
> And air shaped Heaven where souls grow wild
> As horses in the foam.

(Horses are symbolic of innocence or perfection for Thomas, as we can see in "Fern Hill," "In Country Sleep," and "A Winter's Tale"—the "centaur dead," p. 134.) He knows that his life, like that of the "druid" herons, is a "voyage to ruin," but in the midst of his sorrow he sings of the blessings of life. He counts

> Four elements and five
> Senses, and man a spirit in love,

and finally the "triumphant faith" of the whole world of nature. The symbol of this faith is the "mustardseed sun," which, as in the Biblical parable (Matthew 13:31–32), grows from the smallest of seeds to the greatest of herbs:

> the closer I move
> To death, one man through his sundered hulks,
> The louder the sun blooms
> And the tusked, ramshackling sea exults.

The "unbelieving" poet, having sanctified the earth in his service, praises—instead of the light of Heaven, which he knows is closed to him—the beauty of the earth and the angelic, though human, "mansouled fiery islands" as he sails "out to die."

The theme of Thomas's poetry from beginning to end is the reconciliation of life and death. Young Dylan Thomas perceived a world full of suffering, a world moving toward death. This was true both on the natural level and in terms of the Calvinistic preaching of sin and damnation which he had absorbed in his childhood. And his reaction to this world, as we have seen, was one of iconoclastic denial; of questioning, debate, and encounter; and finally of loving affirmation.

The sun roars for Thomas in the last splendid poems of his life. His great odes, so reminiscent of Keats's great burst of creativity, find a similar passionate pitch of acceptance, find joy in the midst of sorrow. "Poem in October," "Fern Hill," "In Country Sleep," "Over Sir John's Hill," "Poem on His Birthday," and "In the White Giant's Thigh" all celebrate the joy of life. Thomas, in commenting once on the meaning of a poem, epitomized the acceptance sung in these final poems when he spoke of a movement "through pity and violence to an unreconciled acceptance of suffering." [21] The word "unreconciled" testifies to the conditional (perhaps dynamic) nature of Thomas's consent. His final consent is dialectical. It is a temporarily accepted synthesis but one which—theoretically, at least—can yield to a new thesis. Thomas rejected and outgrew his obsession with the horror of death and the evil of sex. He also rejected the traditional Christianity of his childhood, but he learned to see nature as holy, faith in life as essential, and love as the best immortality.

[21] Treece (1956 edition) p. 37.

CHAPTER FIVE

"The Legend of Adam and Eve": Total Vision

This story's monster has a serpent caul,
Blind in the coil scrams round the blazing outline,
Measures his own length on the garden wall
And breaks his shell in the last shocked beginning;
A crocodile before the chrysalis,
Before the fall from love the flying heartbone,
Winged like a sabbath ass this children's piece
Uncredited blows Jericho on Eden.

"To-day, This Insect"

ALTHOUGH it appears to be a miscellaneous collection of lyrics, Thomas's *Collected Poems* is a remarkably unified body of work. We have just seen the thematic part of that unity in our examination of the "argument" of the poetry. But a subsuming unity in the poetry can be seen not so much in terms of the "rational line" as in terms of the poetry's symbolic or imagistic cohesion. For, finally, Thomas's poetry creates, as Boris Pasternak says all genuine art does, a symbolic universe.[1]

---

[1] *Dr. Zhivago*, trans. Max Hayward and Manya Harari (New York, 1958), p. 90. Great art "resembles and continues the Revelation of St. John."

Thomas's poetry presents a mythic perception of the human condition which stretches not from origin to death but from origin to regeneration. It is a perception based, finally, not on man the mortal animal, or rational animal, but on man the animal who loves.

In one sense the symbolic unity of *Collected Poems* is accidental, principally a product of what we earlier termed "Thomas's Welshness." But in that this unity represents the fullest expression of the poet's vision, it may be seen as revealing deeper preconceptions and attitudes than even the thematic unity. For the repetition and close relationship between images can reveal associations in the mind of the poet that even he may not have been aware of. Symbolic unity reveals psychic as well as thematic preoccupations. Thomas certainly did not set out to write one long poem nor to create a universe of imagery. At the outset, he felt that the repetition of certain images was a mark of failure. He admitted that his "earlier poems might appear to constitute a section from one long poem," but he felt that it was "because I was not successful in making a momentary peace with my images . . . ; images were left dangling over the formal limits." [2] But at various later points in his career, he expressed the desire to write a long poem and suggested that individual poems might be read as parts of a long "poem in progress." When he sent his first "Altarwise" sonnets to an editor, he said he planned them as the beginning of what would be "a very long poem indeed." [3] In 1950 he said that "In Country Sleep," "Over Sir John's Hill," and "In the White Giant's Thigh" should all be seen as parts of one long poem. [4]

[2] Henry Treece, *Dylan Thomas: "Dog Among the Fairies"* (London, 1956), p. 37.

[3] J. Alexander Rolph, *Dylan Thomas: A Bibliography* (New York, 1956), p. 11.

[4] *Quite Early One Morning* (New York, 1954), p. 178.

"Legend of Adam and Eve"

The symbolic unity of *Collected Poems* is observable in two ways: there are, in Kenneth Burke's phrase, "symbolic equations" in the poetry arising from the repetition of images,[5] and certain poems may be seen as parts of particular symbolic concerns. The major divisions into which we can place both the imagery and the poems are Biblical. There is no doubt that his treatment of the broad aspects of human awareness in the poetry was affected by an enthusiastic sampling of countless works, from Freud to Frazer. But the overwhelming influence on the poetry is clearly that of the Bible.

Every Welsh home, Thomas tells us, has a parlor with its Bible—and the Bible opens automatically at the book of Revelation. It should not be necessary at this point to establish, any further than we have already, Thomas's dependency on the Bible. Nearly two-thirds of the ninety-odd poems are concerned, directly or indirectly, with material related to it. Moreover, both Thomas's concept of divinity and the central "voice" of the poetry are rooted in Biblical concepts and figures. But it is not the mere presence of Biblical material that should be noted; the important thing is that the most comprehensive relationships of imagery, theme, and subject matter are cast in a Biblical mold.

The figures and incidents that struck Thomas's imagination, consciously or unconsciously, were not only those that have intrigued poets for centuries but also those that impart to the Bible its most apparent formal characteristic. As theologians, poets, and critics have long implied, and as Northrop Frye has stated explicitly, the unifying structure of the Scriptures is based on a series of movements, or "rhythms," related to the process of Creation, Fall, and Regeneration. The two most apparent instances of this rhythm are the analogous movements of the Pentateuch and the New Testament, in which

[5] Kenneth Burke, *The Philosophy of Literary Form* (Vintage, New York, 1957), pp. 63, 65.

events in the history of the Jewish people are paralleled by events in the life of Christ: Christ's birth, his flight into Egypt and his "hidden life," and his death and resurrection recapitulate the basic pattern of the Pentateuch—creation, captivity in Egypt and wandering in the desert, figurative death in the death of Moses and entrance into the promised land.[6]

A major point of Frye's treatment of the "Biblical rhythm" is that the Bible, by its primacy in Western thought, has been so impressed on the literate Western mind that almost any attempt to express total vision has recourse to some variation of the Birth, Fall, and Regeneration movement. Since there are also obvious connections to the dying god and Jungian transformation archetypes, it is almost commonplace to point out a "Biblical rhythm" in a literary work—or even in a group of works such as Thomas's poems or those that Frye cites: "the later poems of Eliot, of Edith Sitwell, and many cantos of Pound."[7] But, on the other hand, each artist handles the rhythm differently. Compare, for example, Eliot's apocalyptic vision in the "Quartets" with Thomas's in his volume *In Country Sleep*. The value lies not so much in pointing out the presence of total vision but rather in noting the individuality involved in the poet's vision, in noting the particular metaphors and themes the poet uses to develop his *Weltansicht*.

The publication dates of the books that compose *Collected Poems* have an approximate relationship with the Creation, Fall, Regeneration movement. The relation between the chronology and the "Biblical rhythm" is not precise, nor should we expect it to be. But, generally speaking, Creation (albeit the horror more than the miracle of it) is the prime concern of *18 Poems* (1934), the Fallen world is most

---

[6] Northrop Frye, *Anatomy of Criticism* (Princeton, 1957), pp. 205, 315–326.

[7] *Ibid.*, p. 324.

specifically dealt with in *Twenty-five Poems* (1936) and *The Map of Love* (1939)—with one notable exception, the "Ballad of the Long-legged Bait," which appeared in 1941. The final two books, *Deaths and Entrances* (1946) and *In Country Sleep* (1952), fully develop the concept of Regeneration.

The prose suggests less unity, although it does share a common symbolism. From the short stories written between 1934 and 1938 (later published in *Adventures in the Skin Trade and Other Stories*) through *Portrait of the Artist as a Young Dog* (1940) to *Quite Early One Morning* (1954), there is a progression almost solely chronological. The nightmare world of youth yields to the ironic absurdity of young manhood and climaxes in the comic vision of the mature man looking back on youth as a mixture of Robert Louis Stevenson adventure and Dickensian warmth. The prose is a healthy corrective to our notion of Thomas as a latter-day mystic. His humor and satire, only occasionally obvious in *Collected Poems*, reveal themes and attitudes which help us to achieve a fully rounded appreciation of Thomas the journeyman writer with pervasive comic interests. It also allows us to see the poetry as a particular vehicle for particular emotions and ideas and to perceive the Biblical symbolism as the most appropriate means for expressing these emotions and ideas.

There are, as should be expected, themes and images of Creation, Fall, and Redemption throughout the poetry—just as the Flood and the rainbow covenant of Noah occur in the Old Testament long before the entry into the promised land, and just as the *"Shantih shantih shantih"* of *The Waste Land* anticipates the "Teach us to sit still" of "Ash Wednesday." Thomas did not set out to treat Creation, Fall, and Redemption successively; that there is some chronological relationship between these themes and the publication of the poems must be regarded as the result of unconscious factors. The influence of the Bible certainly had much to do with his treatment of these subjects. And age—his shifts from an obsession with genesis and womb to the objective world that suffers and loves and then to the formulation of a vision of perpetuity—surely had just as much to do with the shape the poetry assumed. In fact, rather than the early poetry building toward the thematic unity of the later poetry, the opposite would appear to be the case: the final poems bring out the thematic and symbolic unity inherent in the early poems. In his world of Creation, for example, Thomas describes not an Edenic universe but—as does Blake—a world which falls in the very act of creation. As the poetry moves along, from "Incarnate Devil" to "Fern Hill," for example, he comes to align his concept of creation more with the Biblical story—he supplies an "Eden" to precede the "Fall." [8] It is relatively late in his poetry ("Ceremony After a Fire Raid") that he comes to realize that

> the legend
> Of Adam and Eve is never for a second
> Silent in my service.
>
> (p. 145)

And it is, finally, in the poem written to introduce *Collected Poems*, that he comes—with hesitation, self-consciousness, and some self-deprecation—to assume the Noah persona, a persona which epitomizes his regenerative vision.

[8] In Blake, the appearance of man was brought about by a separation of the human element from the divine. The creation of man was almost literally a falling away of part of God's being. Men were "Thrown down from their high station/ In the Eternal heavens." See *The Writings of William Blake*, ed. Geoffrey Keynes II, (London, 1925), p. 131. Thomas, of course, is much closer to traditional Christian views of the Fall, but in this regard there is agreement with Blake—man was fallen from the moment his flesh was formed. Thomas's attitude becomes blurred later in his poetry when he has recourse to the story of Adam and Eve. Thereafter, the emphasis is not on the correspondence of Creation and Fall, but rather on a Fall from an Edenic state.

"Legend of Adam and Eve"

I
CREATION

Thomas once described his early work as his "womb-tomb" period.[9] Despite the tongue-in-cheek tone, the remark is apt: birth, and birth's irreversible impetus toward death, dominate the thought and imagery of both the early poetry and the prose. Human generation, however, was not the only creation he was interested in; he was also obsessed by thoughts of the creation of the world and of poetry. These three types of creation are not always clearly separable. In each the work of the other is implied, and in each the procreative functions of man are metaphorically present. Thomas put it this way in his short story "The Mouse and the Woman":

> It is not a little thing, he thought, this writing that lies before me. It is the telling of a creation. It is the story of birth. Out of him had come another. A being had been born, not out of the womb, but out of the soul and the spinning head. He had come to the cottage on the hill that the being within him might ripen and be born away from the eyes of men. He understood what the wind that took up the woman's cry had cried in his last dream. Let me be born, it had cried. He had given a woman being. His flesh would be upon her, and the life that he had given her would make her walk, talk, and sing. And he knew, too, that it was upon the block of paper she was made absolute. There was an oracle in the lead of the pencil.[10]

Since Thomas saw the origin of the universe as analogous to that of man, it naturally follows that cosmic and sexual activities may be seen as comparable functions. Thus the moment of conception is depicted as light breaking "where no sun shines,"

[9] William York Tindall, *The Literary Symbol* (Midland, Bloomington, Ind., 1960), p. 183.
[10] *Adventures in The Skin Trade and Other Stories* (Signet, New York, 1956), p. 111.

and the process of embryonic growth takes place when "the fruit of man unwrinkles in the stars" (p. 29). Similarly, sperm about to fertilize is said to be "from the star-flanked fields of space" (p. 51), much as creative light issues out of the void.

Thomas, however, apparently did not conceive of the universe as entirely anthropomorphic. There is considerable variation and not a little confusion in his views on this matter. Although he is close to Blake's view that "God only Acts and Is, in existing beings and men," [11] his poetry never completely discarded the transcendent and autonomous God of the Welsh Chapel. Tindall observes that Thomas's "God and Christ are . . . metaphors for nature, poet, and their creative powers." [12] This is quite true, yet we must remember that a metaphor for Thomas was sacramental: it was a symbol and a reality, both, and simultaneously.

Language, especially poetic language, is dependent upon metaphor. In any attempt to speak of God, one must use the finite, inevitably metaphoric, terms of human speech. Genesis describes creation as something which was spoken by God, man as the "image" of God (1:26), Eden as "planted" (2:8), and God as "walking in the garden in the cool of the day" (3:8). In Job 38, Jehovah speaks "out of the whirlwind" and asks, "Where wast thou when I laid the foundations of the earth" and "when I made the cloud the garment thereof, and thick darkness a swaddling-band for it"? Although Thomas identifies the Poet with the Word of the Gospels (John 1:1), using each as a metaphor for the other, the first Speaker of the Word, the God of Genesis and the Jehovah of Job, hovers in the background.

---

[11] *The Marriage of Heaven and Hell,* Keynes edition, I, p. 161.

[12] William York Tindall, *A Reader's Guide to Dylan Thomas* (New York, 1962), p. 8. A further discussion of Thomas's relationship to Fundamentalism appeared in Chaps. I and IV.

"Legend of Adam and Eve"

Thomas set out with the hope of creating a total symbology, but by the time he was twenty, he, perhaps unconsciously, discarded any hope of inventing his own symbols. He relied on the archetypes. Thomas had recourse as a poet to traditional ideas of God, before Whom his typical posture is that of petitioner, intercessor, pilgrim (see, for example, *Collected Poems*, pp. 132, 160, 192). The influence of Blake, Joyce, and Lawrence helped to make him something of a vitalist and a pantheist, and he was certainly at times a scoffer—"Every morning I make,/ God in bed, good and bad" (p. 150). But even in this instance he goes on to say, in effect, that if there is no God he might as well be dead:

No Time, spoke the clocks, no God, rang the bells,
I drew the white sheet over the islands
And the coins on my eyelids sang like shells.

(p. 151)

That Thomas rejected the hypocrisy he saw in various forms of Christianity does not *necessarily* mean that he also rejected God or the possibility of metaphoric truth in the Christian "myth." He seems to say as much in his prefatory note to *Collected Poems* (xiii): "I read somewhere of a shepherd who, when asked why he made, from within fairy rings, ritual observances to the moon to protect his flocks, replied: 'I'd be a damn' fool if I didn't!' These poems, with all their crudities, doubts, and confusions, are written for the love of Man and in praise of God, and I'd be a damn' fool if they weren't." We may dismiss this simply as mumble-jumble. But Thomas invoked it; it is the kind of mumble-jumble millions of men still live by. It expresses an awe of the universe and a desire on Thomas's part to express his awe before the mystery of existence.

Despite the fact that Thomas, like most modern poets, never

concerned himself with precise theological points, he did once give a definition of God which is quite distinct and meaningful in terms of the poetry—even if somewhat jocose. He called Him the "godhead, the author, the milky-way farmer, the first cause, architect, lamplighter, quintessence, the beginning Word, the anthropomorphic bowler-out and black-baller, the stuff of all men, scapegoat, martyr, maker, woe-bearer." [13] There are, it may be noticed, three separate groupings in the phrases Thomas uses. He describes a God of creation, a God of attrition, a God of love.

The God of creation is "godhead . . . , the milky-way farmer, the first cause . . . , quintessence, the beginning Word." In general terms this Creator resembles the God of the Old Testament. Thomas's God of creation is further related to Blake's Nobodaddy; it is He who made both the lamb and the tiger, both man and the serpent, both Adam and the devourers of Adam—sex and time. He is an evolutionary God who created life and death out of the sea, "This was the god of beginning in the intricate seawhirl" (p. 44).

The God of attrition, "the anthropomorphic bowler-out and black-baller," is a god of time and destruction, of the wearing-away of life. Thomas ridicules the traditional depictions of such a vengeful God:

> Shall gods be said to thump the clouds
> When clouds are cursed by thunder,
> Be said to weep when weather howls?
>
> . . . . .
>
> It shall be said that gods are stone.
>
> (p. 52)

But Thomas makes of time, if not a god of vengeance, at least a spirit of evil:

[13] *Quite Early One Morning*, pp. 178–179.

with his torch and hourglass, like a sulphur priest,
His beast heel cleft in a sandal,
Time marks a black aisle kindle from the brand of ashes.

(p. 92)

And there are in Thomas's concepts of time certain strong overtones of the Manichean divinity of evil. It is time that "cast forth my mortal creature" (p. 9), it is time that tracks man down "like a running grave" (p. 21), it is time that murders (p. 79).

All three aspects of divinity can be found throughout the poetry, but there is a general shift in emphasis. We perceive a Jehovah, a world spirit of attrition, and finally an immortal spirit of love. The more the God of time gives way to the God of love, the more we recognize His human qualities but, paradoxically, the more *permanent* becomes His presence. Despite this absolutism, the God of love is the "stuff of all men, scapegoat, martyr, maker, woe-bearer." Thomas, for example, merges the God of Genesis and the mythic Prometheus, in the "Ballad of the Long-legged Bait":

He who blew the great fire in
And died on a hiss of flames
Or walked on the earth in the evening
Counting the denial of the grains.

(p. 173)

It is this God of love, Thomas tells us, who stands weeping over His earth as the earth destroys itself ("In Country Heaven").[14] It is He the Poet cannot fathom but knows is true (although he can find no assurance for knowing this truth, p. 191).

Set in and against this theocentric background is a view of

[14] The manuscript of this poem is in the possession of John Malcolm Brinnin.

227

man as spirit, or ghost, imprisoned in flesh. Man's imperfect origin is reflected primarily in a flesh-spirit, metal-ghost antagonism, "the ghost is dumb that stammered in the straw" (p. 36). In dreaming of his rebirth after death, the poet describes the "second/ Rise of the skeleton and/ Rerobing of the naked ghost" (p. 34). It is from the idea of flesh being a prison of the spirit that the images of armor, "flesh's armour" (p. 8), and of man being "forged" in minerals (p. 40) make sense. All men are imprisoned in their contraries, body and spirit, "bonerailed and masterless" (p. 40).

Because he is an imperfect being, a sinner, man is the unwitting source of much of the evil of the world. He does evil, and he prevents the realization of the good. It is in this sense that "the hours' ladder to the sun" has been "monkeyed by the blood of man" (p. 32). Man is Adam, made in the image of God, born out of the sea from "Adam's brine," but inherently sinful:

> The fellow halves that, cloven as they swivel
> On casting tides, are tangled in the shells,
> Bearding the unborn devil.
>
> (p. 37)

In other words, man is part God and part devil; mankind is climbing a ladder of which the sides are "of Adam," made in the image of God, and the rungs are "of Abaddon," inherently evil (as in Sonnet II, p. 80):

> The horizontal cross-bones of Abaddon,
> You by the cavern over the black stairs,
> Rung bone and blade, the verticals of Adam,
> And, manned by midnight, Jacob to the stars.

Thomas found an imagistic link between the God of genesis and the "stuff of all men," between the creator of the universe and the creature of the world, in Christ. It is because Christ is the "stuff of all men" that God is, too. This relationship is both historical—"I who was shapeless as the water/ That shaped the Jordan near my home"—and eternal—"Was brother to Mnetha's daughter/ And sister to the fathering worm" ("Before I Knocked," p. 8).[15] Christ is not only God in human form; he is also a human being who is partly God. And in this sense all men, and especially the Poet, can be seen as Christ figures. "Before I Knocked" is therefore one of numerous instances, of which the Sonnets are the most notable, in which Thomas is describing *both* Christ and himself (as a representative of mankind and as Poet). The "Jack Self" of Hopkins becomes Jack Christ for Thomas: "My Jack of Christ born thorny on the tree" (p. 15). The central figure of *Collected Poems* is an Adam-Christ-Poet composite—the representative of suffering, crucified humanity:

> I hear, through dead men's drums, the riddled lads,
> Strewing their bowels from a hill of bones,
> Cry Eloi to the guns.
>
> (p. 36)

"Eloi, eloi," was the cry of Christ on the cross: "My God, my God, why hast thou forsaken me?" And the "hill of bones" is, of course, an allusion to the hill of skulls, Golgotha. This identification is crucial to an understanding of "Vision and Prayer," for example, which has to do with the birth of a child who is both any human being and also Christ. But, although Christ is an aspect of God and man is a figure of Christ, man is not to be simply identified with God. The "godhead," the "first cause," the "quintessence" are qualities of the divine

---

[15] Mnetha is a character that Thomas evidently derived from his reading of Blake (see Chapter One). S. Foster Damon, *William Blake: His Philosophy and Symbols* (Boston, 1924), p. 72, says, Mnetha is "a woman aged but strong . . . protectress of arts." See also Elder Olson, *The Poetry of Dylan Thomas* (Chicago, 1954), p. 99.

which are above and beyond the created world of man and Christ.

The created world is the physical manifestation of God or, by analogy, a figure of Christ. This is why "the long world's gentleman" can be said to "share my bed with Capricorn and Cancer" (Sonnet I, p. 80). This is why the rainbow of the covenant (Genesis 9:11–15) can be described as extending "from my nipples/ From pole to pole . . . round the snail-waked world" (Sonnet VIII, p. 84). And the evil and suffering in the world are therefore also God's wound, God's pain.

The whole world-body metaphor, which is so basic to Thomas's poetic vision and which has been so often noticed by his readers, is derived from this figural analogy of man-Christ-world. The sea, for example, can be like the blood of man and it can also be seen as the blood of Christ, as in "Lie Still, Sleep Becalmed," "the sea sound flowing like blood from the loud wound" (p. 153).

The retelling of the opening of Genesis (pp. 27–28) takes on characteristics of human generation:

> In the beginning was the three-pointed star,
> One smile of light across the empty face;
> One bough of bone across the rooting air,
> The substance forked that marrowed the first sun.

The light from the star (three-pointed evidently to suggest both the Trinity and perfection) creates with a smile, and the light of that smile breaks across "an empty face"—not empty space, as we might expect. The "bough of bone" is a variation of the rib of Adam from which Eve (and thereby the human race) was created.

While Thomas's universe may begin with a gentle fiat of a three-pointed star, it proceeds by contradictions and oppositions—"Heaven and hell mixed as they spun"—or, like human generation, it proceeds by division or a kind of cellular mitosis—"the substance forked that marrowed the first sun" and "before the pitch was forking to a sun." [16] "Forking" is one of Thomas's favorite images in his early poetry to express the idea of growth by division: "The seed that makes a forest of the loin/ Forks half its fruit" (p. 6). "From the divorcing sky," Thomas says, "I learnt the double,/ The two-framed globe that spun into a score" (p. 26). Sperm and egg are seen as "bisected shadows on the thunder's bone/ [that] Bolt for the salt unborn" (p. 35). In view of the dependence of one substance on another, cell on cell, man on woman, creature on creator, all the halves are imperfect ("My World Is Pyramid"):

> The broken halves are fellowed in a cripple,
> The crutch that marrow taps upon their sleep.

Human beings are cripples because they cannot create alone; they are dependent upon the living marrow in their bones (and, imperfectly, on one another) and thereby subject to death and decay.

The inherent conflict in creation is, then, life versus death. The point of view for Thomas's treatment of creation is like that of Adam when he first perceived death. He is too close to the horror of the revelation to think of how "green" was the beginning. In Thomas's subsequent poetry, the "Eden" of instinctive life, of childhood, and of nature will be depicted. But at the outset "the womb/ Drives in a death as life leaks out" (p. 6).

Divine creation begins when the "twilight locks" are no longer confined to the "long worm" of God's finger:

[16] "Without contraries there is no progression," says Blake in *The Marriage of Heaven and Hell*, ed. Keynes, I, p. 147, and goes on: "Attraction and Repulsion, Reason and Energy, Love and Hate, are necessary to Human existence."

When once the twilight locks no longer
Locked in the long worm of my finger
Nor damned the sea that sped about my fist,
The mouth of time sucked, like a sponge,
The milky acid on each hinge,
And swallowed dry the waters of the breast.

(p. 4)

The universe is created when the waters of death are no longer
confined within God. ("Locks" in Thomas, although Freudian in some cases, are better understood here in their literal
sense of anything that holds or confines something.) Even
calling God's finger a worm (from the pictorial representations of God by both Blake and Michelangelo perhaps)
conveys the creator-destroyer meaning. For the worm is both
creative, "the fathering worm" (p. 8), and destructive, "the
worm beneath my nail/ Wearing the quick away" (p. 14).
Just as foreboding in this description of the beginning of life is
the image of time hungrily nourishing itself on the galactic
breasts of God. This diabolical creature nourished of God
comes shortly to nourish itself on man and the world: "The
lips of time leech to the fountain head" (p. 10).

Time, however, is more important as a symbol in the fallen
world than it is in the world of creation. First come the worm
and its cognates (serpent, maggot, crocodile); these are particular to the world of genesis. What they signify is that inherent
in creation is sin, fall, or—more directly—death.

"Incarnate Devil" (p. 46) is a whole poem dealing with this
concept. Thomas says here that evil is an integral aspect of
creation, that the "circle" (the cycle of life) was "stung
awake" by the "incarnate devil in a talking snake." In mytho-
logical terms he says, "the garden gods/ Twined good and evil
on an eastern tree," but, he goes on, what it all comes down to

is that "a serpent fiddled in the shaping-time." It is important to note that God is characterized in the first stanza as "a fiddling warden" who "played down pardon from the heavens' hill." The creator, too, is indifferent to the inevitable sinfulness of his creation. Good and evil are inextricably intertwined.

The world that divinity shaped and the world that the poet shapes are symbolically joined both by the poet's purpose and by the way he creates. His purpose is to show the *truth* of the created world, to reveal the crocodile.

> I, in a wind on fire, from green Adam's cradle,
> No man more magical, clawed out the crocodile.
>
> (p. 44)

To claw out the crocodile is to reveal sin and death. (This idea is analogous to that of the "biting man," p. 65, and to biting out the mandrake in Sonnet I, p. 80, as well as to Job 41:1, "Canst thou draw out Leviathan with a hook? or his tongue with a cord . . . ?")

The poet has the same task as the Creator. He is "the brassy orator/ Laying my ghost in metal" (p. 40). He who is already aware of being a spirit imprisoned in flesh by God feels the further necessity of expressing his "ghost" in printed form. In terms parallel to the previous stanza's description of the evolutionary creation of man, the third stanza of "I, in My Intricate Image" describes the creation of a poem:

Beginning with doom in the ghost, and the springing marvels,
Image of images, my metal phantom
Forcing forth through the harebell,
My man of leaves and the bronze root, mortal, unmortal,
I, in my fusion of rose and male motion,
Create this twin miracle.

(p. 40)

Craft and Art of Dylan Thomas

Like the evangelical world of St. John and the cosmology of the Cabala,[17] the poetical world of Dylan Thomas begins with the word:

> In the beginning was the word, the word
> That from the solid bases of the light
> Abstracted all the letters of the void.
>
> (p. 27)

The void, Thomas tells us, is the world of letters, unorganized, chaotic. From this *prima materia* comes the word. Words, once they are part of man's being, explain to the heart the elementary facts of human existence—birth and death. In "If I Were Tickled by the Rub of Love," Thomas finds the knowledge of death more deadening than the fact of death itself: "My Jack of Christ born thorny on the tree?/ The words of death are dryer than his stiff" (p. 15).

The flesh of man is the "declension" by which the disorganized body of words is brought into meaningful relationship and the means by which the poet learns "to twist the shapes of thoughts/ Into the stony idiom of the brain" (p. 25). Just as the creations of God (man, world, time) imply death, so also do the creations of the poet. The talking of his "busy heart" makes him shed his "syllabic blood." (p. 19).

The great shaper is naturally God, and the poet in his ancient role of shaper of words also partakes of this creative function. Thus Thomas can say:

> [He] Who gave these seas their colour in a shape,
> Shaped my clayfellow, and the heaven's ark
> In time at flood filled with his coloured doubles;

[17] "The En-Soph creates by means of numbers and letters. The thirty-two 'instruments of God' are the ten primordial numbers to which all numbers can be reduced and the twenty-two fundamental letters of the Hebrew alphabet to which all words can be reduced." John Senior, *The Way Down and Out* (Ithaca, N.Y., 1959), p. 25.

"Legend of Adam and Eve"

O who is glory in the shapeless maps,
Now make the world of me as I have made
A merry manshape of your walking circle.

(p. 70)

Now, Thomas says, you (God) can shape me back to clay, "make the world of me," just as I have taken the sights and sounds of "your walking circle"—the world, round and always turning—and shaped them into poetry, a "merry manshape." (That these lines may also carry a sexual interpretation does not negate the poetic one. As usual, Thomas may be describing all types of creation by means of a single metaphor.)

The poet who "clawed out the crocodile" of life will be turned back into dust by the crocodile's counterpart, the maggot or the worm. Thus "joy is the knock of dust" (p. 22). But the dust of the earth is the source of new life; all the "dry worlds" (p. 38) are constantly flowering again through both human and natural generation. Even the grains of sand are "multiplying"—"Each golden grain spat life into its fellow" (p. 24). They too take part in the whole world's male and female generative impulse, as in "Into Her Lying Down Head"—"Two sand grains together in bed" (p. 127). All of nature is constantly creating.

"Four elements and five/ Senses, and man a spirit in love" (p. 193)—these are the prime images of creating nature. In the perfect creation, creation viewed without the presence of destructive time, all the four elements move in ideal union—"Earth, air, water, fire, singing into the white act" (p. 185). Such a view of creation, however, is not present in the early poetry for the very reason that that world has not yet been redeemed from the scourges of time.

The images of creation drawn from the earth—tree, flower, grass—are secondary to the major symbolic role of the earth, or "dust," which manifests itself especially in the later poems as an image of re-creation or universal renewal. At the outset, the functions and products of earth are used as signs of fertility and productivity of the most ordinary kind:

> I should tell summer from the trees, the worms
> Tell, if at all, the winter's storms
> Or the funeral of the sun.
>
> (p. 53)

(It is in the redeemed earth of the later poetry that "the dead oak walks for love," p. 134). Thomas uses "flower" to indicate the beauty as well as the productivity of nature's creation—"Flower, flower, all all and all" (p. 39)—and he describes the simple renewal of life through the earth, "My second struggling from the grass" (p. 33).

The wind, the seasons, and the weathers are the actions of the air. In creating the world God "set alight the weathers from a spark" (p. 27), and in the created world "a process in the weather of the heart/ Turns damp to dry" (p. 6). Air, in the form of wind, weather, and seasons, is therefore an essential image of creating nature and a part of all creation, including that of Adam-Christ:

> I knew the message of the winter,
> The darted hail, the childish snow,
> And the wind was my sister suitor;
> Wind in me leaped, the hellborn dew;
> My veins flowed with the Eastern weather;
> Ungotten I knew night and day.
>
> (p. 8)

Air, quite naturally, is also associated with the earth to provide clusters of images signifying life. In Thomas the world is life and a ball is a synecdoche for the world, hence for life: "The ball I threw while playing in the park/ Has not yet reached the ground" (p. 72). "Bubble" is metaphorically related to "ball," it too becoming a synecdoche for life. More specifically, it is a metaphoric substitute for breath: "If the unpricked ball of my breath/ Bump on a spout let the bubbles jump out" (p. 108). Life is created by nature out of "blood and bubble" (p. 40), and time is a thief who brings death by stealing bubbles (p. 76).

The wind as the primary movement of the air is another constant metaphor for the breath of the world and of life itself. Whether "four-winded" (p. 24) or "twelve-winded" (p. 69) the created world is a world of blowing winds, the "windy salvage" of God (p. 80). And in the human being "the windy blood/ Slides like a sea" (p. 29) and becomes in death the "clotted wind" (p. 33).

Most of the water imagery has to do with the sea, and, as might be expected, one of the major functions of the sea imagery is to express the idea of evolution. Man is "sea born" (xvi), Adam is "sea-sucked" (p. 35), and woman has been "water-lammed" (p. 63). The begetters of mankind have risen "grimly from the wrack" (p. 54), that is, from seaweeds. From the sea comes all the force of life: "Out of the sea, the drive of oil" (p. 39), or, again,

> Life rose and spouted from the rolling seas,
> Burst in the roots, pumped from the earth and rock
> The secret oils that drive the grass.
>
> (p. 27)

The sea is a "face of voices" (p. 43), and both the sea and a woman can be viewed similarly: "Where once the waters of your face/ Spun to my screws" (p. 12). The unborn Christ was "shapeless as the water/ That shaped the Jordan" (p. 8). The sea is the "nurse of giants" (p. 65). Within man there is an ocean: "Where no sea runs, the waters of the heart/ Push in their tides," and man's "windy blood/ Slides like a sea" (p. 29). When the human seed fertilizes the egg, it is imaged as a hero coming to harbor:

> Let the hero seed find harbour,
> Seaports by a thirsty shore
> Have their drunken sailors hide him.
> (p. 50)

But the sea is not only the source of life; it is the termination of life in Thomas's imagery. This is why his thirty-fifth birthday poem closes with "I sail out to die" (p. 193). Life itself is a "graveward gulf" (p. 76), and man returns in death to the sea, which draws its water from all the corners of the world:

> My grave is watered by the crossing Jordan.
> The Arctic scut, and basin of the South,
> Drip on my dead house garden.
> Who seek me landward, marking in my mouth
> The straws of Asia, lose me as I turn
> Through the Atlantic corn.
> (p. 37)

The sea is also a metaphor for the "voyage of life." Here is an instance of Thomas's handling of the voyage metaphor from "I, in My Intricate Image" (p. 41):

Intricate manhood of ending, the invalid rivals,
Voyaging clockwise off the symboled harbour,
Finding the water final,
On the consumptives' terrace taking their two farewells,
Sail on the level, the departing adventure,
To the sea-blown arrival.

The "invalid rivals" of this stanza are the Philistines of the world who reject the poet. They live (voyage) "clockwise," that is, in a humdrum circle, according to the clock. They see the water of death as annihilation; they are "consumptives," weak and diseased. They do not voyage bravely; instead they take their lingering "two farewells," but they "sail on the level," not on the two levels of the poet. This is their "departing adventure/ To the sea-blown arrival."

The moon and the tides of the sea are Thomas's images for the regularity, the order of life. In this sense the sea tumbles "in harness" to the moon (p. 112), and the moon is "the binding moon" (p. 74). The moon, as the guardian of sleep, dream, romance, also marks the passage of time and, by analogy, the coming of death. The "conceiving moon" of "In the White Giant's Thigh" is, like Keats's Cynthia, a symbol of fertility.

In keeping with universal occult and religious symbolism, Thomas's creation and renewal by fire is of a higher, or at least intenser, kind than that of earth, air, or water. Fire is seen as an aspect of God the creator, as well as of the world he created:

> In the beginning was the mounting fire
> That set alight the weathers from a spark,
> A three-eyed, red-eyed spark, blunt as a flower.
>
> (p. 27)

The whole creating earth turns "on a wheel of fire" (p. 38) which is the sun. The sun is "the mystic sun, the wife of light" (p. 61), and the prime symbol of the created world's dependence on God—the "servant sun," "the rite of light" (p. 65). The sun is associated with the blood and the forces of life: "blood in their suns/ Lights up the living worm" (p. 6); "The secret of the soil grows through the eye/ And blood jumps in the sun" (p. 30). And the poet in the process of creating a poem can say, "Caught by the crabbing sun I walk on fire" (p. 19).

The three types of creation, divine, natural, and poetic, all share one imagistic complex—that derived from spinning. Playing on the dual meaning of "spin," Thomas superimposes the idea of turning on the idea of making thread from raw fiber such as straw. Thus the globe is "of genesis spun" (p. 122); the world is a "spun bud" (p. 137); the earth in its turning makes a musical composition—"the whole world then . . . / Spins its morning of praise" (p. 193); "the two-framed globe . . . spun into a score" (p. 26); and north, south, east, and west winds are a "four-winded spinning." The work of the creating season, spring, is likewise the work of spinning:

> Beginning with doom in the bulb, the spring unravels,
> Bright as her spinning-wheels, the colic season
> Worked on a world of petals;
> She threads off the sap and needles, blood and bubble
> Casts to the pine roots, raising man like a mountain
> Out of the naked entrail.
>
> (p. 40)

The newly created world is called "the first, spinning place" (p. 179). The sun in its mere manifestation is the spinner of the conditions of life (pp. 157, 164), and the world of its making is "spun slime" (p. 193). And the poet, of course, is likewise a spinner (xvi)

> I, a spinning man,
> Glory also this star, bird
> Roared, sea born, man torn, blood blest.

Thomas's tailor and straw imagery are directly connected with his spinning concept. Since the tailor is one who makes things out of cloth and thread, he is a creator. In "Once Below a Time" (pp. 147–149), Thomas describes God as "my maker,/ The cloud perched tailors' master with nerves for cotton"; the "tailors' master" does his sewing with nerves instead of cotton. Man's physical appearance is tailored—

"pinned-around-the-spirit/ Cut-to-measure flesh"—and the poet beneath his pretensions is "the boy of common thread." He characterizes his detractors, conventional mankind, as "the clock faced tailors,"

> The flashing needle rock of squatters,
> The criers of Shabby and Shorten,
> The famous stitch droppers.

Even the tides in their function as the source of life are called the "sewing tides" (p. 65).

Since, however, a tailor cuts as well as sews, and since the "cut-to-measure" flesh is doomed to death, the tailor image, like all images of creation, implies destruction as well as creation. There is an etymological connection between the words "tailor" and "scissors." The middle Latin *scissor* meant "one who cleaves or divides," specifically a tailor.[18] It is in this destructive role that Thomas sees the embryo "crouched like a tailor/ Sewing a shroud for a journey" (p. 110). It is thus that the tailor can be "the green unraveller," green because he creates, an unraveller because his creation is doomed to death, and because he dresses man and nature for death:

> Where once your green knots sank their splice
> Into the tided cord, there goes
> The green unraveller,
> His scissors oiled, his knife hung loose
> To cut the channels at their source
> And lay the wet fruits low.
>
> (p. 12)

This is also why "tailor age" "comes, like a scissors stalking" (p. 21).

[18] Edward A. and Lillian D. Bloom, "Dylan Thomas: His Intimations of Mortality," *Brown University Studies in English*, IV (1960), 143.

This cluster of tailor images explains most of the references to straw, string, bandages, hair, and winding sheets that occur in various places in *Collected Poems*. All of these things are creative when joined, bound, "spun," or sewn, and all are uncreative or symbols of death when they are not united. Unless some definite statement of their union is made, their appearance is a sign of mortality, serving a function similar to the more common "wax." When Thomas says, "from the planted womb the man of straw" (p. 2), he means mortal man. He uses similar images in the opening of "If I Were Tickled by the Rub of Love," where he says:

> A rooking girl who stole me for her side
> Broke through her straws, breaking my bandaged string.
>
> (p. 13)

The breaking through straw is the coming to the surface of sexuality, and the breaking of the bandaged string is the arousing of adolescent sexual desires. The notion of mortality and infertility is apparent in the imaging of the world as "the lying likeness of/ Our strips of stuff that tatter as we move" (p. 17), and in the line "button your bodice on a hump of splinters" (p. 82).

Imagistically associated with strips and straws and threads are the hair and coil images which make occasional appearances. The avenues of love which the fisherman of the "Ballad" had explored when "his loin was a hunting flame" become the snare of the long-legged bait—"Coil from the thoroughfares of her hair" (p. 175). "Sussanah's drowned in the bearded stream" (p. 171), and Samson is "drowned in his hair" (p. 125). Even the forbidden fruit is seen as a "bearded apple" (p. 46). Just as the procreative urge ensnares man—"In the groin's endless coil a man is tangled" (p. 89)—so also does the poetic urge ensnare the poet:

He

In his slant, racking house
And the hewn coils of his trade perceives
Herons walk in their shroud.

(p. 190)

II
FALL

It is not necessary to postulate a specific relationship of
Thomas to any doctrinal or theological position regarding the
Fall or the Garden of Eden. As far as his poems go, he could
just as well have used classical allusions to the Golden Age, or
accounts of the fabled Hesperides, or Freud's first unweaned
state, in order to emphasize the imperfection of his world. But
the fact remains that his symbolism was primarily derived
from an imaginative re-creation of the Bible.

Of the two types of references to the unfallen world in
Thomas, only one is of symbolic importance. The idea of a
historic Eden is present in "Incarnate Devil" (p. 46):

We in our Eden knew the secret guardian
In sacred waters that no frost could harden,
And in the mighty mornings of the earth.

But it is only part of the "cloven myth." The idea of Eden
which is important to the symbolism is that related to
"Edenic" states known to living man—childhood, and rare
moments of tranquillity in nature, and even rarer moments of
sexual bliss.

Referring to childhood, before the "rumour of manseed/
Within the hallowed gland," Thomas can say, "Green was the
singing house" (p. 24). This is also the condition in the later
Edenic descriptions of "Fern Hill," where the memory of
childhood "was all/ Shining, it was Adam and maiden" (p.

179). This joyful memory of Eden's green persists even though the poet now realizes he was "green and dying," now realizes the inevitability of the Fall, of suffering and death (p. 180). Thomas's best picture of the unfallen state, another description of childhood, occurs in "Poem in October" (p. 114):

> And I saw in the turning so clearly a child's
> Forgotten mornings when he walked with his mother
>> Through the parables
>>> Of sun light
> And the legends of the green chapels.

Glimpses of the unfallen state may also be found in rare moments of physical love:

>> in the cool of your mortal garden
> With immortality at my side like Christ the sky.
>>> (p. 121)

He can say to his love, "In your every inch and glance is the globe of genesis spun,/ And the living earth your sons" (p. 120). Love enables the lovers in "Love in the Asylum," (p. 119) to recapture the pristine quality of the newly created world:

> And taken by light in her arms at long and dear last
>> I may without fail
> Suffer the first vision that set fire to the stars.

But the fallen world in its many different aspects is omnipresent. It cannot be avoided. First there is the great Fall which is inherent in the nature of creation and existence:

> The hand that whirls the water in the pool
> Stirs the quicksand; that ropes the blowing wind
> Hauls my shroud sail.
>>> (p. 10)

Because creation is subject to it, time is the most important symbol for the attrition that wears away life—"I saw time murder me," says the poet (p. 79).

The individual, and mankind whom he represents, is enclosed even before birth in an Egyptian pyramid: [19]

> My world is pyramid. The padded mummer
> Weeps on the desert ochre and the salt
> Incising summer.
> My Egypt's armour buckling in its sheet,
> I scrape through resin to a starry bone
> And a blood parhelion.
>
> (p. 36)

Wrapped in the mask of a mummy (as also in "The mummy cloths expose an ancient breast," p. 72), which is also his "Egypt's armour," man weeps in the desert and the "salt/ Incising summer" while he tries to "scrape" through the embalming resin to reach the "starry bone" and the small spot of false light which is life, "a blood parhelion." Sonnet IX has to do with this same process of mummification—"the resurrection in the desert" (p. 85).

Nearly all the early prose draws upon the Biblical symbols, but "A Prospect of the Sea" reveals a remarkably consistent use of "fallen world" imagery. The story is one of several dealing with youthful initiation into sex. At the climactic moment, the girl asks the boy, "Where do you come from?" And he replies: "I come from Amman valley." "I have a sister

---

[19] John Senior, in *The Way Down and Out*, p. 12, says that "the pyramid was a means of ascension. The word for 'pyramid' is derived from a set of hieroglyphics meaning 'place of ascension,' and the glyph for 'ascension' could represent a kind of pyramid. It is therefore reasonable to assume that the pyramid was an Egyptian ziggurat, a tower that stretched to heaven." This idea casts light on Thomas's other pyramid imagery ("my proud pyramid," p. 88), and also connects it to his tower and turret image clusters.

in Egypt, she said, who lives in a pyramid." Shortly afterward she calls him Amman. And then the boy's slumbering mind races:

from history to the thigh, through the thigh in the dark to the first and West print between the dark and the green Eden; and the garden was undrowned, to this next minute and for ever, under Asia in the earth that rolled on to its music in the beginning evening. When God was sleeping, he had climbed a ladder, and the room three jumps above the final rung was roofed and floored with the live pages of the book of days; the pages were gardens, the built words were trees, and Eden grew above him into Eden, and Eden grew down to Eden through the lower earth, an endless corridor of boughs and birds and leaves. . . .

Wake up, she said into his ear; the iron characters were broken in her smile, and Eden shrank into the seventh shade.

Eden has been lost in sexual knowledge. Thereafter the story moves in panic and fearful flight as the now initiated "stumbled on over sand and sandflowers like a blind boy in the sun." [20]

"You shall never go back," a voice says to the boy. And indeed he could not return to innocence. The Biblical way is the only way, and in the last paragraph of the story Thomas says: "On a hill to the horizon stood an old man building a boat, and the light that slanted from the sea cast the holy mountain of a shadow over the three-storied decks and the Eastern timber." One can't go back, but one can go forward. The ark is the symbol of the forward movement.

As might be expected, parchment and calligraphy, pyramid and (as they are in Genesis and Exodus) the Nile and Egypt, are images of time's oppressive captivity: "time, the quiet gentleman/ Whose beard wags in Egyptian wind" (p. 72). Egypt is also the cradle of civilization and therefore an image

[20] *Adventures in the Skin Trade and Other Stories*, pp. 132, 133–134, 135.

of antiquity and, by analogy, the mummified world of propriety and convention. This is one reason why the "crocodile" is described as "Tail, Nile, and snout" (p. 44); its body is human civilization, and mankind weeps for the lost Eden—"All-hollowed man wept for his white apparel" (p. 44).

Thomas describes this loss further in "To-day, This Insect" (p. 47), where he says, now that his symbols have "outelbowed" time and space, he will use the insect "and the world I breathe" as his images. Presumably, he has just killed an insect as it crossed the table where he wrote. The severed halves of the insect are the subject of the particular poem, symbolic of his poetry in general and, also, symbolic of the world which he sees about him. Thus he describes the death of the insect in terms that are meaningful to both poetry and life:

> I divided sense,
> Slapped down the guillotine, the blood-red double
> Of head and tail made witnesses to this
> Murder of Eden and green genesis.

By killing the insect, he has destroyed its Eden and "green genesis" just as time destroys man's. And the central figure of this poem, as of the fallen world, is a "serpent":

> This story's monster has a serpent caul,
>
> . . . . .
>
> Measures his own length on the garden wall
>
> . . . . .
>
> A crocodile before the chrysalis,
> Before the fall from love the flying heartbone.

That Thomas is talking about a caterpillar is apparent from the imagery: the "crocodile" refers to the worm, the caterpillar, which precedes the chrysalis, and before the butterfly's brief life is over it resembles in its flight a "flying heartbone." But these lines are also applicable to the poet, who is the monster that killed the insect, who like the proud serpent visited the garden, who like the butterfly grew from the worm and the chrysalis ("Snail of man in His ship of fires," p. 78), and who before he fell from innocence was a spirit of love. (As he tells us in "Should Lanterns Shine," p. 72, any boy would hesitate before he fell from innocence if he knew what followed sexual knowledge: "any boy of love/ Look twice before he fell from grace.")

The last three lines of the stanza inform us that, like the ass's jawbone, this simple tale, "this children's piece," tells the truth, although unacknowledged; it brings the fate of the destroyed place upon the place of bliss—it "blows Jericho on Eden." Observation of the insect, whose story is the "certain promise," provides evidence of the whole cycle of existence and of the inevitability of death.

Life itself then is by its nature imperfect, "fallen." This is how Thomas can say of the newborn child, the "fallen saint," "Heaven fell with his fall and one crocked bell beat the left air" (p. 105), and again, in " 'If My Head Hurt a Hair's Foot,' " (p. 109):

'Now to awake husked of gestures and my joy like a cave
To the anguish and carrion, to the infant forever unfree,
O my lost love bounced from a good home.'

However, there is another aspect of the Fall that is somewhat closer to the traditional interpretations of the story of Eden. This is the fall that comes with the knowledge of sex and the awareness of suffering. The all-important knowledge, for instance, that Adam and Eve gained from the apple is called in rabbinic commentaries *tob wara*, which means something like adult awareness.[21] Adult life is comparable to the expulsion

[21] I am indebted to Professor Yochanan Muffs of the Jewish Theological Seminary, New York, for observations on the similarity between Thomas's views and rabbinic commentaries.

from the Garden, comparable to the wandering in the desert. It is in this sense that Thomas sees woman as lying "Like exodus a chapter from the garden" (p. 63) [22] and that the images of sex and time come to be the spirits of evil in the poetry. The fallen world of adult life is made up of "time and the crabs and the sweethearting crib" (p. 14). Life is a "boiling circle," it is "the sea and instrument, nicked in the locks of time" (p. 44). And time is "like a running grave" (p. 21), it is

> a man outside with a billhook,
> Up to his head in his blood,
> Cutting the morning off.
>
> (p. 150)

The whole world is seen as the helpless prey of the hunter time, who has a tail like the beast of Revelation:

> Down fall four padding weathers on the scarlet lands,
> Stalking my children's faces with a tail of blood,
> Time, in a rider rising, from the harnessed valley.
>
> (p. 58)

Both the world of nature and the world of human beings move inevitably toward death:

> Curlews aloud in the congered waves
>   Work at their ways to death,
> And the rhymer in the long tongued room,
>   Who tolls his birthday bell,
> Toils towards the ambush of his wounds.
>
> (p. 190)

And the poet mourns the loss of innocence:

[22] This interpretation is in accord with Olson, p. 98, where he says that "exodus" is "not a reference to the biblical Book of Exodus but to the exodus itself, which is part of the story of the Garden of Eden in that the captivity and the exodus resulted from the Fall."

But time has set its maggot on their track.

. . . . .

Under the sky signs they who have no arms
Have cleanest hands, and, as the heartless ghost
Alone's unhurt, so the blind man sees best.

(p. 59)

Above all, time for Thomas was a thief and the source of grief. "Grief thief of time" is a "knave of pain" and also the "time-faced crook,/ Death flashing from his sleeve." And this "knave of pain steals off/ The sea-halved faith that blew time to his knees" (p. 76)—time and grief steal our faith which is our only means of defeating time. "Birth and death, the two sad knaves of thieves," are the offspring of time (p. 11). In Sonnet VII (p. 83), "time's tune" fixed "in a naked sponge . . . sucks the bell-voiced Adam out of magic"—steals mankind's faith. And in "In Country Sleep" Thomas associates the "Thief" and his inevitable coming with the fallen state of the whole world:

This night and each night since the falling star you were born,
Ever and ever he finds a way, as the snow falls,

As the rain falls, hail on the fleece, as the vale mist rides
Through the haygold stalls, as the dew falls on the wind-
Milled dust of the apple tree and the pounded islands
Of the morning leaves, as the star falls, as the winged
Apple seed glides,
And falls, and flowers in the yawning wound at our sides,
As the world falls, silent as the cyclone of silence.

(p. 183)

But "the country is holy" where the child lives. It is a kind of Eden in which all of nature worships God, and she in her innocence is still in a state of grace: "Be shielded by chant and flower and gay may you/ Lie in grace" (pp. 182–183). But time, the Thief, comes in this poem also "to take/ Her faith" so that her death will leave her in a meaningless world ("the lawless sun"), grieving for the loss of time (p. 186).

The drive of time to create new life and to overcome death is the source of the "urchin grief" (p. 92):

Time's coral saint and the salt grief drown a foul sepulchre
And a whirlpool drives the prayerwheel.

The "coral saint," ever multiplying life, and the "salt grief"—the suffering of existence—make us forget the fact of death for a while, and our worship of God is conditioned by the "whirlpool" of our fallen existence. New life is the death knell of the living. It leads to the recognition that the living are being replaced, and thus the poet cries, in "Ballad":

> *Time is bearing another son.*
> *Kill Time! She turns in her pain!*
> *The oak is felled in the acorn*
> *And the hawk in the egg kills the wren.*
>
> (p. 173)

The fallen world is a world of "wounds." [23] Man's mortality is his wound that cannot be healed. It is the "tide raking/ Wound" (p. 186) which is "the turning of the earth in her holy/ Heart" (p. 185). Without creation and mortality, time, the Thief, would be meaningless and powerless, would "fall on the dead like the willy nilly dew." The womb is a "bowl of wounds and weed" (p. 101) because it brings forth mortal

---

[23] Some idea of the antiquity and the universality of the "wound" image may be gathered from Tertullian's use of the word. Speaking of Christ, he calls his wound, *de iniuria*, a figure not only of the Church but also of all mankind. Cited in Erich Auerbach, *Scenes from the Drama of European Literature*, trans. Ralph Manheim (Meridian, New York, 1959), p. 30. Auerbach's whole discussion of figural interpretation of Scripture (pp. 11–76) is generally relevant to Thomas's use of Biblical material.

creatures. But the joy of sex may at times make even mortality beautiful:

> But blessed by such heroic hosts in your every
> Inch and glance that the wound
> Is certain god.
>
> (p. 120)

The wound as an image of the suffering of life and the inevitability of death is crucial to the "Sonnets," "Vision and Prayer," and "Lie Still, Sleep Becalmed." The "gentleman of wounds" of Sonnet I is Christ, a figure for suffering humanity. This is why he can say (Sonnet VIII):

> The world's my wound, God's Mary in her grief,
> Bent like three trees and bird-papped through her shift,
> With pins for teardrops is the long wound's woman.
>
> (p.84)

God's world is the whole of creation, which is, by its mortal, fallen nature, a "wound." But the world of creation is also the mother of Christ, "God's Mary in her grief." The trees and birds of nature are her body, and she is the spouse of the "long wound," the "gentleman of wounds," God. In each of the five sonnets in which it appears, "wound" has a slightly different meaning (such usage being a habit of Thomas's which we discussed in Chapter Two). For example, in Sonnet VI, the "wound of manwax" has a much more specific connection with sex.

The figure which dominates Thomas's fallen world is a voyaging or wandering figure. He is variously a Samson, a Christ, Ishmael, Cain—all figures of suffering humanity, "the stuff of all men, scapegoat, martyr, . . . woe-bearer." The sea, as the primordial archetype of chaos, is the favorite place of wandering. Other places, common to numerous poets besides Thomas—Blake especially—are "the forest, the fallen garden . . . the labyrinth, the wilderness and the pathless blanket of winter snow." [24] In "A Winter's Tale" it is the trackless new-fallen snow that symbolizes the wilderness in which the man is "torn and alone in a farm house in a fold/ Of fields" (p. 131). In this fallen world no one can escape; whoever is born into the "flat cities" is sure to fall "to His green myths."

> Who in these labyrinths,
> This tidethread and the lane of scales,
> Twine in a moon-blown shell,
> Escapes to the flat cities' sails
> Furled on the fishes' house and hell,
> Nor falls to His green myths?
>
> (p. 78)

The poet prays (in "Vision and Prayer," pp. 161–163), "In the name of the wanton/ Lost on the unchristened mountain" "that he [the Savior] let the dead lie though they moan." He prays this because

> Forever falling night is a known
> Star and country to the legion
> Of sleepers whose tongue I toll
>
> . . . . .
>
> And we have come
> To know all
> Places
> Ways
> Mazes
> Passages
> Quarters and graves
> Of the endless fall.

Although the child is its parents' hope of immortality ("Ceremony After a Fire Raid," pp. 143-146),

[24] Northrop Frye, *Fearful Symmetry* (Princeton, 1947), p. 380.

the serpent's
Night fall and the fruit like a sun,

her dead body is the symbol of the death of innocence:

White as the skeleton
Of the garden of Eden,

and her death an evidence of the Fall, a return to chaos:

Man and woman undone,
Beginning crumbled back to darkness
Bare as the nurseries
Of the garden of wilderness.

The "Altarwise" sonnets (pp. 80–85) are Thomas's most complete depiction of the fallen world, the world of exodus or wilderness, the world of the lost wanderer, the outcast voyager. The sonnets are also the epitome of Thomas's obscurity. The whole sequence, and every word within it, is intended to be meaningful on so many different levels that it may almost be said that the ambiguity itself is an image of the fallen world which it depicts.

The sonnets have a loose chronological framework based on references to various periods in the process from birth to maturity. Thus in the first sonnet Christ scrapes at "my cradle," while in the second "the child that sucketh long is shooting up" and "soon sets alight a long stick from the cradle." Sonnet III marks youth and the earliest stages of adolescence. It describes the loss of innocence in terms of the murder of Abel ("the lamb") by Cain ("Adam's wether" and "the black ram"). Sonnet IV marks the age of questions, the first awareness of death and passing time. Sonnet V signifies the discovery of the hypocrisy of conventional religion and the revolt against it. Like Jonah, God's prophet to Nineveh, the hero is cast into the sea and swallowed by the whale:

"Legend of Adam and Eve"

> A climbing sea from Asia had me down
> And Jonah's Moby snatched me by the hair.

The initiation into life (which is also an initiation into poetry) through the experience of sex occurs in Sonnet VI, where the voyager blows tallow "from the wax's tower/ The fats of midnight when the salt was singing." In Sonnet VII the voyager-poet is aware of the nature of reality, the "bell-voiced Adam" has been sucked "out of magic/ Time, milk, and magic, from the world beginning." And what is the result of this view of life (Sonnet VIII), the inevitable end of the voyager?

> the crucifixion on the mountain,
> Time's nerve in vinegar, the gallow grave.

Sonnet IX then describes the mummification and burial of the crucified one. This is the end of the voyage; this is the meaning of man's odyssey:

> With priest and pharaoh bed my gentle wound,
> World in the sand, on the triangle landscape,
> With stones of odyssey for ash and garland
> And rivers of the dead around my neck.

The end of life, both its penance and victory wreath, is death. What meaning has this for the speaker, the man brought up in the knowledge of Christian teachings, the man at whose cradle Christ scraped "in a walking word"? Sonnet X answers the question:

> Let the tale's sailor from a Christian voyage
> Atlaswise hold half-way off the dummy bay
> Time's ship-racked gospel on the globe I balance.

The "tale's sailor" will, like Atlas, "hold half-way off" the false harbor balancing "time's ship-racked gospel," the world, on the "globe" of his poetry. He will not, in other words, commit himself. If the believer, imaged by Peter, wishes to believe, let him. Thomas, the Poet, will describe "the blown word" and "December's thorn screwed in a brow of holly"—the pain of life in the midst of its joy.

> Let the first Peter from a rainbow's quayrail
> Ask the tall fish swept from the bible east,
> What rhubarb man peeled in her foam-blue channel
> Has sown a flying garden round that sea-ghost?

Peter, of course, became an apostle of Christ after nets, empty during a day of fishing, were miraculously filled upon Christ's command (Matthew 4:18–20, Mark 1:16–18, Luke 5:1–11). Also, an early Christian symbol for Christ was the fish. Peter can ask "the tall fish," Christ, about the "rhubarb man," Thomas, who has produced such a "flying garden" out of the "sea-ghost" of Christianity and life. And, as for the Poet, he hopes that his "garden," with its own "two bark towers" of personal Eden and Calvary," will, by dying, find regeneration at the Day of Judgment. The Day of Judgment is seen as organic decay and reintegration of the body into the natural cycle, by means of the worm, the maggot of death:

> Green as beginning, let the garden diving
> Soar, with its two bark towers, to that Day
> When the worm builds with the gold straws of venom
> My nest of mercies in the rude, red tree.

What makes the sonnets so opaque is that the relatively simple chronological progression is often obscured by the shifting point of view and the shifting and multiple identity of the narrator. The narrator is above all the Poet who is archetypally associated with Christ, especially in Sonnet VIII (where Christ is also personified by the earth, so that the rainbow of the covenant made with Noah is seen as emanating from his nipples, the two poles of the earth). But the Poet is also associated with Adam as the prototype of the human race, and in his role as Poet he is "Adam, time's joker," who "on a witch of cardboard/ Spelt out the seven seas, an evil index." [25] And the Poet is also one with all the outcasts and rebels of history and literature—Cain and Rip Van Winkle, Ishmael, Jonah, and Christ crucified. The sonnets deal not only with the voyage of an individual but also with the man-Christ-poet composite that we have seen continually in the poetry.

While the voyage of the sonnets is essentially that of a young man and a poet seeking to learn the purpose and meaning of life, the "Ballad of the Long-legged Bait" is the voyage of a man and husband seeking fulfillment in marriage. As Richard Condon has said, the theme of the "Ballad" is "the loss of Eden." [26] The hero of the "Ballad" is closely identified with Samson (the original title was "Ballad of Samson-Jack"),[27] and the poem is a comprehensive treatment of the sex-time-death trap which for Thomas epitomized much of the human condition. In loving we reproduce, and in reproduction we prepare for our own death—this is the dilemma of the wanderer in the fallen world. (The same idea is crucial to numerous other poems of Thomas's middle period, for example, "It Is the Sinners' Dust-tongued Bell," "I Make This in a Warring Absence," "Unluckily for a Death," "Into Her Lying Down Head.")

In the "Ballad" Thomas takes the basic sea-voyage, life-journey analogy and adds a new dimension: fishing voyage,

[25] These lines may have a specific relationship to Thomas's own working methods. Vernon Watkins describes the manuscript of one of Thomas's stories, "The Orchards." "The whole story was written in minute handwriting on the inside cover of a cardboard box. He told me that it helped him to see the whole story in one place as he wrote it, and pages were less good for this than box-covers." *Dylan Thomas: Letters to Vernon Watkins*, ed. Vernon Watkins (London, 1957), p. 14.

[26] Richard Condon, "Thomas' BALLAD OF THE LONG-LEGGED BAIT," *Explicator*, XVI (March, 1958), 37.

[27] In the work sheets, Lockwood Memorial Library, University of Buffalo.

reproduction. The "Ballad" is thus the story of marriage or the fulfillment of sexual desire, told in a kind of Freudian dream about a fisherman who uses a woman for bait. Literally, the poem describes a man who goes to sea, casts his line, hears "his bait buck in the wake/ And tussle in a shoal of loves" as "she longs among horses and angels,/ The rainbow-fish bend in her joys" (p. 167). Shortly the fisherman sees

> the bulls of Biscay and their calves
> Are making under the green, laid veil
> The long-legged beautiful bait their wives.
>
> (p. 169)

The fisherman is next described as satiated, purged of lust:

> Oh all the wanting flesh his enemy
> Thrown to the sea in the shell of a girl.
>
> (p. 170)

Afterward, the fisherman begins reeling in his bait and finds that not only is the whole of the sea clinging to his bait, but that

> Round her trailed wrist fresh water weaves,
> With moving fish and rounded stones
> Up and down the greater waves
> A separate river breathes and runs;
>
> Strike and sing his catch of fields
> For the surge is sown with barley,
> The cattle graze on the covered foam.
>
> (p. 174–175)

Finally, his catch and bait leads him nightmarishly home:

> And terribly lead him home alive
> Lead her prodigal home to his terror,
> The furious ox-killing house of love.
>
> (p. 175)

"Legend of Adam and Eve"

And at the poem's end the fisherman stands

> lost on the land.
> He stands alone at the door of his home,
> With his long-legged heart in his hand.

(p. 176)

When we analyze this dreamlike sequence of events, we find it a symbolic description of courtship, marriage, pregnancy, and parenthood. In essence we find it a modern variation of the Samson story—a man daringly marries the woman he most desires and is brought by the deed into servile captivity; he becomes a sacrifice in "the furious ox-killing house of love."

As might be expected, this fantastic voyage occurs at night under the spell of the moon. At the outset "the moon swam out of its hulk," it is a "moonstruck boat," and nothing shines "on the water's face/ But the oil and bubble of the moon." The raw animality, the brutish urge which Thomas associated with sex (as in "Into Her Lying Down Head"), is conveyed by a host of violent images, especially images of sea life. The fisherman has "his hooks through her lips," and "all the fishes were rayed in blood." The world is turned upside down; the cathedral lost under the sea floats, and "the anchor rode like a gull" (p. 167). A storm smokes "out to kill/ With fuming bows and ram of ice." The sexual act is described in terms of the woman bait fleeing, "in a weaving dip," "humpbacked tons" of whales. Now innocence is lost: "Oh, Jericho was falling in their lungs!" (p. 168).

The one clear piece of evidence that the fishing tale is an allegory of sexual experience occurs in the seventeenth stanza, when the "whirled boat" is located "in the burn of his blood." All the monstrous and nacreous sea creatures, then, are aspects of sexual desire. It is in stanza eighteen that the "boatsized brood . . . the bulls of Biscay and their calves"

259

> Break the black news and paint on a sail
> Huge weddings in the waves.

The wedding here is the wedding of sperm and egg; it signals the result of sexual union—progeny. Then time becomes central—"My mast is a bell-spire" (p. 169)—and

> The long, laid minute's bride drifts on
> Old in her cruel bed.

There is no victory over the twin evils of flesh and time. In the very act of destroying one devil—lust—he has created a worse one. He has conquered flesh:

> Oh all the wanting flesh his enemy
> Thrown to the sea in the shell of a girl.
>
> (p. 170)
>
> The tempter under the eyelid
> Who shows to the selves asleep
> Mast-high moon-white women naked
>
> Walking in wishes and lovely for shame
> Is dumb and gone with his flame of brides.
>
> . . . . .
>
> Sin who had a woman's shape
> Sleeps till Silence blows on a cloud
> And all the lifted waters walk and leap.

And the prince of devils himself, Lucifer (appropriately associated with snow and ice—"Out of the sides of the north"),

> Has melted away and is lost
> Is always lost in her vaulted breath.
>
> (p. 171)

He has, in other words, satiated his sexual hunger. The fisherman has "no more desire than a ghost" (p. 172). But in achieving that sexual tranquillity he has sown his seed, he has thrown out "his line," he has cast forth his "gold gut." Now as he winds his reel he finds the miraculous multiplication of loaves and fishes being re-enacted in the monstrous progeny of time; out of the womb,

> Out of the urn the size of a man
> Out of the room the weight of his trouble
> Out of the house that holds a town,

comes new life. Time is reborn.

> The centuries throw back their hair
> And the old men sing from newborn lips:
> *Time is bearing another son.*
> *Kill time!*
>
> (p. 173)

The great god-devil Time possesses the fisherman through the instrument by which he sought to evade time—sex. In this dream sea of the unconscious, of the womb, the fisherman's "rod" becomes a dowser's willow twig. But instead of divining water his rod divines land. That land is the fallen world, Jericho blown on Eden. It is Eden's green and virgin land populated with the world as we know it:

> A garden holding to her hand
> With birds and animals
>
> With men and women and waterfalls
> Trees cool and dry in the whirlpool of ships
> And stunned and still on the green, laid veil
> Sand with legends in its virgin laps
>
> And prophets loud on the burned dunes.

But it also has the serpent-insect, "insects and valleys," "Time and places," "seasons and clouds" (p. 174). It is not the paradisiacal world he sought. The catch is the world of generation and destruction—"Rome and Sodom To-morrow and London"—it is a world ruled by time and time's symbol, the steeple: "steeples pierce the cloud on her shoulder" (p. 175).

There is nothing left of the womb dream, the sea. There is nothing left of the Edenic orchards and the country of innocent childhood wishes:

> There is nothing left of the sea but its sound,
> Under the earth the loud sea walks,
> In deathbeds of orchards the boat dies down
> And the bait is drowned among hayricks,
>
> Land, land, land, nothing remains
> Of the pacing, famous sea but its speech.
>
> (p. 176)

The anchor which once "rode like a gull/ Miles over the moonstruck boat" (p. 167) now "dives through the floors of a church," and the fisherman is "lost on the land" (p. 176).

Another poem built around a voyage metaphor, which deals with the Man-Christ-Poet figure in contact with and in combat against time and suffering, is "Lie Still, Sleep Becalmed" (p. 153). Thomas identified the world as Christ's wound both in the "Sonnets" and in "Vision and Prayer." The sufferer of this poem is both Christ and mankind, and the wound is creation itself and the fallen world of life. The sea then is the "salt sheet," the bandage that wraps the wound of God, and it is also the place of voyage and the grave of the "drowned" who died on the voyage:

> And when the salt sheet broke in a storm of singing
> The voices of all the drowned swam on the wind.

Man's passage through this "wound wrapped in the salt sheet" is also the passage of a wound through salt. It is imaged as a "slow sad sail . . . of the wandering boat." The speaker calls life "my voyage . . . to the end of my wound." But he asks

the sufferer, both God and mankind, to "lie still, sleep becalmed, hide the mouth in the throat," so that the rest of us will
not be condemned or tempted to join the drowned, to give up
the voyage.

In Thomas's world, like the world of St. Paul, "all creation
groaneth and travaileth in pain until now," and, also like St.
Paul, both mankind and creation wait for regeneration: "And
not only it, but we ourselves also, who have the first-fruits of
the Spirit—we ourselves groan within ourselves, waiting for
the adoption as sons, the redemption of our body" (Romans
8:22, 23). As we have seen, a large portion of Thomas's poetry
is concerned only with the "sound flowing like blood from the
loud wound" (p. 153), the groaning of mankind and creation.
But Thomas's hope and vision of redemption becomes more
and more evident as *Collected Poems* progresses. Almost in
spite of himself he finds

> That the closer I move
> To death, one man through his sundered hulks,
> The louder the sun blooms
> And the tusked, ramshackling sea exults.
>
> (p. 193)

III
REGENERATION

The plethora of rebirth imagery which marks the final
quarter of *Collected Poems* is one of the most striking develop-
ments in Thomas's poetry. Nearly every one of the major
poems written after 1941—the war poems, the poems to his
children, the birthday poems, the incomplete "Country
Heaven" trilogy—each has perpetuity or regeneration as its
central theme. There are notable exceptions to this general
movement: "Fern Hill" concludes that "time held me green
and dying/ Though I sang in my chains like the sea" (p. 180),

which is more in keeping with the view of the earlier poetry, as is the "revolt" theme previously noted in "Lament." But the dominant tone of the later poetry is restorative; it presents a view of life regenerated. The anguish of a creation whose end is decay, and of a fallen world characterized by a fatal marriage to sex and time and by the opposition of flesh and spirit, becomes reconciled in a gigantic body which creates and recreates deathlessly.[28]

Although the final poems are overwhelming in their symbolic promise of a regenerated world, they do not present a completely realized paradise. We have nothing comparable to the *Paradiso* and Dante's vision of the redeemed enthroned as petals of the divine rose, nor do we even approximate Blake's "Night the Ninth" in *The Four Zoas*, where all the dead awake to the last judgment and men walk through flames and live. We have in Thomas, rather, a poet continually striving to transmute, out of the natural signs of perpetuity, a vision of man's own immortality. By the use of movements from dark to light, from winter to spring, by instances of sexual fulfillment and religious rituals, by such traditional symbols as the phoenix, and by pastoral and Edenic analogues, Thomas gives us glimpses of what that "other" state of existence might be like. But it is a condition which he as poet and we as readers must look upon from afar. Like Moses, we all stand atop Mt. Pisgah and gaze toward a promised land. It is a land which owes much to literary tradition, to the Bible, to modern psychology, to animism, and to numerous other occult and theological positions whose presence is more a matter of tone

[28] Frye, in *Fearful Symmetry*, p. 423, commenting on modern literature being part of a "great mythopoeic age," says that in *Finnegans Wake* and numerous other modern works "we are being told once more that the form of reality is either that of a gigantic human body or of an unending series of cycles, and that the artist's function is to achieve an epiphany of the former out of the chaos of nature and history."

than of demonstrable certainty. Although the land is not clear in all its particulars, we know its outlines, and, more important, we know that it is a symbolic world toward which the poetry has been moving.

At the outset, Thomas saw birth as the beginning of death; toward the end, he came to view birth as the beginning of a cycle which culminated in an entrance into "the sundering ultimate kingdom of genesis' thunder" (p. 146). By 1939 the more optimistic view was beginning to be manifest. Although he sees his son being bullied into the "rough seas" of existence by the "witchlike midwife second," he admonishes him (in an obvious counterpoint to Shakespeare's "Cry Havoc!") to "Cry joy" (p. 107).[29] And in a companion poem, " 'If My Head Hurt . . . ,' " the woman marks the birth of her son by saying, "the endless beginning of prodigies suffers open" (p. 109).

This shift of attitude toward birth, and consequently toward life and death as well, is the substance of "Vision and Prayer." It reveals the tension of the "common lazarus" (cf. John 11) who "prays/ Never to awake and arise" (p. 163) but who nevertheless is "found" (p. 165) and comes

To   dumbfounding   haven
And the finding one
And the high noon
Of his wound
Blinds my
Cry.

(p. 157)

The movement from dark to light—the poem begins with the dark running "over the ghost" (p. 154) and ends with light-

---

[29] Thomas himself said of this work, "It's an optimistic, taking-everything, poem. The two most important words are 'Cry Joy.'" Watkins, p. 45.

ning and sun (p. 165)—is underlined by a subtle adaptation of baptism imagery. The speaker of the poem, contemplating the birth of his child, says in the first stanza:

> In the birth bloody room unknown
> To the burn and turn of time
> And the heart print of man
> Bows no baptism
> But dark alone
> Blessing on
> The wild
> Child.

At the poem's end, however, the rite of incorporation into the *élan vital* has been accomplished. It is not effected by the pouring of ordinary water but by the fiery liquids from the heart of the theocentric universe—the sun:

> But the loud sun
> Christens down
> The sky.
> I
> Am found
> O let him
> Scald me and drown
> Me in his world's wound.

Although this is an expression of Thomas's affirmation, of his belief in the worth and value of human life, it is an agonizing expression. What he announces here is the movement from the horrible confusion of the purposeless world to the horrible reality of the purposeful world, what Blake speaks of as "the terrors of Creation and Redemption and Judgment." For he prayed "In the name of the wanton/ Lost on the unchristened mountain" (p. 161), and his prayer was that they not know the suffering and terror of rebirth, that they be allowed to remain "In the interpreted evening/ And the known dark of the earth" (p. 164). The whole poem, then, turns on the analogy between the birth of a child out of the safety and darkness of the womb into the terror and pain of the birth process and the blinding sun of life, and the rebirth or redemption of man out of the "known dark" into the "dazzling prison" and lightning of the "blinding/One." Despite the magnificence of the goal, the process is painful and terrifying. But the wonder of creation startles him into love of life and desire for redemption:

> I turn the corner of prayer and burn
> In a blessing of the sudden
> Sun.

And "the sun roars at the prayer's end" (p. 165).

Love is the transmuting element that turns the fallen world into the redeemed world. Thomas says as much in nearly all of his later poems, but each time he uses a slightly varied combination of symbolic equations. "A Winter's Tale," for example, employs winter-spring, sexual fulfillment, the phoenix, and the cup and bread as prime metaphors for saying that a man may achieve a state of bliss, Nirvana, release from the "crest of grief" (p. 132), fulfillment for his hunger and need.

"A Winter's Tale" is the tale of rebirth which nature tells even in the dead of winter, and it is likewise the tale told about desiring man, "the believer lost and the hurled outcast of light" (p. 133). The "winter's tale" is told by the "snow blind twilight" as the poem opens. It is told by the voices of the remembered spring—the nightingale, the "voice of the dust of water from the withered spring" (p. 133), "the wizened/ Stream," "the gristed leaves," and even the "carved mouths in the rock" (p. 134). The telling of nature is the answer to the man "torn and alone" (p. 131), "forsaken and afraid" (p. 132).

It is a gesture or a sound in the telling that reveals the meaning of death—"It was a hand or sound/ In the long ago land that glided the dark door wide." The "dark door" is perception, and when it is thrown open there appears the mystic bride, the "she bird" who combines the symbolic red and white of fulfillment, perfection, the ideal state, "her breast with snow and scarlet downed." [30] Once the knowledge or awareness of the symbol of rebirth appears, all that had been seen as dead comes alive. "The dancers move/ On the departed, snow bushed green," the "centaur dead, turn and tread the drenched white/ Paddocks" (p. 134). (In "Poem on His Birthday" Thomas says Heaven is a place "where souls grow wild/ As horses in the foam," p. 192).

The bird has come to make life meaningful to the "hurled outcast of light" and to bring him with her. In this meaningful life, everything is done for love: "The dead oak walks for love," "For love, the long ago she bird rises" (p. 134). Now that the man has seen the fulfillment of life, release from his sorrows, he follows her. In this pursuit of the ideal all the fallen world rejoices, for in the prayer and the bird who came in answer to the prayer all nature sees its redemption: "all the elements of the slow fall rejoiced/ That a man knelt alone in the cup of the vales" (p. 135).

Now, as is customary in fairy tales and legends of wish-fulfillment, the man follows the bird.[31] "He ran like a wind after the kindling flight" in his quest for immortality:

[30] Evelyn Underhill, *Mysticism* (Meridian, New York, 1955), p. 146.
[31] Søren Kierkegaard, in *Fear and Trembling and The Sickness unto Death*, trans. Walter Lowrie (Anchor, New York, 1954), p. 170, refers to this in his discussion of possibility: "Fairy-tales and legends so often relate that a knight suddenly perceived a rare bird, which he continues to run after, since at the beginning it seemed as if it were so very near—but then it flies off again, until at last night falls, and he has become separated from his companions."

"Legend of Adam and Eve"

All night lost and long wading in the wake of the she-
Bird through the times and lands and tribes of the slow flakes.

(p. 135)

Thomas does not leave the bird symbol without sufficient synonym. In fact, he supplies the reader with some of the numerous ideals she typifies. Some of these are sexual, but that they are meant allegorically Thomas makes very apparent:

The sky, the bird, the bride,
The cloud, the need, the planted stars, the joy beyond
The fields of seed and the time dying flesh astride,
The heavens, the heaven, the grave, the burning font.

(p. 136)

In death the man and the bird are united. The "door of his death" opens to a second and completed vision which he had sought after the opening of the first "dark door" (p. 134). The man who had "knelt alone in the cup of the vales" is now "on a bread white hill over the cupped farm" (p. 136)—he has attained his vision. And the earth, the world of nature, is seen as the sacramental cup and bread, the ritual foundation of his vision. This is why the whole tale takes place "Once when the world turned old/ On a star of faith pure as the drifting bread" (p. 131), and after the tale ends "The rite is shorn" (p. 136).

The final four stanzas of the poem are an intense recapitulation of the preceding twenty-two stanzas. The first two of these concluding stanzas bring us back to the condition in the poem before the apparition of the bird; the final two relate the final effect of the bird's appearance. Everything that had come alive with the bird—the village, the minstrel dead, the nightingale, and the centaur—disappears back into death and winter, still waiting for the resurrection, the "trumpeting dawn."

The rite is shorn
Of nightingale and centaur dead horse. The springs wither
Back. Lines of age sleep on the stones till trumpeting dawn.
Exultation lies down. Time buries the spring weather
That belled and bounded with the fossil and the dew reborn.

(p. 136)

But the man does not return to the winter of his hunger and
need; he is reborn. Joined with the bird in the nuptials of
death, brought to the bridal chamber of the grave, the man
finds the mystic "still point of the turning world." He lay with
the bird "bedded/ In a choir of wings . . . and he was
hymned and wedded." This "woman breasted and . . .
heaven headed/ Bird" (p. 137) is now clearly a figure of androgynous divinity. (In Genesis, for example, the Hebrew
word for Almighty God, "El Shaddai," means "woman
breasted." "Heaven headed" speaks for itself.) The man
who had knelt and wept and prayed

> By the spit and the black pot in the log bright light
> And the cup and the cut bread in the dancing shade,
>
> . . . . .
>
> At the point of love
>
> (p. 132)

has now been

> brought low,
> Burning in the bride bed of love, in the whirl-
> Pool at the wanting centre, in the folds
> Of paradise, in the spun bud of the world.

And from this death he rises in the spring of resurrection:
"And she rose with him flowering in her melting snow" (p.
137).

Thomas regarded three of his last poems—"In Country
Sleep," "Over Sir John's Hill" and "In the White Giant's

Thigh"—as parts of a single poem-in-progress.[32] Considered as parts of one long poem, these three works reveal a complete development of Thomas's redemptive concepts. They form a complete picture of the god-universe and the man-divinity being merged and yet, paradoxically, still carrying on their respective man or God functions. In order to see more clearly this penultimate development of Thomas's regeneration myth, it is best we begin by looking at the unity of these poems through Thomas's own eyes.

In 1950, during a B.B.C. reading, Thomas described the plan into which the three poems would fit as "grand and simple." The "grand" part of the design is that he fashioned an optimistic and a regenerative view of human existence. The "simple" part of the plan is, as might be suspected, the account Thomas gives of it. The description is not of the poems as they actually exist, and does not very well explain their relationship, but it does provide invaluable insights into what Thomas was striving to achieve.

Thomas explained the grand design by saying the "godhead . . . black-baller . . . woe-bearer" weeps when one of his worlds (the earth) murders itself. At the outset of the proposed long poem, which he called "In Country Heaven," God weeps "and Country Heaven is suddenly dark. Bushes and owls blow out like candles." The human inhabitants of heaven wonder which of the worlds has destroyed itself, and, when they learn it is their former home, they begin to exchange stories of earth. "And, one by one, these heavenly hedgerow-men, who once were of the Earth, call one another, through the long night, Light and His tears falling, what they remember, . . . what they know in their Edenie [sic] hearts, of that self-called place. They remember places, fears, loves,

---

[32] *Quite Early One Morning*, pp. 178–179.

exultation, misery, animal joy, ignorance and mysteries, all *we know and do not know.*" [33]

Thus, it seems, Thomas would have us regard "In Country Sleep," "Over Sir John's Hill," and "In the White Giant's Thigh" as remembered tellings of inhabitants of country heaven. (Thomas is not using "remembered" in the conventional sense—as we mentioned in Chapter Two. Instead "the rememberer may live himself back into active participation in the remembered scene, adventure, or spiritual condition.") Thomas's explanation of God weeping and heavenly men telling of their earth serves as a frame for the poems in that it puts all the poems *sub specie aeternitatis* and, consequently, allows us to connect the Thief and child, the sparrow and hawk, the women and the hill. For all finally become meaningful under a concept of a divinity who is both within nature and outside of nature.

When Thomas made these comments about these three poems being "separate parts of a long poem," he also said that "some of the long poem is written down on paper, some of it is in a rough draft in the head, and the rest of it radiantly unworded in ambitious conjecture." [34] Fortunately, at least one copy of "In Country Heaven" has survived (see footnote 14), and that manuscript fragment forms an interesting complement to Thomas's remarks on the grand design into which the final three long poems fit.

"In Country Heaven" equates God, the human heart, and nature, and even more particularly the hill, and yet at the same time retains the perception of God as an individual spirit. This poem shows maker and first cause of Creation subsumed under a God of love and of pity who cosmically prays and weeps for man. At the opening of the poem God

[33] *Ibid.*, p. 179.   [34] *Ibid.*, p. 177.

Crosses the breast of the praising East, and kneels,
    Humble in all his planets,
      And weeps on the abasing hill.

The symbol of heaven is nature; heaven is "the canonized valley," where "angels whirr like pheasants." Heaven is a place of "seraphic fields," with "God's bright, flocks, the belled lambs leaping,/ (His gentle kind)," and the hawk is a shooting star who is "locked blind in a lame cloud." "Heaven's cities" are also sacred, they are "the twelve apostles' towns," and though the marauding fox still prowls there, the "farms of Heaven's keeping,/ . . . sleep sound." They sleep sound because the final element of existence is pity:

    For the fifth element is pity,
      (Pity for death);
No fowl or field mouse that night of his kneeling
    Lies in the fox's fires
  Or twice dies in the screechowl's eyes.

This glimpse of paradise that Thomas fashioned sometime between 1946 and 1949 was apparently put aside in order to view eternity through human eyes, rather than the world through God's eyes. Eventually, Thomas might have gone back to the "In Country Heaven" manuscript and completed the "long poem." But it is not necessary that he should have done so in order for us to see how he would bring man from mortality to immortality. In the "remembered" tales of "In Country Sleep," "Over Sir John's Hill," and "In the White Giant's Thigh," he sufficiently developed his mythopoeic vision of the regenerated world.

"In Country Heaven" describes eternity as the world without death—but Thomas did not find it so easy to banish death from the world. It is this problem that the three "remembrances" try to resolve. The first, "In Country Sleep," is a

poem directed at a sleeping child. The poem moves from the child and her protected innocence to nature and its sanctity to the "Thief" who falls upon the world "Silent as the cyclone of silence" (p. 183). The second part begins by reaffirming the miracle of life as manifested in nature, repeats the constant efforts of the Thief to steal her faith, and concludes with an assertion that the child "shall wake, from country sleep, this dawn and each first dawn" (p. 186). At first glance, the poem appears repetitious and contradictory. The repetition is certainly part of the poet's effort to enchant the reader, to spellbind him by a Whitmanesque piling up of description. The contradictions would appear to lie in the poem's opening by admonishing the child not to "fear or believe" that the wolf shall devour her, and concluding with the warning that she must always "believe and fear" that the Thief "comes to leave her in the lawless sun awaking/ Naked and forsaken to grieve he will not come."

The resolution to this apparent contradiction and to the meaning of the poem lies in the identification of the half-dozen major images of the poem. The "country sleep" which the child experiences is a symbol of death. And the meaning of the final confusing lines turns on a distinction to which we have previously alluded. The thing the child should fear is that the Thief will leave her in a "lawless sun." If, however, she retains her faith in nature, she need not fear.

The religious imagery associated with nature and the country becomes a kind of catechism of the faith the poet would confer on the child. Nature is heaven because, as we saw in discussing "In Country Heaven," all the attributes of nature except *death* become a description of eternity. In "In Country Sleep" we still have death (symbolized by the Thief), but we should know by the sacramentality of nature that it will transcend death:

"Legend of Adam and Eve"

A hill touches an angel! Out of a saint's cell
The nightbird lauds through nunneries and domes of leaves
Her robin breasted tree, three Marys in the rays.

The "holy of holies," the "*Sanctum sanctorum* [is] the animal eye of the wood/ In the rain telling its beads" (p. 182). There is a "beat of blood through the laced leaves," and a "surpliced/ Hill of cypresses." The whole of nature is a miraculous prayer. It is a "saga from mermen/ To seraphim," it is "Music of elements, that a miracle makes!" (pp. 184–185).

The speaker is telling his daughter to have faith in this miracle of life, not to fear the wolf but to fear the Thief who can steal her faith. The Thief is time and, consequently, death. In calling time a Thief he is also drawing attention to the New Testament descriptions of Christ as the Thief—"The Lord will come as a thief in the night" (Peter II, 3:10)—and especially Revelation 16:15 where Christ says: "Behold, I come as a thief! Blessed is he who watches and keeps his garments, lest he walk naked, and they see his shame." The garments which Revelation would have the believer keep are the garments of faith. The Thief of the Apocalypse does not, however, come to steal the faith of the believer, as Thomas's Thief does. The Thief of "In Country Sleep" comes to steal her faith in "the saga of prayer." If the adult believed as fervently as the child in the fairy magic of nature, he would finally want the Thief to come; he would want to wake "from country sleep" to find that deathless faith of which miraculous nature is but a figure.

The primary law of animal existence is cannibalism. All living matter from the amoeba to man devours other living organisms in order to live. If "the country is holy" (p. 182), if all the elements of nature are miraculous and eternal, some judgment is necessary concerning this fundamental cannibal-

275

ism. This judgment is given in "Over Sir John's Hill." The
hawk symbolizes devouring nature; he is the executioner who
"pulls to his claws/ And gallows, up the rays of his eyes the
small birds of the bay" (p. 187). The hawk, like all nature,
calls, "Come and be killed." And the poet, like St. John who
heard a "voice from heaven like the sound of many waters"
(Revelation 14:2), opens "the leaves of the water at a passage/
Of psalms" and finds the meaning of his fable about the
sparrows' death.

First of all, death is not blamed on the slayer: "all praise of
the hawk on fire in hawk-eyed dusk be sung." The emphasis
falls rather on the innocent victims, "who cluck, 'dilly dilly,/
Come let us die!'" (p. 188). But in their slaughter they
become "blest," although they, at the same time, are judged
guilty of death by the forces of nature:

> the heron and I, under judging Sir John's elmed
> Hill, tell-tale the knelled
> Guilt
> Of the led-astray birds.
>
> (p. 189)

The judgment of Sir John's Hill is Thomas's judgment of the
world. It is a judgment of the beauty and value and purpose of
life. The poem announces praise for the hawk, guilt for the
sparrows. The hawk is praised because he continues the life
process, and, although the sparrows must die (they have been
led astray and are guilty because of the nature of life), they too
are of infinite worth. Thus the poet (and the heron—because
the heron is sacerdotal and a symbol of the holiness of nature)
asks mercy for the souls of the slain birds. The appeal for
mercy, and the religious attitude of the speaker, echoes
Matthew 10:28–29 (a passage which also shows the thematic

relationship of this poem to "In Country Sleep"): "Fear not them which kill the body, but are not able to kill the soul: but rather fear him which is able to destroy both soul and body in hell. Are not two sparrows sold for a farthing? and one of them shall not fall to the ground without your Father." This is the basis for the poet's prayer that God

> for their breast of whistles,
> Have mercy on,
> God in his whirlwind silence save, who marks the sparrows hail,
> For their souls' song.
>
> (p. 189)

The implication is, clearly, that there will be mercy. For the poet says at the poem's end that he has engraved these words "for the sake of the souls of the slain birds sailing." If the birds are "sailing," then there is already some note of regeneration implied.

Thomas, in "In the White Giant's Thigh," reverses the common platitude about human beings continuing to live through their children. He takes here as his subject those women who in their lifetime never conceived and finds that they do produce new life in death. Although the most pan-theistic of Thomas's rebirth poems, even this poem cannot be regarded as *simply* pantheistic. For from these dead women he not only draws the knowledge of man's participation in the ever-creating earth, but he also learns of a love that survives the grave. These "dead and deathless . . . women of the hill" teach him the "love that is evergreen" (p. 199).

There has been considerable confusion over just what the "white giant" is that the poem refers to. That it is a landmark in Wales is clear enough. But one critic has insisted that it is also the locale of some Welsh legend and marks the spot from which a group of young women leaped to their deaths rather than be taken away from their husbands.[35] If it is a real landmark, it is not included in the usual guidebooks to England and Wales. Thomas himself said that he had "never seen the White Giant and had no idea of its location, if any." But he understood that "barren girls" came to the Giant in the cause of fertility and that boys were waiting there to oblige—without success.[36] The question of legend or of allusion to a "real" geographical landmark seems slightly irrelevant. Thomas thought that there was such a place, and he embellished it for his own purposes, forming the hillside landmark into a living creature—in whom and by whom the dead women were now deathless.

The first eleven lines of the poem picture the poet walking at night in a graveyard on the side of a hill where he imagines the long-dead women still longing for creativity. These women, however, are yearning not only "to labour and love" but also for "the unconceived/ And immemorial sons of the cudgelling, hacked/ Hill." Their yearning, then, is analogous to the creative urge in all nature, and the poet perceives their yearning within nature, specifically in the cries of the curlews.

The central section of the poem carries the analogy further. The women's love-making is described in terms of animal and vegetable life, suggesting that even in life the human creative urge is the same as that of nature. The women were "a hedgerow of joys" (p. 197); they had "buttermilk manes" and were like the blooms on the hawthorn bushes. Their flesh was "rooted" by the swineherd and "trounced" by the wings of their "gander king." Furthermore, their love-making was il-

---

[35] Marlene Chambers, "Thomas' IN THE WHITE GIANT'S THIGH," *Explicator*, XIX (March, 1961), 39.
[36] Tindall, *Reader's Guide*, p. 293.

licit, amoral, like that of nature. They were "wayside brides in the hawed house" (p. 198). Nevertheless, for one reason or another, they all remained barren—they were all a "boulder of wives."

The line, "Now curlew cry me down to kiss the mouths of their dust" (p. 199) is essentially a restatement of the earlier line, "Now clasp me to their grains in the gigantic glade" (p. 197). Not only is this a call to the poet to respond to the elemental creative drive reflected in nature, and an aspect of his own death-wish. It is also part of the "remembering" of the "heavenly hedgerow men."

In the final section of the poem (p. 199), the poet asks these women to teach him "the love that is evergreen" not only after the burial itself but also after the names have been worn off the gravestones and even those who loved them are dead and part of the "fox-cubbed streets" and "crumbling wood." And the answer is given: the women love their dead lovers who are now, like the women, free of death because they are beyond life—"dead and deathless." Their love is forever culminated in the meridian of the earth from which grow the "courters' trees" to shelter new lovers, as they themselves were once sheltered "in the courters' lanes." And life goes on; "The daughters of darkness flame like Fawkes fires still."

In the course of spelling out the Biblical rhythm, we have encountered these figures: Jehovah, Satan, Adam, Abraham, Cain, Jacob, Samson, Jesus, and, finally, Noah. The Adam-Christ-Poet composite is constant, but in each phase of the poetry it takes on slightly different overtones. The three modifying figures of the poetry are Jehovah, Samson, and Noah. The jealous God, the first cause, is the figure under which the early poetry labors—in awe, in mockery, in creation. Samson, although only explicit in two poems, is nevertheless the representative figure of the fallen world. Finally, it is Noah, the savior of mankind and nature, who epitomizes the poetry of regeneration.

In the "Author's Prologue" Thomas invokes the primitive archetype of the flood to symbolize metamorphosis from the natural cycle to a new and a higher kind of life. That the sea in this poem is not primarily a Freudian sea and that Thomas is not simply imaging a return to the womb is indicated by the use that Thomas makes of the ark figure. Thomas the man and the poet is the Noah's ark which sails into the primordial flood. ("Man is the Ark of God," said Blake.) [37] This is the explanation for the baffling lines toward the end of the poem (xviii)

> We will ride out alone, and then,
> Under the stars of Wales,
> Cry, Multitudes of arks.

What Thomas sees as he sails out to die, alone with all his poetic creations, are the stars. At the poem's opening the day was "winding down," a third of the way into the poem "the salmon, sucked sun slips," shortly thereafter the moon appears and, finally, the stars. The stars, then, are what caused Thomas to shout "Multitudes of arks." He identifies them with men. (He times the birth of his daughter, "since the falling star you were born," p. 183, and he describes the stars as "mansouled fiery islands," p. 193.) Thus Thomas not only sees himself as Noah saving his world, he also sees each man as a Noah:

> Across
> The water lidded lands,
> Manned with their loves they'll move,
> Like wooden islands, hill to hill.

This is the summation of Thomas's vision of regeneration, the thematic and symbolic climax of the Biblical rhythm that

[37] Keynes ed., I, p. 108.

"Legend of Adam and Eve"

unites his poetry. It is epitomized in the ending of "Prologue," where the faith he found for his daughter, the mercy he found for the sparrows, and the perpetuity he found for the barren women becomes a symbolic regeneration for himself:

> My ark sings in the sun
> At God speeded summer's end
> And the flood flowers now.

CHAPTER SIX

Beyond Good and Evil

We are not wholly bad or good
Who live our lives under Milk Wood,
And Thou, I know, wilt be the first
To see our best side, not our worst.
Rev. Eli Jenkins in *Under Milk Wood*

Before the sun sinks I'll lie there in their arms
For they're *good* bad boys from the lonely farms.
Polly Garter in *Under Milk Wood*

AT first encounter, the disparity between the "high serious-ness" of *Collected Poems* and the music-hall quality of *Under Milk Wood* is apt to be shocking. The prophetic Noah of the poetry's "Prologue" seems to have yielded to an almost vaude-villian interlocutor; the poet is replaced by the comedian. But in point of fact, *Under Milk Wood* was neither a radical shift in Thomas's creative effort nor a complete departure from the regenerative vision expressed in so much of the last poetry.

Obviously, *Under Milk Wood* does indicate a shift in style and attitude. But what must be stressed is that this "Play for Voices" was a long time in preparation, that it was the culmination of a significant aspect of Thomas's art. Daniel

Jones, in his Preface to *Under Milk Wood*,[1] explains the appearance of the work in this manner: "The publication of Thomas's *Collected Poems* in 1953 marked the end of one period of his literary development; after this, according to his own words, he intended to turn from the strictly personal kind of poetry to a more public form of expression, and to large-scale dramatic works, in particular, where there would be scope for all his versatility, for his gifts of humour and characterisation as well as his genius for poetry."[2]

The truth of the matter, however, is that Thomas's "genius for poetry" is not evident in any of his dramatic works, and what we admire in *Under Milk Wood*, specifically, is its comedy. In terms of poetry, there is in *Under Milk Wood* a good deal of what we earlier referred to as the merely decorative use of auditory techniques:

> By Sawddwy, Senny, Dovey, Dee,
> Edw, Eden, Aled, all,
> Taff and Towy broad and free,
> Llyfnant with its waterfall,
>
> Claerwen, Cleddau, Dulais, Daw,
> Ely, Gwili, Ogwr, Nedd,
> Small is our River Dewi, Lord,
> A baby on a rushy bed.[3]

And if the reader is prone to add that these lines are a perfect parody of sentimental Welsh verse sometimes heard at an Eisteddfod, so much the better. It is sentimental verse that exaggerates sound in expressing the commonplace. And more importantly, it is precisely the whole network of parody—along with a folk earthiness—that enables *Under Milk Wood* to escape the pall of sentimentality which threatens all the folk

---

[1] *Under Milk Wood* (New York, 1954), vii–xi.
[2] *Ibid.*, vii.   [3] *Ibid.*, p. 28.

of Llareggub. Because everything in the world of the play is parodied, even the poet himself, the final effect is not one of ridicule or rejection but rather of a completely unreal world, a completely comic world.

Jones's Preface likewise touches on the genesis of *Under Milk Wood*. He was the first to point out that the play went back more than ten years before its 1953 production in New York City, back to a B.B.C. script called, like the book, "Quite Early One Morning." The work passed through a succession of forms and titles before it reached its final form in October, 1953.

The proper background of *Under Milk Wood*, however, is Thomas's humorous prose—the mildly grotesque humor of such stories as "After the Fair" (1934) and "Adventures in the Skin Trade" (1939). As early as 1940, with the publication of *Portrait of the Artist as a Young Dog*, Thomas's "gifts of humour and characterisation" were fully revealed. The stories in that volume—"The Peaches," "A Visit to Grandpa's," "Patricia, Edith, and Arnold"—won for Thomas his first large reading audience, *this* long before the more direct poetry of his final period saw print. Almost all the best comic touches of *Under Milk Wood* can be found in earlier Thomas writings, and these touches are there without the commercial jingo and barroom bawdry of *Under Milk Wood*. These stories, like the play, have their origin in Thomas's life in and knowledge of the Carmarthenshire country.

Under Milk Wood is neither good poetry nor good drama; it has touches of great comedy (Mr. Pugh's feeble plotting against his wife and Mrs. Ogmore-Pritchard's cleanliness, for example). If only for this reason, it is a fitting work for Thomas's farewell to the world of creative expression. A writer's last works of art tell us neither more nor less than what his state of mind was when he reached the end of his career. Thus *The Tempest* crowns Shakespeare's comic vision, and James's *The Golden Bowl* completes the moral esthetic that his last novels were moving toward. Thomas did not know that *Under Milk Wood* would be his last work, but he could not have planned it better if he had. With all its incompleteness, its romantic and overblown rhetoric, its man-of-the-pub wit and fairy-tale timelessness, it summed up Thomas: the man and the work.

What Thomas hoped to achieve with *Under Milk Wood* he set forth very clearly in a letter to Countess Caetani, the first publisher of the work:

Out of my working . . . came the idea that I write a piece, a play, an impression for voices, an entertainment out of the darkness, of the town I live in, and to write it simply and warmly & comically with lots of movement and varieties of moods, so that, at many levels, through sight and speech, description & dialogue, evocation and parody, you came to know the town. . . .

As the piece goes on, two voices will be predominant: that of the preacher, who talks only in verse, and that of the anonymous exhibitor and chronicler called, simply, 1st Voice. And the 1st Voice is really a kind of conscience, a guardian angel. Through him you will learn about our Edwards, the draper, and Miss Price, the sempstress, & their odd and once it is made clear, most natural love: Every day of the week they write love letters to each other, he from the top, she from the bottom, of the town: all their lives they have known of each other's existence, and of their mutual love: they have seen each other a thousand times, & never spoken: easily they could have been together, married, had children: but that is not the life for them: their passionate love, at just this distance, is all they need. And Dai Bread the baker, who has two wives, one is loving & mothering, sacklike & jolly: the other is gypsy slatternly and, all in love, hating: all three enjoy it. And Mrs Ogmore-Pritchard who, although a boardinghouse keeper, will keep no boarders because they cannot live up to the scrupulous & godlike tidiness of her house and because death can be the only boarder good enough for her in the end. And Mr Pugh, the schoolmaster, who is always nagged by his wife and who is always plotting her murder. This is wellknown to the town, & to Mrs Pugh. She likes nagging; he likes plotting, in supposed secrecy, against her. He would always like plotting, whoever he lived with; she would always like nagging, whoever she lived with. How lucky they are to be married. And Polly Garter has many illegitimate babies because she loves babies but does not want only one man's. And Cherry Owen the soak, who likes getting drunk every night; & his wife who likes living with two men, one sober in the day, one drunk at night. And the cobbler who thinks the town is the wickedest place to live in the world, but who can never leave it while there is a hope of reforming it; and, oh, the savour his cries of Gomorrah add to the pleasure of the little town wicked. And the old woman who every morning shouts her age to the heavens; she believes the town is the chosen land, & the little river Dewi the River of Jordan; she is not at all mad: she merely believes in heaven on earth. And so with all of them, all the eccentrics whose eccentricities, in these first pages, are but briefly & impressionistically noted: all, by their own rights, are ordinary & good; and the 1st Voice, & the poet preacher, never judge nor condemn but explain and make strangely simple & simply strange.[4]

Little more needs to be said about the drama itself. It needs only to be re-emphasized that the play is both humorous and comic—comic in the fundamental sense of being a presentation of a happily constituted society, life commodious and harmonious. It pictures a town, mankind, under a dreamlike dispensation which makes good and evil, right and wrong, superfluous terms.

There are some critics, and Holbrook is the best example, who feel that *Under Milk Wood* is amoral, salacious, a parody

[4] *Botteghe Oscure*, XIII (1954), pp. 94–96.

of all serious and civilizing forces. They charge that the work shows no character change or development. Such a view is about as relevant as saying Captain Ahab had no sense of humor. True, the play is a direct outgrowth of Thomas's rebellious immaturity; it is a final slap at the establishment, a thumbing of his nose at society. But it is to miss the spirit of the play, even its *donnée*, to judge it in terms of a morality it repudiates and not to consider the structure of its own morality.

Under Milk Wood does not simply create a dream world, it also creates an ideal world. It is a world which dotes on foibles and follies, selfishness and indulgence, but concludes that the ridiculous things are wonderful and the shortcomings have a rationality which justifies—as Thomas explained in discussing the "odd" but "most natural love" of Mr. Edwards and Miss Price. It is not that *Under Milk Wood* does not see the failures of men; it sees them all too well, but it tells us to laugh at them.

What is most real in this stage town is that the ugly and the beautiful, the innocent and the guilty, are rendered from the view of an indulgent parent. The town prostitute is not so much a prostitute as a lover of babies who ever longs for her one true love, no matter what man she lies with. The "no-good" boy of the town really wants "to be *good* Boyo, but nobody'll let me." [5] Sinbad Sailors watches the coquettish Gossamer Beynon and sees her, "demure and proud and schoolmarm in her crisp flower dress and sun-defying hat, with never a look or lilt or wriggle, the butcher's unmelting icemaiden daughter veiled forever from the hungry hug of his eyes." [6] And Sinbad romantically sighs, "Oh, beautiful beautiful Gossamer B, I wish I wish that you were for me. I wish you

[5] *Under Milk Wood*, p. 80.   [6] *Ibid.*, pp. 67–68.

were not so educated." Contrary to his name there is no evil in "Sinbad."

The town drunk likewise is not a reprehensible figure—just the opposite, he is twice-loved. He is loved by his wife as a sober man and loved by her as a drunkard. And the nagging wife nags because she loves nagging, and the nagged husband plots her murder not because he will ever kill her but because he loves to plot. "How lucky they are to be married," comments Thomas. "And so with all of them, all the eccentrics . . . all, by their own right, are ordinary and good." There is no judgment or condemnation in *Under Milk Wood*.

One of the most interesting aspects of *Under Milk Wood* is what it points back to in Thomas's work and what it points forward to as the future course of his work. It points back to all that was entertaining in Thomas; it emphasizes comedy over concern, parody over poetry, wit over vision. It marks the end of Thomas as a romantic visionary. Whatever there was of the young poet who called himself a spiritualist seems to have vanished in *Under Milk Wood*. Even the romantic proclivities disappear. Childhood, for example, is more realistically presented in the drama than anywhere else in Thomas. The Reverend Eli Jenkins remembers, sadly, the drunken father of his boyhood. Mr. Waldo sings:

> In Pembroke City when I was young
> I lived by the Castle Keep
> Sixpence a week was my wages
> For working for the chimbley sweep.
>
> . . . . .
>
> Did you ever hear a growing boy
> To live so cruel cheap
> On grub that has no flesh and bones
> And liquor that makes you weep? [7]

[7] *Ibid.*, p. 91.

Beyond Good and Evil

The claims of *Under Milk Wood* are significant only because they are the claims of a great lyric poet. By itself the play would be a fine, gusty work by a richly talented writer. As the final work of an important lyric poet, it has received—and probably will continue to receive—unusual attention. It is a very important part of Thomas's final attitude of mind and an important example of his genius for comedy. Before speculating about where *Under Milk Wood* was leading Dylan Thomas the poet, it is necessary that we make a few summary judgments about the more important matter—about the value of the poetry itself.

Dylan's mother, Mrs. D. J. Thomas, once recounted this reminiscence for an interviewer:

> I said, "You know, you must try and get to the University—what are you going to do? Anybody'd think you were a Keats or something." He looked at me—and he wasn't the cheeky type, he wasn't even a big talker—and he said, "I'll be as good as Keats, if not better." I went to his father and said, "I'll never tell him anything again." [8]

Keats continually comes to mind as a poet with whom Thomas may be compared. I doubt, however, that Thomas's reputation will ever equal that of Keats. Thomas's place on that specious and fickle exchange known as the literary stock market would probably be midway between Herrick and Keats—if any such point could be said to exist. Any comparison of poets seems necessarily to involve a good deal of special pleading, but the difference between Keats's love poetry and Thomas's is singularly significant. A good deal of the difference is a reflection of their respective historical positions; nevertheless, Keats was able to convey ranges of emotion that Thomas was unable to convey. In Keats, love has the charm of

---

[8] John Ackerman, *Dylan Thomas: His Life and Work* (London, 1964), p. 25.

"magic casements, opening on the foam/ Of perilous seas, in faery lands forlorn." It has the sensuousness of "warmed jewels" and "rich attire rustling to her knees." It has the anticipation and yearning of "a God in pain." Thomas's love is more often a generic emotion; he loved "Adam." For him, love of man and woman includes the constant presence of warfare and of lustful bestiality. In Thomas there is the contemporary fascination for the clinical, there is undeniable passion, and, there is a romantic idealism invariably presented in terms of some imagined state of childhood innocence. The child continually crops up at the end of a Thomas love poem, and the implication is that he has the better part.

Further, Thomas cannot lay claim to having been an innovator. Hopkins anticipated nearly all of Thomas's auditory practices. Yeats had a marvelous clarity of idiom lacking in Thomas, Stevens's rhetorical practices revealed fresher modes of perception, Eliot caught the mind of a generation midstream in its agony—whereas Thomas too early despaired of the mind. But while Thomas may not have been one of the geniuses of the language, one of those by whom the history of literature is altered, he was, indisputably, a master of the lyric. It is no exaggeration to say, as David Daiches does, that "no poet of his time had a keener sense of form," or to say, as Karl Shapiro does, that of all the poets of his age only Thomas "could be called a singer." [9]

It is this mastery of form that makes one labor through the intricate process of reading Thomas at his most obscure, and that gives one the sense of supreme accomplishment in his fully realized poems. Thomas's mastery of his medium is evident in nearly every poem he wrote, and in a number of poems he

[9] David Daiches, "The Poetry of Dylan Thomas," *College English*, XVI (October, 1954), 2; Karl Shapiro, *In Defense of Ignorance* (New York, 1960), p. 172.

achieves true greatness. No poet in English has written a better series of birthday poems than the four Thomas wrote: "Especially When the October Wind," "Twenty-four Years," "Poem on His Birthday," and "Poem in October." Among the finest brief elegies in the language, we would have to include "Do Not Go Gentle . . ." "A Refusal to Mourn," "Ceremony After a Fire Raid." "To-day, This Insect," "On No Work of Words," and "In My Craft or Sullen Art" must be considered memorable achievements as poems on poetry. Surely, as long as English poetry is read, some of these poems will be read. This by no means exhausts the list of Thomas's best poems. Such a list would also have to include "The Force That through the Green Fuse," "Fern Hill," "Over Sir John's Hill," "Vision and Prayer," "In Country Sleep," "A Winter's Tale," "Ballad of the Long-legged Bait," "We Lying by Seasand," "And Death Shall Have No Dominion," "The Hand That Signed the Paper," "Conversation of Prayer," "Lie Still, Sleep Becalmed," and "In the White Giant's Thigh."

When we consider only the score or so of brilliant poems, we are likely to exaggerate the importance of Thomas. In this we are like Alissa, in André Gide's novel *Strait Is the Gate*, who says, "I would give nearly all of Shelley and all of Byron for Keats's four odes . . . just as I would give all Hugo for a few of Baudelaire's sonnets. The words 'great poet' have no meaning—what is important is to be *pure* poet." [10] It was for a few lines of "associated" sensibility in *Hyperion* that the younger Eliot praised Keats above all the other romantics. Such a judgment, based on indefinable terms ("pure" poetry, for example) and a good deal of subjectivity, is the kind that makes it so difficult properly to appraise Thomas. One comes

[10] André Gide, *Strait Is the Gate*, trans. Dorothy Bussy (Vintage, New York, 1956), pp. 77–78.

quickly to realize that a vital but evasive quality of exultation, of incantation, is central to Thomas's poetry. A less physical poetry, or a poetry with a broader philosophical base, is not so dependent on precise sensibility. And the evasiveness of the quality of poetic vitality makes it difficult to come to a conclusive judgment about Thomas. When the emotional quality is successfully handled, as in the poems just cited, Thomas rises to a stature comparable to Keats's or Hopkins's. When, however, that quality is lacking, Thomas seems either pointlessly obscure or full of overblown rhetoric.

Even Thomas's most severe critics, Steiner, for example, do not deny him moments of brilliance, flashes of rare lyric achievement. Where critics disagree about Thomas is in regard to the number of great poems and the value and legitimacy of his vision. If our examination of Thomas's rational and symbolic expression has served no other purpose, it should have served to demonstrate that Thomas was no Druid delighting only in passion and vehemence. Rather than a howling iconoclast raging in his animality, Thomas was—and I am here concerned only with his poetry—the celebrant of a secular *hieros gamos* (Revelation 19:7, 21:2), a unified state of existence between man and nature where there is no death.

In his attempt to fashion a comprehensive view of existence, Thomas was one with all the major poets of the century, and his efforts are comparable to theirs in kind, although admittedly not in degree. Hart Crane with his "Bridge"; Pound with myth, history, and economics; Eliot with Frazer, philosophy, and Christianity; Yeats with occultism and Byzantium—all were seeking symbols whereby they might present a total and unified perception of human life. In the sense that Thomas attempts much the same ends with his adaptation of a Biblical *Weltansicht*, he makes larger demands upon history than would an author of a handful of exquisite lyrics. He is, then, to be viewed finally not simply as a writer of particular poems but as a poet of comprehensive vision.

It is perhaps possible—though it does not seem likely—that the longer view of history will discover qualities of visionary excellence where the contemporary critic has been unable to discover them. If we are to judge by the examples of Blake, Smart, and Whitman, it would seem prudent to conclude that what are for us the most obscure poems may be the most interesting to subsequent generations. It may be, for example, that such opaque poems as "I Dreamed My Genesis" and the "Altarwise" sequence will be regarded as wells of richness.

The limitations of Thomas, however, for our own age, remain those poems which seem like gibberish to the occasional reader and remain a quagmire to the persistent explicator. Because Thomas's most obscure poems were written before he was twenty-five, and because his most generally acclaimed poems were written after that time, one is tempted to see Thomas as a maturing poet whose career was cut short by death. The truth would seem otherwise. Thomas matured early, and by thirty-eight he was anxious to turn from lyric poetry to other forms of art. The poems Thomas was working on at the time of his death seem to me noticeably inferior to most of his other work. The "Elegy" Vernon Watkins reworked, for example, despite suggestions of new metrical interests by Thomas, cannot be compared to the earlier poem to his father, "Do Not Go Gentle." Philip Burton recalled that Thomas, a few days before his fatal journey to America, had lost interest in *Under Milk Wood* because "he was on fire with a new work . . . —a stage play." The play was tentatively entitled *Two Streets*. Burton describes it this way:

Two Streets was to be "a simple love-story." It was to be set in a small industrial town in South Wales, and it would tell of the lives of two families who live unknown to each other in neigh-bouring streets. The play would begin with the birth of the boy in one family and the girl in the other, and it might possibly end with their first meeting, in a dance-hall. There was to be little realism in the presentation, and the families would live their separate but unconsciously interwoven lives at separate ends of the stage, until at last the boy and the girl met in the middle. The first character to form a link between the families would be the midwife attending both mothers.[11]

Then there was, in this same evening with Burton, talk of the projected libretto for Igor Stravinsky. Here is the plot for that work:

The setting of the opera was to be the world destroyed by atomic warfare. Almost all life had disappeared. The scene was to be a cave in completely barren surroundings. Miraculously two young people had survived, and they had to find life again in an almost total absence of it. . . . The incident that made Dylan's imagination glow was when the boy tried to remember and explain to the girl what a tree was. Another character was to be an old prophet who had survived the doom he had foretold. As I listened, it suddenly struck me that Dylan was feeling to-wards a sort of Garden-of-Eden story. When I told him this, he was momentarily surprised and then he seized excitedly on the idea and began to embellish and develop it with brilliant spon-taneity. The theme of the opera was clearly to be one that under-lies much of Dylan's work—life is stronger than death.[12]

One has the feeling that Thomas was ready to begin from that mature position of acceptance, the position of praiser of life, that we have traced in the poetry, and to put into libretto and poetic drama much of the feeling and sentiment that ex-

[11] *Dylan Thomas: The Legend and the Poet,* ed. E. W. Tedlock (London, 1960), p. 68.
[12] Tedlock, pp. 69–70.

isted in the later poetry. He seemed, in other words, ready to rework Genesis once again, only this time in terms of the popular stage rather than in a "Biblical rhythm" of lyric poetry.

By 1952 Thomas had, for all practical purposes, completed his vision of the human condition, the unity of birth, fall, and regeneration. Imperfect, truncated, and ambiguous in many particulars, *Collected Poems* nevertheless marks a completed esthetic. The highly imaginative existence revealed in this esthetic, together with his singular importance as a neo-romantic poet and his score of superb lyric poems, mark Dylan Thomas as one of a half dozen major poets writing in English in the first half of our century.

Thomas himself provided the metaphor that joins his work as lyric poet and poetic dramatist—it is that recurrent metaphor of sound-shape discussed earlier.[13] What he so often described as a desire to give sound to the shapes of the world sums up the design of everything he ever wrote. His universe—in distinction, say, to Blake's highly intellectualized embodiments—aims at something hardly more intellectually profound (albeit more magical) than shaping the sounds of existence and giving articulation to the mute shapes of the universe.

Silence for Thomas was death, sound was life. Thus the war against silence that his poetry waged and the ever-increasing desire to utilize more and more voices, as in the manner of *Under Milk Wood*, are both parts of one purpose. Thomas shows his dread of silence most clearly in "Do Not Go Gentle . . . ," where the inability of his father to speak is the equivalent of death, nonentity; it is Blake's "black incessant sky," the cosmic silence neither defied nor praised. This end of

---

[13] See Chapters One and Two.

existence Thomas would not accept. Though the whole world every instant dies, "silent as the cyclone of silence" (p. 183), the poet will cry from his "long tongued room" (p. 190), though he "cry with tumbledown tongue" (p. 192). He will tell what the "good bells jaw" (p. 196) with resentment, for he would rather at his very end do what he had set out to do at the beginning: make magical spells out of "the spider-tongued, and the loud hill of Wales" (p. 20). Thus it is that his "ark" of poetry ("Prologue") gathers the sounds of woods, hawks, sparrows, mice, owls, trees, and ocean. Thus it is that the dead women of "In the White Giant's Thigh" are given the voices of rivers and curlews. And thus it is, finally, that Thomas gathered all the sounds of his world, all the memorable voices a *blind* man could hear, and shaped a world of sound: *Under Milk Wood*. Blind Captain Cat of *Under Milk Wood*, unlike the father of "Do Not Go Gentle . . . ," does not go toward death in silence. He goes, like Dylan Thomas, savoring all the sounds of life. He goes with the shadows of the world shaped in sound and with that sound loud in the praise of existence.

Index

Index

Index

Index

Index

301

Index

Index